Native American Roots

Native American Roots: Relationality and Indigenous Regeneration Under Empire, 1770–1859 explores the development of modern Indigenous identities within the settler colonial context of the early United States.

With an aggressively expanding United States that sought to displace Native peoples, the very foundations of Indigeneity were endangered by the disruption of Native connections to the land. This volume describes how Natives embedded conceptualizations integral to Indigenous ontologies into social and cultural institutions like racial ideologies, black slaveholding, and Christianity that they incorporated from the settler society. This process became one vital avenue through which various Native peoples were able to regenerate Indigeneity within environments dominated by a settler society. The author offers case studies of four different tribes to illustrate how Native thought processes, not just cultural and political processes, helped Natives redefine the parameters of Indigeneity.

This book will be of interest to students and scholars of early American history, indigenous and ethnic studies, American historiography, and anthropology.

Christian Michael Gonzales is Assistant Professor of History at the University of Rhode Island, USA. His research interests lie in Native American cultural and intellectual histories, settler colonialism, race relations, and early American slave systems. He lives in Connecticut with his wife and two sons.

Native American Roots

Relationality and Indigenous Regeneration
Under Empire, 1770–1859

Christian Michael Gonzales

Routledge
Taylor & Francis Group

NEW YORK AND LONDON

First published 2021
by Routledge
52 Vanderbilt Avenue, New York, NY 10017

and by Routledge
2 Park Square, Milton Park, Abingdon, Oxon, OX14 4RN

Routledge is an imprint of the Taylor & Francis Group, an informa business

Library of Congress Cataloging-in-Publication Data
Names: Gonzales, Christian Michael, author.
Title: Native American roots : relationality and indigenous regeneration under empire, 1770–1859 / Christian Michael Gonzales.
Description: New York : Routledge, 2021. | Includes bibliographical references and index.
Identifiers: LCCN 2020013084 (print) | LCCN 2020013085 (ebook) | ISBN 9780367479862 (hardback) | ISBN 9780367479855 (paperback) | ISBN 9780367479855 (ebook)
Subjects: LCSH: Indians of North America—Ethnic identity. | Indians of North America—Colonization. | Indians of North America—History—19th century. | Indians of North America—History—18th century. | Indians of North America—Social conditions—19th century. | Indians of North America—Social conditions—18th century.
Classification: LCC E98.E85 G66 2021 (print) | LCC E98.E85 (ebook) | DDC 970.004/97—dc23
LC record available at https://lccn.loc.gov/2020013084
LC ebook record available at https://lccn.loc.gov/2020013085

ISBN: 978-0-367-47986-2 (hbk)
ISBN: 978-0-367-47985-5 (pbk)
ISBN: 978-1-003-03749-1 (ebk)

Typeset in Times New Roman
by Apex CoVantage, LLC

To Erin, Owen, and Hayden — may we continue to experience love, connection, purpose, and renewal.

Contents

Illustrations

Figures

Tables

Acknowledgments

I would like to thank all of those who have helped me write this book. Rachel Klein gave me invaluable feedback on my writing, and Ross Frank helped me better understand Indigeneity. I want to give my appreciation to my Wesleyan University colleagues Kehalauni Kauanui and Patricia Hill and my fellow Mellon Fellow Amelia Kiddle. My La Guardia Community College colleagues, Karen Miller, Robin Kietlinski, and Lorraine Cohen, were always supportive of my research and writing. I would also like to thank the multitude of archivists and librarians from the Houghton Library, the Gilcrease Museum, the University of Oklahoma, the Special Collections at Northeastern Oklahoma State University, the Special Collections at Haverford College, the Cornwall Historical Society, and the Connecticut Historical Society who helped me conduct research. I also greatly appreciate the insightful comments and constructive criticism from the anonymous reviewers of my manuscript. Their critiques helped me make the book a far better piece of scholarship. I want to thank all of my colleagues in the Department of History at the University of Rhode Island. I give particular gratitude to my Department Chairs Tim George and Rod Mather, and to those who read and critiqued chapters in progress, including Alan Verskin, Erik Loomis, and James Ward. Finally, I want to especially thank all of my family members and friends who have been supportive throughout my academic career: my mother Linda Gonzales and father Gilbert Gonzales; my mother-in-law Theresa Horan and father-in-law Michael Horan; my friend Professor Tom Massey; my siblings Garrett Gonzales, Nicole Gonzales, Janet Paul, and Clark Paul. My deepest gratitude to my wife, Erin Horan Gonzales, and to my sons, Owen Gonzales and Hayden Gonzales, who always enthusiastically supported me during those long hours of writing. Without their love this book would have never come to fruition.

Introduction

What does it mean to be Indigenous under empire? Not in the initial and developmental stages of empire when Indigenous peoples might choose to ignore, trade with, or incorporate newcomers into their worlds; or later when an imperialistic, settler society[1] is young and Natives might have recourse to the use of force to shape relationships with, or to expel, settlers. Rather, what does it mean to be Indigenous under a dominant and powerful settler state in which viable options for Native peoples to resist or disconnect from such a civilization have all but evaporated? The latter was the situation for Natives living on the eastern seaboard at the founding of the United States, and it would be the condition Indigenous peoples throughout the continent would confront by the end of the nineteenth century.[2]

How Natives lived as Indigenous peoples under the imperialistic settler societies of the late colonial era and the early United States forms the central query of *Native American Roots*.[3] While scholars have produced important work on some of the fundamental cultural values and characteristics seminal to Indigeneity,[4] this book begins its inquiry with the Indigenous *idea* that the world fundamentally functions as a system of relationships and social bonds. For Native peoples, such a view envisioned webs of individuals and communities linked to each other through relationships that developed from reciprocal exchange and interaction.[5] Identifying Indigenous ways of being through this type of examination of Native thought, rather than through analysis of Indigenous cultural expressions, can be particularly fruitful. Indigeneity in a settler context is often subject to substantive cultural change. Attention to culture and cultural change can consequently obscure or overlook other ways that Natives conceptualized and enacted Indigeneity. *Native American Roots* therefore focuses its analysis on Indigenous thought in order to negotiate this problem. Its examination is based on the assumption that the Native ontological understanding that relationships formed the basis of reality was vital to the reproduction of Indigeneity under colonialism and empire. Natives peoples' persistent adherence to the idea that relationality was foundational to the nature of being distinguished them from others, and indeed laid the base from which they would reproduce their Indigeneity, even as they continued to live under the oppressive presence of a settler colonial society.

The methodological basis of this study rests upon examination of the interplay between Indigenous understandings of relationality and Native self-actualization; (here defined as Native efforts to reproduce Indigenous peoples and communities). Simply put, the study focuses on how Natives' cultivation of social bonds directly intersected with attempts to ensure the persistence of their peoples.

We see an example of this dynamic in the actions of a mid-nineteenth-century Seneca leader named Solomon Lane. In 1849 Lane wrote to the Society of Friends (or Quakers) who had been long-standing allies of the tribe. At this point in time, a central goal of the Senecas was to secure their lands and to remain economically viable within the boundaries of New York State. Lane perceived the Quakers as useful political allies who could aid in this goal largely because they had proven to be indispensable allies in the fight against Removal during the late 1830s and early 1840s. However, Lane also understood that one of the central filaments — shared Christianity — that had bound the Senecas and Quakers might, from the Friends' perspective, be strained by the fact that the majority of Senecas were not Christian. Perceiving the need to strengthen and reaffirm the Seneca–Quaker alliance so as to best strengthen Seneca efforts to remain in New York, Lane wrote to the Philadelphia Yearly Meeting and asked for the Quakers' continued support. "Be guardians to my people," wrote Lane, "though it is true that but very few of us are Christian." Lane continued "many of us are pagans, and also many Christian pagans." Lane's classification of the Senecas into a tripartite structure of religious belief — Christian, pagan, and Christian pagan — revealed his efforts to balance the broad political goals of the Senecas with the religious proclivities and identifications of three main factions of the tribe, as well as with the colonialist objectives of the Senecas' Quaker allies. That Lane strove to maintain the Quaker alliance as the Senecas worked to secure themselves in New York is clear from his manipulation of the chauvinism with which the Quakers viewed their relationship with the Senecas. He wrote: "Our dear guardians we hope you will not withdraw from us in our infancy to perish."[6] Such words do not demonstrate the Senecas' acceptance of the Quakers' colonialist construct of their alliance with the Senecas. Rather, they reveal that Lane understood Seneca efforts to secure their future in New York as embedded within and as unfolding within a web of relationships that required *balancing* the interests of many — including the Senecas as a tribe, the various factions of Seneca religious groups, and the Quakers. Lane's perception of the world was one in which the power to achieve his community's ongoing presence on its New York lands was directly connected to the complex relationships between constituent groups of Senecas, as well as between the Senecas and the Quakers.

***

Native American Roots is at base of an intellectual history that investigates the expression of a fundamental element of Indigenous thought among the substantial cultural changes that derived from the presence of a powerful settler society. The book analyzes Cherokee, Choctaw, Seneca, and Mohegan involvement in non-Indigenous cultural institutions as case studies of Native efforts to contend with settler colonialism from the early 1770s to the onset of the Civil War. It investigates Native incorporation of non-Indigenous cultural constructs because the phenomenon provides a window into how Natives expressed Indigenous ways of being within a settler colonial environment. For one, Natives infused Indigenous values and epistemologies into structures adopted from the settler society and thereby created paths for elements of Indigenous ways of being to persist despite the genocidal forces unleashed by colonialism. Just as importantly, Natives used non-Native cultural practices as media through which they could establish relationships that they perceived as generating the connections or power needed to realize their social and political goals. As such, non-Native cultural structures became loci both for the expression of the Indigenous idea that relationships produced power and for enacting other centrally important values that underwrote, and continue to underwrite, Native ways of being.

The book's central argument is that Natives expressed Indigenous conceptualizations inside of the cultural institutions they adopted from the settler society. Indigeneity centers on cultivating relationships in a given place in order to regenerate life. Natives applied this basic conceptual paradigm to govern their involvement with, and behavior within, borrowed cultural practices. In addition to this foundational paradigm of Native thought, Natives enacted other seminal concepts of Indigenous ontology within non-Native cultural constructs. These included ritual kinship, alliance, peoplehood, reciprocity, and balance. The enacting of Indigenous concepts manifested in concrete practices, all of which distilled down to Natives pursuing their interests by using non-Indigenous cultural structures as media to build specific relationships and social bonds — both with other Natives and with white Americans — that worked to benefit and reproduce Native communities. Through borrowed institutions, Natives worked to rebuild intragroup social bonds, forge new intergroup connections, and to protect Indigenous lands. They also strove to acquire white American allies who could support Natives by aiding their efforts to safeguard Native lands.

Natives thus embedded or "planted" Indigeneity into the cultural structures that the settler state supposed would erode Native cultures and eventually erase Indigenous peoples. The very instruments of Native annihilation thereby became places where Natives re-rooted Indigenous life. Cultural constructs became, at times, surrogates for the land itself in settler colonial environments in which the lands upon which Natives usually enacted Indigenous ways of being were either reduced in size or under threat of usurpation and Native dispossession. This surrogacy was extremely significant as it became an important avenue through which Natives regenerated Indigenous people and communities inside of the American settler state. The regeneration of Indigenous life happened because Natives had "places" in which they could live out the epistemological and ontological values that defined Indigeneity. In other words, one reason why Natives were able to remain Indigenous despite the massive degree of disruption to Indigenous life wrought by the presence of settler colonialism was because they explicitly used new cultural forms to incubate the values and practices of Indigenous ontologies. Living by these ontologies reproduced Indigenous people and regenerated Indigeneity in the face of genocidal forces that had been unleashed against them.

This argument has important ramifications for our understanding of the historical development of Indigenous modernity in the first decades of the United States. First, it reveals that Natives worked to experience modernity in certain ways that contradicted understandings held by the dominant society. Natives, for instance, rejected the settler colonial ethos that had underpinned white visions of the relationship between Indigenous peoples and modernity. These visions had posited that Natives would "fade away" as they became modern. Indeed, for white Americans of the late eighteenth and nineteenth centuries, modernity represented the antithesis of authentic Indigeneity as they saw Native movement into modernity as tantamount to the erasure of Native cultures and peoples. However, by relying on their own ontologies to contend with modern cultural institutions, and with a modern settler state, Natives found novel routes to reproduce Indigeneity despite the generalized hostility modernity as conceived by the dominant society posed to them. Because of this, Natives were not simple imitators of white American modernity, nor were they only refugees fleeing the violence inflicted upon them from modern constructs like colonialism. Rather, by finding a way to apply important Indigenous precepts within a modern context, Natives became to a degree architects of modern Indigeneity despite the fact that settler colonialism ominously dominated that very context. Simply put, Natives made efforts to craft their experiences with modernity in ways that aligned with, rather than were antithetical to, Indigeneity.

Second, Natives applied a different conceptual habitat to govern their pursuit of self-actualization within a modern context. The Enlightenment model of social relations pedaled by the settler state had sanitized the pursuit of self-actualization by characterizing the world as populated by atomized individuals and communities who, while seeking their self-interest, did not really need to take into account the consequences to others derived from the actions of the self-seeker. In comparison, self-actualization as imagined by Natives relied not on atomization of individuals or groups, but rather upon connections between them. Relationships and social bonds were foundations upon which Native self-actualization occurred. As such, Native self-actualization was mediated and delimited by the web of relationships which an Indigenous group inhabited. It was therefore Indigenous because it rested upon the importance of social bonds and relationality to health and the reproduction of Indigenous life, yet also modern because it sought these goals through the exercise of human agency specifically through borrowed modern cultural institutions. In sum, Natives were not simply thrust into modernity by an assimilatory settler society. Because they rejected the idea that modernity was antithetical to Indigeneity and because they intertwined Native self-actualization with an understanding that placed enhanced value on relationality, Native peoples made strides toward shaping their modern experience in ways that subtly, but significantly, differed from the dominant construction of modernity inside of the United States.

Finally, Natives leveraged important elements of liberal thought that emerged during the modern era. Scholars have recently explicated significant insights regarding how liberalism functioned in the eighteenth and nineteenth centuries. Duncan Kelly has argued that liberal-minded Enlightenment philosophers understood liberty as containing something he calls "propriety of liberty." Propriety referred to the capacity to self-restrain and self-constrain within a free society. According to Kelly's reading of thinkers like John Locke, Adam Smith, and John Stuart Mill, only the person possessed of propriety or the ability to restrain himself was truly free.[7] Others like Christopher Castiglia have argued that an opposite trend became increasingly powerful, particularly in the antebellum United States. Castiglia has asserted that the inner conflict between opposed forces like desire and deferral, and self-interest and constraint, increasingly came to dominate and eventually replace arguments about modern liberal democracy that had earlier been voiced through the public sphere. As such arguments receded and indeed as the public sphere came to vanish, the inner conflict experienced by American individuals was resolved in a way that saw them eschew "reform" and instead move to an embrace of democracy. By this democratic turn, Castiglia meant that Americans, men in particular, came to see themselves as freed to pursue their individual interests with a greatly reduced consideration of the effects of those pursuits on others.[8] Others have uncovered additional important processes in modern America. For example, Elizabeth Dillon has considered the ramifications of the twin processes concerning the historical development of "the commons." In reference to land, the commons became privatized; but in relation to people, the demos, the commons expanded. She has argued that these two processes converged and became mutually constitutive in a process that she has termed the "virtualization of the commons." According to Dillon, virtualization was concerned with "how to represent the virtual body of the people, and most particularly, the political will of the people."[9]

It was into these contexts that Indigenous peoples expressed their desires and sought their interests. Their efforts in waging antiremoval campaigns, for instance, were premised in part on working to remind Americans of the "propriety" needed for the moral and ethical functioning of American civilization. And as will be discussed in the following chapters, Natives over the course of late eighteenth and early nineteenth centuries would continually intercede into the "virtualization" of the commons by means such as disseminating alternative racial constructs of "Indians" and by foregrounding Native involvement with Christianity in their political relations with the United States. Yet in so doing, Natives did not simply replicate white American ways of being. Rather, what they did was to insert their own ontic into structures of modern liberal America.

Let us call such processes "neo-autochthonous." Neo-autochthony is defined by application of Indigenous ontological values that have migrated from expression primarily on the land to manifestation of such values both on the land and *also* within non-Indigenous constructs. The historical development and expression of neo-autochthony from the late eighteenth through late nineteenth centuries is a central pillar of Indigenous modernity that was created by Indigenous peoples themselves, rather than borrowed from the dominant society through a simple mimesis of dominant practices.

In their examinations of Indigenous history, historians have often assumed a perspective that investigates the pragmatic ways that Natives negotiated colonialism.

By contrast, this study looks at Native actions from a different view; one that turns the scholar's gaze away from an effort to discern what Natives were doing in *practical* reaction to colonialism to one in which Native historical negotiation of colonialism is examined from a perspective that privileges Indigenous ways of being, and asks how those ways of being drove Native behavior under a settler colonial context.

The difference between these two perspectives is clear in how this book understands relationality. The first perspective would see the relation-building Natives engaged in with white Americans as primarily a pragmatic response to colonial impositions because it represented, in praxis, a way to ultimately "survive" settler colonialism. This is obviously true on one level, but again it is a level that is deeply informed by a rationalist outlook that can easily lead contemporaries to assume that the way Natives enacted relation-building derived almost entirely from the need to survive the presence of a settler society. In contrast, the perspective assumed by this book posits that an equally important force (beyond and in addition to the pragmatic need to negotiate colonialism) shaping Indigenous relation-building was a preexisting Native ontological belief that relationality was foundational to the world's structure. Consequently, even though white Americans often dominated the economic and sociopolitical contexts investigated by this book, it would be a mistake to assume that Native–white relations were generally indicative of Native reactionary responses to colonialism, or of their capitulation to the assimilatory pressures of American civilization. Rather, Natives conceptualized their efforts to build relationships with white Americans in accordance with Indigenous views of the world. Because Natives continued — after the establishment of the settler state — to see the world as comprised of interconnected communities, it was illogical for them to work toward their interests without considering how relations with all the groups that were linked to a Native community could be leveraged to contribute to those interests. Another way to see this is to understand that when Natives negotiated settler colonialism by establishing and maintaining relationships with white Americans, they were motivated in large part by an interpellation that placed value on relationality and connection. In this way, the relationships became vectors for the reproduction of, not instruments for the negation of, Native ways of being. This process of Indigenous renewal, though, is obscured if one looks at Native relation-building from a perspective that assumes pragmatism as the singular or most prominent driving force behind Native responses to colonial impositions.

In arguing that pragmatism was not the only factor driving Indigenous behavior, this book also uncovers historical occurrences of the reproduction of a Native way of being derived from an Indigenous, place-centered ethic.[10] Scholars have various terms for this land-centered ethos. Glen Sean Coulthard has called it "grounded normativity," which is in essence the set of ethics, specific to a place, that arise from and govern the relationships among the various groups of people that inhabit the area. Leanne Betasamosake Simpson has used the Anishinaabemowin term *aki* to describe the same phenomenon. The Native actors examined in this study also grounded themselves in a conceptual paradigm in which relationships are the foundation of a larger, living entity comprised of the interconnections between people. However, they did not limit their application of this paradigm to a given geographic area, but rather enacted it in other "spaces."[11]

Indigeneity consequently also existed in "spaces" that were non-landed or outside of geography. As already stated, the enacting of Indigeneity could and was performed within cultural and perceptual arenas. As a settler colonial civilization, the United States articulated deadly associations and binaries: "Indians" should be confined on reservations, land was privately owned, and "Indians" existed in antithesis to "civilized" citizens. All of these worked to erase Indigenous peoples and cultures by attacking Natives' connection to land, specifically through dispossession, Removal, and confinement to reservations. By enacting Indigenous ontology in new spaces, Natives worked to counter the intended consequences of colonial policies and practices, and strove to ensure the renewal of Indigeneity. Though Indigeneity is at its roots place and land based,[12] Natives expressed the ontologies of Indigeneity in other spaces when their connections to land and place were threatened or attenuated. They worked to keep alive land-based ways of being in an environment in which the connection between the land and the people was explicitly targeted. In so doing, Natives engaged in a counter-colonialism in which their weapon was a simple ongoing adherence to living as Indigenous people that was expressed in new "places."

Since the publication of Richard White's *The Middle Ground*, historians have lavished much attention on how Natives partnered with non-Natives to build institutions that would allow them to relate to each other in ways that would help each group achieve its objectives or work toward its interests. A recent manifestation of this historiographical trend is Andrew Lipman's *The Saltwater Frontier*,[13] which explained how Natives and Europeans produced and interacted within coastal maritime frontiers. Middle ground studies have greatly enhanced our historical knowledge, but they fall short in explicating what happened after a given "middle ground" disintegrated. This leaves open questions about the expression of Indigeneity after the fall of the middle ground and after the balance of power had shifted decidedly in favor of non-Native historical actors. Unfortunately, this can inadvertently lead back to the myth of the "disappearing Indian." After power shifts to the favor of white Americans and the middle ground collapses, Natives are left to a process of decay in which their Indigeneity is erased through dispossession or sociocultural "assimilation." Seeing the history of the expression of Indigeneity in non-landed spaces provides historians a historiographical pathway out of this predicament because it does not implicitly assume that Natives always needed a land base or the persistence of "traditional" cultural institutions to enact Indigeneity.

In addition to middle ground studies, scholars over the last few decades have made much progress in explicating the complexities in the relationship between Native peoples and colonialism.[14] Most relevant to this study is work that has contributed to the larger decolonizing project that scholars of Indigeneity have recently worked to develop. Crucially important here is Audra Simpson's *Mohawk Interruptus*, which argued that Mohawks of Kahnawake have "refused" to accept the political boundaries imposed upon them by settler states. Such refusal has been key, she asserted, to maintaining Indigenous identity in the face of settler societies that seek the erasure of Native people. This refusal is one reason why the colonial project is unfinished and ongoing.[15] Others have complicated this narrative by identifying important processes that have reinforced Native subordination under colonial or imperial contexts. Scholars like Taiaiake Alfred, Jodi Byrd, and Glen Sean Coulthard have all explained various ways such processes have worked.[16] Alfred has argued that Native accommodationism derived from colonized mentalities among Indigenous actors, which in turn aided assimilation efforts and thereby contributed to cultural genocide. Byrd has examined how the United States has repeatedly designated various populations as "Indians," so as to justify the expansion of its hegemony over those populations. She has further described how this process has at times co-opted Native Americans as colonizers in alliance with white American colonizers. She pointed to the use of a Native reservation as a site at which Natives would help the United States "assimilate" Japanese Americans interned during World War II for instance. And Coulthard has explicated how "recognition" in the twentieth century followed on the heels of the outright use of force to subordinate Natives. He has explained that in seeking recognition from the dominant society, Natives place themselves in a position that relies on the dominant society to grant acknowledgment of Native peoples and rights, in effect giving control over the future of Indigeneity to non-Native peoples and the settler society.

To combat the historical and ongoing subordination Native communities have experienced due to settler colonialism, many scholars of Indigeneity have called for Indigenous "resurgence." Resurgence refers to Native peoples' use of Indigenous precepts, understandings, cultural constructs, epistemologies, and ontologies to strengthen and build Indigenous communities. Moreover, resurgence is not reliant on recognition or reconciliation with dominant societies to proceed, though it does welcome alliance-building with non-Natives. This study engages directly with this body of scholarship by showing that Natives in the past used a variant of resurgence to deal with colonialism. By embedding Indigenous ways of being into cultural constructs that were either forced upon them or that they borrowed from the settler society, Natives opened space within that society, and the empire it supported, for their persistence and for the re-creation of Indigeneity. Through examination of this past, this study reveals how what we today call resurgence has historically been part of Indigenous responses to colonization.

∗∗∗

Natives worked — to the extent that they could under settler and imperial contexts — to apply and express Indigenous worldviews and to live as Indigenous people. This occurred as they articulated foundational Indigenous ontological concepts within borrowed cultural institutions. They sought to carve out space for expressions of Native ways of thinking, and thus to promote the perpetuation of Native peoples within a modern era dominated by the suffocating presence of colonialism and empire. Such efforts by Native peoples deeply affected their involvement in some of the most significant developments of late eighteenth and early nineteenth century American history. It influenced new understandings of race among Natives in southern New England, it was a factor in motivating the infamous Cherokee Treaty Party to sign the Treaty of New Echota (which paved the way for the Trail of Tears), it was used as an ideological foundation upon which Natives and their white allies formed arguments against Indian Removal, and it led Cherokee and Choctaw political leaders to work to prevent the development of antislavery within their respective Nations.

This book traces these developments through five chapters, each of which analyzes Indigenous participation in a cultural institution whose origin is non-Indigenous. These include race, black slavery, formal education, political protest in the public sphere, and Christianity. In addition, each chapter examines how Natives embedded a particular Indigenous concept within a non-Native cultural structure so as to pursue their interests and reproduce their communities. The book purposefully revisits some of the well-known ways that Natives became deeply involved with the cultural constructs of the American settler society. It does so because the stories usually told about these processes have not sufficiently accounted for the ontological viewpoints of Native actors. Again, this leads us to assume that Native behavior was only motivated by a pragmatic need to survive colonialism or to mimic the behaviors of the dominant society, thereby leading us to miss how Natives used those cultural constructs as critical sites for Indigenous (re)creation. The reader is invited to understand the retelling of these histories from this latter vantage point so as to comprehend them anew.

Chapter 1 examines how the Mohegans of Connecticut conceptualized race during the late eighteenth century. It argues that they shaped ideas of race around Indigenous notions of *ritual kinship*, and then leveraged the precept of Christian brotherhood to support newly created kin relations between unrelated Natives. Their understanding of what it meant to be "Indian," moreover, purposefully contradicted the pejorative connotations white Americans had attached to "Indians." This process demonstrated that the Mohegans were racial thinkers who used racialization to their benefit. They crafted characterizations of "Indian" that helped them to exercise a degree of self-determination in the years leading up to the American Revolution. In this case, their goal was to exercise increased social authority over themselves, while simultaneously weakening the social authority wielded over them by white Americans.

Chapter 2 focuses on Cherokee and Choctaw relations with white missionaries from the Boston-based American Board of Commissioners for Foreign Missions. It analyzes how the institution of slavery complicated Native–missionary relations. It argues that the Cherokees and Choctaws each leveraged slavery in their interactions with missionaries to the benefit of Indigenous goals and interests. Primarily, Natives understood their relations with missionaries as *alliances*. They hoped that such alliances could be used to help Natives protect their lands. The central role slavery would play in Native–missionary relations produced significant consequences. Namely, the importance of slavery to the interested parties would lead to substantial efforts to block the emergence of antislavery sentiment within the Cherokee and Choctaw nations during the antebellum period.

Chapter 3 reviews the development of formal education systems in the Cherokee, Choctaw, and Seneca nations. It sees Indigenous conceptualizations of the *people* as a central motivator to their willingness to create new formal education systems. Initially, it was missionaries who sought to establish boarding or day schools for Native children. Natives, however, co-opted these efforts and became partners in the formation and running of the schools. This chapter contends that Indigenous leaders supported the schools because they wished to give their children an enhanced ability to re-create "the people" through time. On the surface, this meant producing educated, English-literate Natives who could effectively engage in diplomatic relations with the settler society and with white Americans. Native leaders viewed the ability to protect their interests as largely dependent upon the possession of capable tribal members who were well-prepared to negotiate with the US government and with various state governments. However, on a deeper level, Natives understood these abilities as crucial to the protection of Native societies. Indigenous communities would more easily reproduce themselves if they contained cadres of educated youths who could protect and advocate for the interests of their communities as they simultaneously navigated the sociopolitical and economic contexts inherent in living within a settler colonial environment. In this way, the people would persist in the future. Yet they would also be connected to the people of the past as educated youth, it was hoped, would possess the knowledge to protect dwindling or threatened Native land bases that housed the bones, stories, and places inhabited by their ancestors. Because of these stakes, Natives, far more than white missionaries and teachers, were the principal agents who did the work to incorporate formal education into their communities.

Chapter 4 surveys two important Jacksonian Age political efforts to prevent Indian Removal: the attempt to thwart passage of the Indian Removal Act of 1830, and the effort to stop the removal of the Senecas under the auspices of the 1838 Treaty of Buffalo Creek. The chapter claims that Natives used antiremoval campaigns to characterize "Indians" as rights-bearing peoples. Natives repeatedly cited and relied on their understandings of *reciprocity* to support their arguments concerning the validity of their rights. Simply put, they asserted that their actions to make treaties, sell land, and adopt cultural practices like Christianity, western style farming, and formal education demonstrated that Natives had worked to meet the needs and demands of white Americans. In return, Indigenous leaders and authors expected white Americans to reciprocate through respecting Native rights, particularly land rights. Consequently, Natives promulgated antiremoval literature through the public sphere in attempts to persuade white Americans to reject the policy of forced relocation. In the case of each antiremoval campaign examined, Natives allied with white evangelical antiremoval activists who generally believed that the outcome of the Removal question would create an indelible indictment of, or a shining example of, the moral character of the United States. Finally, the chapter asserts that, despite the ultimate failure of antiremoval, the campaigns were nonetheless significant because they reinforced Natives' adherence to the precept of reciprocity in their post-Removal relations with the United States. Even though Removal sought the destruction of Indigeneity by targeting its source — Native peoples' place on the land — it failed in an important way. It inhumanely ripped Natives from their lands, but Indigenous peoples' antiremoval efforts ensured that a central principle of Indigenous thought persisted beyond Removal's horrors.

Chapter 5 investigates Choctaw involvement with Christianity. It argues that the Choctaws used Christianity as an instrument in tribal social redevelopment in the wake of Removal. Specifically, the Choctaws employed understandings of *balance*, or healthy relationships, to regain security in the wake of Removal. This meant security from social disorder within the Choctaw nation and also security from further land dispossession at the hands of the United States. This chapter demonstrates how these processes of rebalancing occurred through the actualization of social bonds created via the medium of Christianity.

The Native peoples examined in this study could not repel or avoid the colonialism and imperialism that the Euro-American settler societies of the late eighteenth and early nineteenth centuries created. They consequently found themselves living under a colonial and imperial civilization in which the majority of non-Native politicians and citizens alike envisioned and strove for the end of Indigeneity. In such circumstances, Native people had to find novel ways to be Indigenous and to express and live by the values and behaviors that had long been elemental to the Native societies of North America. One way they did so was to co-opt some of the cultural practices of the settler society and use them as media to enact seminal conceptualizations of Indigenous ontologies. The stories that follow trace how such processes regenerated Indigeneity as Natives expressed ontologies that rested on a foundation of relationality and the power of social bonds.

Notes

1. A settler society is one that arises from a process scholars generally call settler colonialism. Settler colonialism is defined by two main characteristics. First, it is a colony in which the colonizing group seeks permanent settlement for themselves and for their posterity. Second, the settler colony works for the displacement, erasure, or subordination of the people indigenous to the place in which the colony is planted. For a study of settler colonialism, see Patrick Wolfe, *Settler Colonialism and the Transformation of Anthropology: The Politics and Poetics of an Ethnographic Event* (London: Continuum, 1998).
2. Throughout the book there are references to empire and imperialism. For our purposes, empire means geographic expansion with attendant efforts to either establish or maintain political, social, and economic hegemony. The book understands the United States as an imperialistic settler society. In other words, it is a settler society that seeks expansion and/or maintenance of its hegemonic power over territories and the peoples who inhabit those territories.
3. Though this book asks what Indigeneity was under American settler colonialism, it does not intend to provide an exhaustive answer to what constituted Indigeneity. Rather, it focuses on one important process for the expression and reproduction of Indigeneity.
4. For discussions of widely shared beliefs and values of North American Indigenous cultures, see the following works: Daniel Richter, *The Ordeal of the Longhouse: The Peoples of the Iroquois League in the Era of European Colonization* (Chapel Hill, NC: University of North Carolina Press, 1992); Richard White, *The Middle Ground: Indians, Empires, and Republics in the Great Lakes Region, 1650–1815* (Cambridge, UK: Cambridge University Press, 1991); Betty Bastien, *Blackfoot Ways of Knowing: The Worldview of the Siksikaitsitapi* (Calgary, Canada: University of Calgary Press, 2004); James Brooks, *Captives and Cousins: Slavery, Kinship, and Community in the Southwest Borderlands* (Chapel Hill, NC: University of North Carolina Press, 2002);

and Ramon A. Gutierrez, *When Jesus Came the Corn Mothers Went Away: Marriage, Sexuality and Power in New Mexico, 1500–1846* (Palo Alto, CA: Stanford University Press, 1991).

5. See Lisa Brooks, *The Common Pot: The Recovery of Native Space in the Northeast* (Minneapolis, MN: University of Minnesota Press, 2008).

6. Solomon Lane to Philadelphia Yearly Meeting, March 30, 1849, AA41, Box 1, #156, Philadelphia Yearly Meeting Indian Committee (hereafter referred to as PYMIC) Correspondence, Records of PYMIC, Quaker Collection, Special Collections, Haverford College, Philadelphia, PA.

7. Duncan Kelly, *The Propriety of Liberty: Persons, Passions, and Judgement in Modern Political Thought* (Princeton, NJ: Princeton University Press, 2010).

8. Christopher Castiglia, *Interior States: Institutional Consciousness and the Inner Life of Democracy in the Antebellum United States* (Durham, NC: Duke University Press, 2008).

9. Elizabeth Dillon, *New World Drama: The Performative Commons in the Atlantic World, 1649–1849* (Durham, NC: Duke University Press, 2014), 3.

10. Here I mean that Natives continued to understand the world as a system of interconnected relationships. Retention of seeing the world as interconnected was by no means the only way that Natives continued to exist as Indigenous under colonialism, but I am arguing that it was a vital signifier of Indigeneity that persisted under settler colonialism.

11. Glen Sean Coulthard, *Red Skin, White Masks: Rejecting the Colonial Politics of Recognition* (Minneapolis, MN: University of Minnesota Press, 2014); and Leanne Betasamosake Simpson, *As We Have Always Done: Indigenous Freedom Through Radical Resurgence* (Minneapolis, MN: University of Minnesota Press, 2017).

12. Connection to ancestral lands was and is important to Indigenous people. Moreover, contemporary Native peoples who have been displaced from their lands should be reconnected to them. The argument here is not that Indigeneity ever fully became divorced from place, nor should it be.

13. Andrew Lipman, *The Saltwater Frontier: Indians and the Contest for the American Coast* (New Haven, CT: Yale University Press, 2015).

14. We have gained insight into Native identity formation through examinations of race, material culture, and biological markers like blood and DNA. See, for instance, Circe Sturm, *Blood Politics: Race, Culture and Identity in the Cherokee Nation of Oklahoma* (Berkeley, CA: University of California Press, 2002); Fay A. Yarbrough, *Race and the Cherokee Nation: Sovereignty in the Nineteenth Century* (Philadelphia, PA: University of Pennsylvania Press, 2008); Craig N. Cipolla, *Becoming Brothertown: Native American Ethnogenesis and Endurance in the Modern World* (Tucson, AZ: University of Arizona Press, 2013); and Kim Tallbear, *Native American DNA: Tribal Belonging and the False Promise of Genetic Science* (Minneapolis, MN: University of Minnesota Press, 2013). For work on how Natives shaped or created empire, see Pekka Hamalainen, *The Comanche Empire* (New Haven, CT: Yale University Press, 2009) and Michael McDonnell, *Masters of Empire: Great Lakes Indians and the Making of America* (New York City, NY: Hill and Wang, 2015). And for studies that have investigated ways Native agency worked to weaken colonial power and control, see Scott Richard Lyons, *X-Marks: Native Signatures of Assent* (Minneapolis, MN: University of Minnesota Press, 2010); and for time, see Mark Rifkin, *Beyond Settler Time: Temporal Sovereignty and Indigenous Self-Determination* (Durham, NC: Duke University Press, 2017).

15. Audra Simpson, *Mohawk Interruptus: Political Life Across the Borders of Settler States* (Durham, NC: Duke University Press, 2014).

16. See Taiaiake Alfred, *Peace, Power, Righteousness: An Indigenous Manifesto*, 2nd edition (Oxford, UK: University Press, 2009); Jodi A. Byrd, *The Transit of Empire: Indigenous Critiques of Colonialism* (Minneapolis, MN: University of Minnesota Press, 2011); and Coulthard, *Red Skin, White Masks*.

1 Family Ties

Ritual Kinship and Christianity in the Making of Indigenous Conceptions of Race

By the late colonial period, Natives living on the eastern seaboard were not only racial thinkers,[1] but they had also begun to use race in an instrumental fashion just like other groups in America. For example, the Lenni Lenape prophet Neolin employed a nativistic conceptualization of race that envisioned separation between "Indians" and "whites." But Indigenous people of immediate prewar southern New England utilized race in other ways that reflected the circumstances they encountered living in colonies like Massachusetts and Connecticut. In southern New England, settler colonialism had become well-entrenched, and white Americans had worked with increased vigor since the end of Metacom's War to ensure that they occupied a position of social dominance. From such a position, white Americans took the initiative to define what the "Indian" race was. Their descriptions reinforced white paternalism and, more ominously, worked toward the general erasure of Indigeneity through "assimilation" ideology that pictured Natives becoming Christians and yeomen farmers while their tribal and ethnic identities simultaneously faded. One way Natives negotiated these forces was to devise their own conceptions of "Indian" that produced an outcome of the persistence of Indigenous people rather than the gradual disappearance of Indigeneity.

This chapter focuses on the intersecting lives of three Mohegan men as examples of one way Indigenous people of southern New England understood race as it pertained to being "Indian." Indigenous conceptualizations and uses of "Indian" revealed a process in which Natives worked to redefine themselves based in part on long-standing understandings of Indigenous practices centered on ritual kinship. Moreover, Native efforts to utilize Indianness sought to strengthen Native standing in late colonial society vis-à-vis white Americans, and it more particularly strove to strengthen Mohegan social authority and undercut the authority that white authority figures wielded. Finally, this process unfolded upon a conceptual schema that took the power of relationships as its base. Working from these premises, Natives used ritual kinship in conjunction with their participation in Christianity as the central ingredients in formulating Indigenous understandings of what it meant to be "Indian."[2] Ritual kinship and Christianity were the filaments that bound Natives to each other under the larger aegis of race. The Native racial construction of the "Indian" examined here served multiple purposes, but the most important is that it directly linked Natives to each other through the enacting of ritualized kinship. The ongoing reenactment of ritual kinship was both a literal regeneration of Indigenous people as they purposefully cast themselves as "Indians" and a reification of their conception of the power of social bonds, which they sought to manifest and harness through the links forged to each other.

The sincere embrace of Christianity by the Native actors explored here should not be understood as evidence of their capitulation to the dominant society or their abandonment of Indigenous ways of being. Rather, Christianity worked extraordinarily well as a conduit for Native expressions of kinship, precisely because it provided a context that made it easy for Natives to enact ritual within a colonial environment in which Indigenous rituals had either been lost or suppressed. In addition, Christianity had the added benefit of acceptability to the dominant society. As such, Christianity helped Natives from various ethnic groups to gather and form social units without arousing much suspicion or concern on the part of white authorities. Members of such groups forged interpersonal bonds as ministers to congregants or simply as members of the same church. Christianity helped Natives from disparate ethnic backgrounds to come together as they strove to remake and rebuild Indigenous communities that had been disrupted by settler colonialism. Natives would bridge ethnic identities and begin to envision themselves as "Indians" almost as much as they thought of themselves as "Mohegan," "Pequot," or "Narragansett." At the deepest level, it was the kinship bonds created through ritual practices like preaching and ministering that bonded Native individuals and groups to each other. So while older rituals that Natives had used in earlier centuries to create kinship bonds had become rarer, the practice of using ritual to create kinship had not.

Native reliance on ritual kinship to bind them together under the racial category "Indian" makes sense when we consider Native understandings of people. A group or people, or an ethnos, could not cohere without some sort of personal and affective element that signified and explained how they were "related" to each other. Put another way, groups of people were a group *because* they were kin. Consequently, applying race as it functioned in the Euro-American consciousness — as an intellectual category defined by factors like phenotype, culture, and shared history — was to Indigenous psyches simply insufficient to tie together whole groups of Native peoples. But because ritual kinship was a near ubiquitous Native ontological construct, it supplied a ready and capable mechanism that went a long way toward helping formulate "Indian" identities, particularly when those identities brought together people who saw themselves as originating from different ethnicities.[3] The new kinship ties that resulted from the practice of ritual supplied the bond that linked individual "Indians" together as they conceived of themselves as a "race." Natives may have indeed approached each other under the auspices of Christianity as they established interpersonal bonds under a new racial identity category, yet the forging of this new identity was conducted through and upon the older, Indigenous social framework of ritual kinship because it maintained Native understandings of what criteria needed to be met in order to construct a "people."

To make this case, this chapter examines the actions of the Mohegan ministers Joseph Johnson and Samson Occom, using an example from the lives of each of these men. The first event involves Johnson's efforts to become a resident preacher in a Pequot community. The second surrounds both Johnson's and Occom's involvement with the case of the Mohegan Moses Paul, who was convicted for the murder of a white man. The chapter also asserts that the aforementioned cases demonstrate that Natives used the idea of race instrumentally to counteract the more pejorative characterizations of Indians disseminated by white Americans. In this way, Natives, like white Americans, used race as a tool for their own social interests. The difference of course was that white Americans wielded it as a tool of domination, whereas Natives used it as an instrument to resist such efforts.

Joseph Johnson and the Pequot

Ritual kinship's ability to help Natives of different ethnicities bond under the racial category "Indian" is clear in the life of the Mohegan Joseph Johnson. Johnson led an interesting, and for the Indigenous peoples of southern New England, a consequential life. He was well ensconced within eighteenth century colonial society, was literate in English, had studied at Eleazer Wheelock's Indian Charity School, became an ordained minister, worked as a hand on a whaling vessel, and had labored as a missionary to other Indigenous peoples, including the Oneidas in New York.[4]

Though Joseph Johnson was well familiar with white society and culture, his experience in 1772 of taking up missionary work among the Mashantucket Pequots in Connecticut illuminates important divergences between white and Native conceptions and uses of race. In general, white racial prejudices had cast Indians as "uncivilized" and characterized them as possessed of uncultivated intellects. In relation to Johnson's desire to minister to the Mashantuckets, this translated into a requirement that he undergo extra scrutiny by white authorities before he could serve as preacher. Despite his established credentials as a preacher and regardless of his previous experience working as a missionary among the Oneidas, Joseph Johnson was to be vetted before a white minister before he could preach among the Pequots. On one of his initial visits to the Pequots, Johnson needed to "get [the] Approbation" of the resident white preacher, the Reverend Timothy Pitken. Johnson was subsequently "Examined by . . . Pitkin, preaching." After witnessing Johnson perform his craft, Pitkin pronounced that he found Johnson to be "Capable of the business"[5] of serving as missionary to the Pequots.

Pitkin however was not the only one who examined Johnson on that day: also present were "the headmen of the Indian tribe," who had their own way of vetting Johnson for incorporation into their community. A week after Johnson gave his sermon, one of these "headmen" approached Johnson to speak privately with him. Johnson recorded their conversation in his journal:

> He told me that he was very intimate with my father in time of war. He exprest much Regard for him . . . and told of Several Engagements, where

he accompanied my father . . . and after all he acquainted me most freely the Special regards he had for me also, and assurd me that I had more that loved me now, truly than Ever I had [in] my life time before.[6]

The most obvious purpose of this conversation was to let Johnson know that he had won Pequot approval and that they were consequently extending him a welcome to their community. What is even more important, however, is that the Pequots' acceptance of Johnson as their missionary flowed through an Indigenous conceptualization of what it meant to be "Indian," one that centered on ritual kinship. Johnson's acquisition of white approval was governed by capability — was Johnson sufficiently knowledgeable of Christianity to preach? But to the Pequots, Johnson's race meant something quite different because their understanding of "Indians" was different. They connected "Indianness" to shared ontological conceptions that governed how people created interpersonal relationships. Because Johnson was an "Indian," both he and the Pequots understood that he would be made a member of the Pequot community through the forging of ritual kinship bonds. While for Pitkin the foundation of Johnson's relationship with the Pequots rested on his knowledge base, this for the Pequots and Johnson was insufficient ground upon which to tie Johnson to his would-be parishioners.

A closer look at the Pequot headman's conversation with Johnson reveals that Johnson's incorporation into the community was principally governed by ritual kinship rather than by something else like the ability to competently preach the Christian faith. The headman plainly pointed out that he had had a relationship with Johnson's father. They were "intimate . . . in a time of war," implying that they had been like brothers to each other. The headman then used this past connection to explain to Johnson that they too were linked. This is why the headman declared that he held "Special regards" for Johnson. The headman's previous relationship with Johnson's father coupled with his statement of regard for Johnson worked in tandem to place the headman and Johnson into a would-be father–child relationship. The relationship between the headman and Johnson's father had invested the headman with the authority to create a familial bond with Johnson. In the past when he had been an "intimate" of Johnson's father, the headman had been by extension like an "uncle" to Johnson. But in the present, the headman — given the absence of Johnson' father — could assume and elevate himself to the role of Johnson's father. This newly created parental bond was extremely important because it provided the ground upon which the whole tribe could welcome Johnson. By becoming a member of the headman's "family," Johnson became immediately eligible for membership in the people or the tribe. This is why the headman informed Johnson that he now "had more that loved" him. Johnson's trial sermon to the Pequots had served as the ritual that would ultimately bind Johnson to the people. The headman's conversation with Johnson was the confirmation of this ritually created bond. In one fell swoop, Johnson became kin to the headman and a member of (or kin to) the people, and as such was able to readily assume a place as resident minister within this Pequot community.

Johnson's incorporation into the Pequot community reveals a case in which Indigenous peoples had constructed conceptions of "Indian" on their own terms and for their own purposes.[7] Johnson's exchange with the Pequot headman shows that these particular Native peoples perceived a mutual "Indian" identity, in part, through a shared ontological understanding of kinship that manifested in particular interpersonal and social practice. What defined "Indians" apart from others was not "savagery," "heathenism," or "barbarity" as some white Americans had assumed, but rather shared cultural knowledge. In the case of Johnson and the Pequot headman, both men understood ritual kinship as a mechanism designed to forge the emotional ties needed to create strong interpersonal (or intergroup) bonds between unrelated persons from different ethnic backgrounds. In this light, Johnson's sermon, the Pequots' examination of Johnson preaching, and Johnson's subsequent conversation with the headman should all be read as acts in a larger ritual performance. These events formed the constituent parts of an adoption ritual that had been refashioned within the framework of an Indigenous racial consciousness. The shared ability of the Pequots, the Pequot headman, and Johnson to invoke and understand the usage of ritual kinship converged to make them all "Indian," and in the process allowed them to understand and relate to each other as such. By becoming the son of a Pequot "father," Johnson in turn could become a spiritual "father" to the Pequots as a community. This process proved empowering for all involved as it skirted the religious authority wielded by Pitken and placed it into the hands of Johnson.

The Moses Paul Case

Johnson's experience with the Pequots reflected a process in which Natives used their understanding of "Indian" to form new bonds with each other while circumventing the authority of a designated white authority figure. The Moses Paul case provides another example of the same basic phenomenon, except that in this case the creation of new relationships was the first step in Native efforts to publicize characterizations of "Indian" that ran counter to widely held pejorative views of Indians. Natives involved in the case leveraged ritual kinship and Christianity to define the "Indian" in ways that showed a keen awareness of the significance of both their relationships with each other and with white Americans. Both Joseph Johnson and Samson Occom established relationships with Moses Paul by drawing on kinship, Christian ritual, and the idea that they were "Indians." They then exploited the public attention the case drew to create and disseminate characterizations of "Indians" that were designed to speak to both Native and white audiences.

The events of the Moses Paul case are as follows: in late November or early December of 1771, the Mohegan man Moses Paul rented a room in Clark's Tavern in Bethany, Connecticut. On the night of December 7, Paul went down to the bar where he encountered a white man named Moses Cook. Cook lived in Waterbury, Connecticut, where his family had established roots.[8] Paul became intoxicated and found himself in an argument with Cook. This argument escalated and Paul eventually grabbed what was described as a "club" and struck Moses Cook in the

head. Moses Paul subsequently ran from the tavern, but was pursued and appre-
hended that night. Cook clung to life for a few days, but ultimately died of his
wounds. After a short "fair and impartial Hearing," Moses Paul was convicted of
murder and sentenced to be hanged.[9]

The case generated a great deal of attention from white Americans. By the
late eighteenth century, white Americans in New England had a long history of
defining Indians as "dangerous."[10] Paul's actions of killing a white man therefore
provided fodder to feed the stereotype of the "violent Indian" whom white Americans needed to keep subdued. Playing their part, several white Americans camped
outside of Paul's jail and subjected him to harangues of "Hang the Indian, Hang
him! Hang him!"[11] which he heard shouted outside of his prison. But because
the case brought these social tensions and animosities to the forefront, it also
provided Natives with a good opportunity to develop a counter-narrative to the
one white Americans assumed the case proffered. Instead of an affirmation of
white stereotypes of "Indians," Johnson and Occom used the case, and specifically their relationships with Paul, to develop a characterization of "Indian" that
denoted traits such as "moral," "intelligent," "pious," "industrious," and "repentant." While these characteristics were meant to speak to white audiences, the
two Mohegan men also worked to reach an Indigenous audience by imbuing their
construction of "Indian" with the ideology and language of kinship.

Joseph Johnson leveraged his position as a Christian minister to create an opening to enter into the drama of the Paul case. Shortly after Paul's conviction, and
while he sat in jail in New Haven, Johnson penned a letter to Paul urging him to
repent and accept Jesus. "I tell you that there is no other Name given unto men
under heaven, whereby they may be saved but by the name of Jesus! . . . Therefore seek his favour," urged Johnson.[12] Ostensibly, Johnson approached Paul as a
Christian minister seeking to save Paul's soul as he was about to be put to death.
To hammer home the pastoral nature of his relationship to Paul, Johnson ended his
letter with "I am your soul's well-wisher."[13]

Yet Johnson was not simply fulfilling his ministerial duties. He took care
to explain that his desire to save Paul's soul found its motivation in great part
from the affinity he felt for him due to the racial and ethnic connections he and
Paul shared. From his point of view, Johnson was coming to the aid of a fellow
"Indian" and a fellow Mohegan. In the second sentence of his letter, Johnson
pointed out their common racial and ethnic identities. "I am an Indian . . . a native
of this land and of the Mohegan tribe." He then immediately wrote: "I am one
who am truly sorry for your misfortune."[14] The implication of Johnson's pairing
of his racial and ethnic identities with his feelings of sympathy for Paul was that
Johnson's empathy derived from witnessing the dire circumstances surrounding
his compatriot. What Johnson had carefully and skillfully achieved through his
letter was an exploitation of their Christian identities (Johnson was a minister, and
Paul had been brought up as a Christian in the home of a white family) in order to
articulate and affirm the two men's shared "Indian" and Mohegan identities. But
the significance of these shared religious, racial, and ethnic identities was to form
the foundation upon and through which the two men would establish kinship. On

the surface, they were "brothers" because they both were Christian, Indian, and Mohegan.

While a sense of brotherhood between Paul and Johnson found its ostensive genesis in shared Christian, racial, and ethnic identities, Johnson solidified this brotherhood through a constructed and ritualized kinship built through Johnson's efforts to support Paul. As an Indian who had been convicted of murdering a white man, Paul was isolated and subjected to a deep and angrily voiced anti-Indian racism. Johnson became "family" to Paul because he fulfilled the roles a family member would normally play in such circumstances. Johnson served as confidant, well-wisher, supporter, and provider of empathy. In other words, he put himself in a place to share, if only obliquely, in Paul's distressing situation. He acted and felt like Paul's "brother" would feel upon witnessing Paul's conviction and upon learning that he had been sentenced to death. But what reified the fabricated "brother" relationship between Johnson and Paul were the public "performances" Johnson undertook in relation to Paul and his case. By visiting Paul in jail, by publishing the letter he wrote asking Paul to repent, and by urging and then helping Paul to write and publicize his autobiography before his execution, Johnson publicly linked himself to Paul. Johnson's open show of support for Paul and his purposeful positioning of himself as at Paul's side were the performative actions that ritualized the "brother" relationship Johnson had initially articulated as formed from shared ethnic, racial, and religious identities. In other words, because Johnson willingly assumed a place by the side of the compromised Paul, he proved in an open and public forum his fealty to and feeling for Paul — actions that served as the "ritual" performances that proved Johnson's genuine sympathy for Paul, and that consequently cemented affective ties between Johnson and Paul.

The other Mohegan man who connected himself to the Paul case followed a similar script to the one Johnson had pursued. Samson Occom had become involved with Paul because the condemned man had asked him to deliver his execution sermon — a request Occom agreed to fulfill. After agreeing to give the sermon, Occom undertook the process of ritually constructing a kin relationship with Paul through the performance of his ministerial duties, and most importantly, upon and through race. Race's role as the medium through which Occom forged kinship with Paul is clear through Occom's implicit expressions of the two men's shared Indian identity. The published account of Occom's sermon shows that he spoke directly to Paul before he begun the lecture that would immediately precede Paul's hanging. He addressed him as "My poor unhappy brother, MOSES" and then continued "You are the bone of my bone, and flesh of my flesh. You are an Indian."[15] In using words that intermixed logics of kinship, the physical body, and race, Occom made clear that the two were bound by a variety of common ties. On one level they were kin. In Occom's words, they were "brothers" who shared in a sense a "body" as they were built from the same "flesh and bone." But on another level, Occom made the point that they also shared a racial identity as "Indians." So like Johnson, Occom took advantage of his authority as a Christian minister to use it to articulate kinship that was built upon the foundation of a racial link. Like Johnson and Paul, the shared "Indian" identity between Occom the preacher and the condemned man Paul mediated their constructed relationship as "brothers." The ritual of this constructed kinship came from the public performance of Occom's deliverance of the execution sermon.

Ritual kinship worked to link Paul both to Johnson and to Occom in yet another way. Beyond bonds as "brothers," the two preachers each assumed a paternal, savior role in relation to Paul. This role derived, on the one hand, from the pastor–supplicant relationship each man created with Paul. The ministers' performances of caring for and advising Paul before and at his most desperate hour would have been what the greater public would have expected as such actions on the part of the ministers generally followed the script of late eighteenth-century practices concerning crime and punishment. The accused's wrongdoings were clearly articulated by a moral authority figure to the public, the accused was then admonished for these transgressions, he was advised to repent, and then he was punished. All of this was based on the theory that such performances would help heal the society from the disruptions of the accused's particular criminal acts through the exacting of publicized ritual justice.[16] On this front, Johnson and Occom played their parts.

On the other hand though, the ministerial roles the two men assumed in regard to Paul were informed by and followed another logic: that of savior to the captured. Most Algonquin peoples Native to southern New England had similar traditional practices relating to the ability of a captor to "save" a captive after that captive had undergone some form of public torture ritual. The torture ritual was meant to destroy the captive's identity. The captive would assume a new identity if he was saved from death. This salvation moreover would connect the captive to his savior by making the savior the one who figuratively gave "life" to the captive person. This giving of life could in some cases lead to the captive's incorporation into the savior's larger extended kin group, particularly if such incorporation was deemed to be helpful or ameliorative to some form of imbalance within the group. The captive's new identity, in other words, could be one that aided the savior's larger kin group. By the late eighteenth century, groups like the Mohegan were no longer engaging in captive raiding and torture, but the understandings of kin that such rituals had in the past manifested were not entirely gone. Consequently, Paul was not a torture victim plucked from imminent death by Johnson and Occom, but the underlying logic that he was, at the moment of his impending death, made a new kin member to a savior figure so as to benefit the savior's kin was in force.

Consider reading Johnson's and Occom's actions along the lines of the aforementioned torture ritual script rather than just seeing their behavior as mimicking the dominant society's punishment practices. First, both Johnson and Occom opened their performances by expressing admonishment and shame for Paul and his discretions. For instance, Occom stated to Paul: "Remember that you have deserved a thousand deaths . . . by reason of your sins."[17] These actions were denigrations of the old Paul. They were verbal not physical assaults. However, both men next took care to express concern for Paul. They then each made it clear that he would not abandon Paul, but on the contrary demonstrated that he would stand by him and provide aid regardless of Paul's culpability. They played, in other words, the role of savior to Paul. And Paul too assumed his role as the spared captive. He obeyed each of his savior's or his "father's" wishes. For instance, at Johnson's urging, Paul, in the short autobiography he authored before he died, publically admitted his culpability for the killing[18] of Moses Cook and he repented for his wrongdoings. He also followed Occom's advice and accepted the consequences of his misdeeds by playing his role as the doomed but repentant condemned man who dutifully listened to the accounting of his misdeeds during his execution sermon and his walk to the gallows.

But most important was the culminating act in this neo captive–savior ritual. Johnson and Occom would use Paul and his new identity as the repentant and "saved" captive in order to help "Indians" or their larger extended kin group. This is one major reason why each man spent energy and time cultivating a relationship with Paul and ensuring that their relationships with him were publicized. That they desired to reach larger audiences is clear from the fact that Johnson and Occom published and disseminated the central documents (Occom's execution sermon, Paul's autobiography, and Johnson's letter to Paul) generated by the case. The form of ritual kinship Johnson and Occom employed to build their relationships with Paul facilitated their ability to more easily reach and be of benefit to a larger Indigenous audience. They used the Paul case as an instructive example to other Natives of what "Indians" should or should not be.

Johnson, for instance, clearly wanted Paul's individual act of repentance to speak to a broader Indigenous audience. Johnson pleaded with Paul to "repent and believe" so that he could "bring forth fruit meet for repentance." On the surface, the fruit to which Johnson referred was the salvation of Paul's soul. "If you have JESUS CHRIST for your friend and advocate, it will be well with you after death and the second death will have no power over you," counseled Johnson. But Paul's repentance would also bear fruit for Indigenous peoples broadly, a proposition Johnson made clear by linking Paul's decision to repent or not to consequences for "Indians." "And be assured," he wrote:

> [that] if you fall short of heaven, into hell you must be turned: and I doubt not, but this is the earnest prayer and desire of many, who have a prejudice against the *Indian* nations . . . and [would] even rejoice that one of the devilish *Indians* (as many express themselves) are suffered to act such a part; and wish that all were as nigh their end.[19]

If Paul failed to accept Christ, he would be condemned to damnation, but the effects of his failure would be even more pernicious when viewed from a wider perspective. Paul's failure would affirm the racial beliefs of those who held "a prejudice against the Indian nations" and who wished that the Indians were "nigh their end." From Johnson's perspective, much was riding on Paul's choice as it was inflected with ramifications for the racialized environment of late colonial society — Paul would either lend credence to white racist beliefs in Indian moral inferiority and would thereby validate the settler colonial objective of the subordination of Indigenous peoples, or he would provide proof for Johnson's assertion that the "Indians" could be repentant and ethical. The hope was that the latter might influence and alter for the better non-Natives' conceptions of "Indians." The element though that made such connections between Johnson, Paul, and Indians relevant to the Indigenous audience Johnson wanted to instruct was the kin connections established between Johnson and Paul, and by extension Johnson and the "Indians." In this way the kin connection between Paul and Johnson established was meant to benefit Johnson's larger extended kin group, "Indians." The kin link was the reason why Johnson could use Paul and his new identity as a repentant "Indian" as an exemplar of the choice all "Indians" had to make.

This dynamic is clear from the way Joseph Johnson sought to paint Moses Paul as an example of the high moral standards to which "Indians" could adhere. He would use the violence of Paul's crime ironically to highlight the strength of "Indian" character. If Paul would "turn to Jesus" before his execution and thereby show genuine contrition for his killing of Moses Cook, it would act as powerful evidence that Natives possessed a strong moral compass. So Johnson's exhortations to Paul to repent, along with Johnson's ensconcing of the entire Paul case within a Christian cosmology, was more complex than one Native trying to get another to articulate what white Americans wanted to hear. Rather, it was a powerful yet nuanced effort to empower Natives by using a particular Native to recast the "Indian" through the kin relations Johnson established between them all. Moses Paul, in other words, had it in his power to demonstrate the moral proclivities of Indigenous peoples generally. And Natives in turn had the ability to prove him correct. In this way, Johnson, Paul, and "Indians" could all work toward decoupling the pairing white Americans commonly made between "Indian" and inherent moral depravity. "Indian" would be redefined as a moniker that denoted an ethical race whose presence in colonial society was not threatening. The creation of connections through ritual kinship was the foundational key to this strategy.

Occom likewise used Paul to speak to a Native audience in the hopes of convincing them to make choices that would improve their social standing. Again, what gave this strategy force among Native peoples was the ritualized kin connections Occom made between himself, Paul, and the larger Native community. Directly leveraging kinship by calling the Native audience of Paul's execution sermon "My poor Kindred," Occom counseled that Paul was an example of what "Indians" should not do. He stated: "You see the woful consequences of sin, by seeing this our poor miserable countryman now before us, who is to die this day for his sins."[20] Occom then argued that the collective decisions of Native peoples had contributed to the racial prejudices with which white Americans had labeled them. Using "drunkenness" as an example to prove his point, he explained: "This beastly and accursed sin of drunkenness. . . . By this sin we have no name nor credit in the world among polite nations; for this sin we are despised in the world."[21] Paul of course fit this description perfectly as he had been drunk when he killed Cook. Occom continued again using the language of kinship, "My poor kindred, God made us men, and we chuse to be beasts and devils; god made us rational creatures, and we chuse to be fools."[22] Kinship here functioned to give the correlation validity. Paul was not alone in his proclivity to make destructive choices, so too were his "kin," the wider Native population. But like Paul, his kin were also able to change course and create a more positive place for themselves. In this way, Paul's kinship to Occom was again a benefit to his wider kin, the "Indians."

The primary way, in other words, that the kin relations established among the Native actors examined here would be of benefit to them all was through using those relations to disrupt pejorative conceptions of "Indians" held by white Americans. Johnson and Occom exploited the normative juridical course through which the Paul case unfolded to provide a new characterization of "Indians" for a white audience. Johnson, Occom, and Paul acted not like "savages," but rather as rational Christian men who experienced shame, contrition, and for Paul, acceptance of the retribution required to pay for his erstwhile violent behavior. This was a picture of "Indians" that was designed to show that "Indians" could and did transcend the logic that whites had used to equate Indigeneity with "savageness."

To make this point, Occom used himself as an exemplar to convey to his white audience what "Indians" were. He cast himself as a rational and moral Native man in order to convey the idea that all Indigenous people had the same capacities. He began this process early in his sermon when he acknowledged the general prejudice that existed against Indians. "You are an Indian, a despised creature," he stated to Paul. Occom established a couple of key points with thus admonishment. First, he illuminated anti-Indian prejudice by pairing "Indian" and "despised creature," thereby recognizing the negative conceptualization of Indians that white Americans held. Second, he established his own rational and moral nature. Occom saw the logic behind why Paul had been condemned, and he readily perceived the ethical failing in Paul's actions. However, the remainder of the sermon was a performance that built up the themes of Indigenous capacity for rationality, contrition, and morality. Occom identified the reasons for Paul's predicament, explained why Paul had acted immorally, and through repeated arguments for Paul to "repent" and accept his fate, worked to show that Paul's culminating act of submission to death was proof of his contrition. By playing these roles, both Occom and Paul became incarnate examples of "Indians" who were rational and moral, so much so that Occom could assume the vital public duty of explaining ethical behavior and taking part in the execution of justice, and Paul could accept his fate. Occom no doubt understood these positions, and used them to disseminate to his white audience the notion that "Indians" had the same capacity as white Americans to hold and live by the virtues of rational thought and moral behavior.

Race and Modern Indigeneity

Both the Moses Paul case and Joseph Johnson's introduction to the Pequot show that Natives used race to navigate the social dominance white Americans wielded in late eighteenth century southern New England. When Johnson sought to become a resident preacher to the Pequot, Natives artfully subverted the authority and control of the Pequots' local white preacher. So while whites had developed a racial hierarchy designed to augment their authority and control over "Indians,"

Natives in this instance used an alternative perception of "Indian" that was based on ritual kinship and that worked to undermine the very power that white constructions of "Indian" were designed to place in the hands of white authorities. And in the Moses Paul case, we see an example of how Natives explicitly drew upon expressions of ritual kinship under the cloak of the performance of Christian duties in order to articulate a racialization through an alternative Indigenous construct of "Indian" that served their interests. The Paul case provided Natives with the opportunity to publicize a particular Indigenous conception of race that worded to undermine the racial edifice colonial society had built to subjugate Native peoples. Within the social, economic, political, and military contexts that had developed by the latter part of the eighteenth century, this was of tremendous significance because it showed that one way Natives lived as Indigenous people was through forging social bonds, primarily ritualized kinship, through an institution, race, that the settler society used to subordinate them. As such, race acted as an ambivalent construct. Settlers envisioned and used it as means to justify social dominance. Yet this was not all that was happening as Natives used this same construct in support of a degree of Indigenous self-determination.

These stories consequently reveal an important insight into modern Indigeneity under settler colonialism. Through the development of racialist thought, Natives participated in a quintessential element of the modern experience: they envisioned humanity in a way that subsumed diverse ethnic groups under the larger banner of race. Mohegan, Pequot, and other Natives were all "Indians." Racial thinking of this kind was modern, but because it used ritual kinship to create Native constructions of "Indian," it was also distinctly Indigenous.

Additional evidence of the intermixing of ritual kinship and race, again within the modern context of late eighteenth century Indigenous southern New England, can be found in other instances concerning Occom's attitudes toward race. It is well known, for example, that Occom maintained correspondences with Phillis Wheatley and with Phillis' owner Susannah Wheatley. Moreover, in such correspondence, Occom chastised ministers for holding slaves and advocated for the rights of enslaved people. Yet Occom also displayed attitudes that seemed complicit with black subordination. On one occasion in 1765, he asked Eleazer Wheelock to borrow "a negro girl," and on another he excoriated Wheelock for having "no Indians at present, except two or three Mollatoes," in his Charity School.[23] He also supported the Mohegans' denial of land rights to blacks living within their community. One possible explanation for the ambiguity in Occom's attitudes toward race may lie in kinship. More specifically, it was kinship more than, or at least in addition to, phenotype, which shaped Occom's understanding of race. One was fully "Indian" only through a combination of kinship and biological markers. Consequently, Occom could, on the one hand, generally support the rights of African Americans, yet, on the other hand, deny them those rights when they impeded on Mohegan rights specifically because blacks were not fully kin and therefore not completely Mohegan. And, Occom could accuse Wheelock of having no Indians, even though he had two mixed race or black Indians, because perhaps those "Indians" were only connected to a Native community through ties that were less substantive than kinship connections. Kinship, in other words, was required for belonging to "the people."[24]

***

For most white Americans, race had functioned to differentiate whites from Indians in a clear hierarchy in which Natives were subordinate. And for many white Americans, race reified the supposed inferiority of Indians by casting that inferiority as an inherent and inheritable trait. Race therefore proved quintessential to how whites conducted the work of settler colonialism by justifying in their eyes the subjugation and eventual dispossession of Indigenous people. But though these attitudes would help underwrite the horrors of colonialism on the American scene, it is vital to remember that Natives did not simply accept these racist attitudes, nor did they meekly submit to the racism they faced. Rather, they engaged in efforts to use race to their advantage. In this light, our understanding of the Brothertown project[25] takes on new meaning. Brothertown was the culmination of Indigenous people from several different ethnicities coming together as "Indians" to create a new community. Rather than just a reaction to the racial prejudice of white Americans in which Natives sought protection for themselves by voluntary removal, Brothertown was also a constructed community of "Indians" and a physical manifestation of Native efforts to live as Indigenous people, both under empire and within the increasingly racialized, settler colonial context of the late colonial period.[26] It was a manifestation of Native attempts to navigate the potency of colonization with an end goal of giving Natives, rather than just whites, some power and authority to determine what Indigenous communities would be within a settler colonial environment. This is exactly what Johnson and the Pequots were doing, and what Johnson and Occom were enacting through the Paul case. Brothertown was an outgrowth of the same idea. So the founding of Brothertown should not be read simply as Native capitulation to, or a doomed Native effort to avoid, settler colonialism. Rather it was the product of a strategy designed to facilitate Native ability to improve their immediate future and to reproduce themselves under persistent settler colonialism. From this perspective, Brothertown reveals a reemergence of an Indigenous people born from the Indigenous belief in the power of social bonds formed in ritual kinship (hence the name Brothertown) and expressed beneath the settler colonial environment under which they lived.

Race acted as a vital medium of this process. Natives came together as "Indians" so as to negotiate the subordination of Natives that settlers sought in part through white understandings of "Indians." Lisa Brooks has argued that in earlier times, land (or place) was the primary mediator of the interconnections between Native communities and between families, leaders, and individuals within a given Native community. In her words: "Native understandings of land 'rights' were always relational. Native land tenure was rooted in the interdependent relationship between a community and its territory. Families had particular relationships to hunting and planting grounds within the village territory."[27] By the time of the migration to Brothertown, the ravages of colonialism had made it extraordinarily difficult for the Mohegans and other Natives in southern New England to use land to facilitate and maintain such relationships.[28] Race filled the void and took over this function by becoming the medium through which Natives connected to each other in interdependent and interconnected kin relationships. This process, in which Natives used ritual kinship to produce a different racial understanding of themselves as "Indians," was in this case vital to the regeneration of southern New England's Indigenous people.

Notes

1. For a discussion of Natives as racial thinkers, see David J. Silverman, *Red Brethren: The Brothertown and Stockbridge Indians and the Problem of Race in Early America* (Ithaca, NY: Cornell University Press, 2015). Silverman argued that by the latter quarter of eighteenth century, the many southern New England tribes that would eventually comprise the Brothertown Indians viewed themselves as racially distinct from Anglo-Americans. According to Silverman, these various groups of Indigenous peoples coalesced into a new discreet unit by bridging their ethnic differences through the development of a racial ideology that neatly delineated peoples along lines of red, white, and black.
2. When I write of race here, I do not refer to Mohegan understandings of race as a universal category that applied to humanity broadly or to different racial groups like black and white. Rather, the Mohegan notions of race examined in this chapter refer to Mohegan understandings of the Native peoples they encountered in the northeast.
3. This is why we see evidence of ritual kinship's centrality in words such as "brethren" and "kindred" that Natives used when employing racial discourse or talking about "Indians."
4. See Laura Murray, ed., *To Do Good to My Indian Brethren: The Writings of Joseph Johnson 1751–1776* (Amherst, MA: The University of Massachusetts Press, 1998).
5. See Ibid., 152.
6. Ibid., 154–5.
7. Other scholars have made similar points. Scott Lyons, for example, in *X-Marks: Native Signatures of Assent* (Minneapolis, MN: University of Minnesota Press, 2010), has argued that scholars should reject the idea that "Indian" and what it signified was solely a product created by whites. I concur with this position.
8. The Day Book of James Whitney, M-35, Box 1, Archive Collection, Mattatuck Historical Society, Waterbury, CT.
9. "Moses Paul, Sketches of His Life and Character, collected chiefly from his own Mouth," in Samson Occom, "A sermon, preached at the execution of Moses Paul, an Indian; who was executed at New-Haven, on the second of September, 1772; for the murder of Mr. Moses Cook, late of Waterbury, on the 7th of December, 1771: Preached at the desire of said Paul," no. 12910, Evans Early American Imprint Series I, Evans 1639–1800, Readex, America's Historical Newspapers, https://docs-newsbank-com.uri.idm.oclc.org/openurl?ctx_ver=z39.88-2004&rft_id=info:sid/iw.newsbank.com:EAIX&rft_val_format=info:ofi/fmt:kev:mtx:ctx&rft_dat=0F2FD32CE0C13548&svc_dat=Evans:eaidoc&req_dat=1BBE3C44083D49AAB2957FA37457B25A. Accessed February 28, 2020.
10. For the history of this type of racialization of Natives, see Jill Lepore, *The Name of War: King Phillip's War and the Origins of American Identity* (New York: First Vintage Books, 1999); and Peter Silver, *Our Savage Neighbors: How Indian War Transformed Early America* (New York: Norton, 2009).
11. Moses Paul to the Superior Court of New Haven, August 26, 1772, in "Hang the Indian, Hang Him, Hang Him: The Sad Tale of That Christian Indian Moses Paul" (Waterbury, CT: The Mattatuck Historical Society, 1946). Found in the Mattatuck Museum Archives, Attic, wall shelf, the Indian Moses Paul, Mattatuck Museum, Waterbury, CT.

12. Letter from J–h J–n, one of the Mohegan Tribe of Indians, to his Countryman, Moses Paul, under Sentence of Death, in New-Haven Goal," March 29, 1772, Readex Digital Collections, Archive of Americana, Early American Imprints, Series I. Evans 1639–1800, number 12496. http://infoweb.newsbank.com
13. Ibid.
14. Ibid.
15. Samson Occom, "A sermon, preached at the execution of Moses Paul, an Indian; who was executed at New-Haven, on the second of September, 1772; for the murder of Mr. Moses Cook, late of Waterbury, on the 7th of December, 1771: Preached at the desire of said Paul," Evans Early American Imprint Series, Evans TCP, https://quod.lib.umich.edu/e/evans/N09814.0001.001?rgn=main;view=fulltext, 21. Accessed January 27, 2020.
16. For a discussion of executions as performance in eighteenth-century America, see Michael Meranze, *Laboratories of Virtue: Punishment, Revolution, and Authority in Philadelphia, 1760–1835* (Chapel Hill, NC: University of North Carolina Press, 1996).
17. bid., Samson Occom, "A Sermon, Preached at the Execution of Moses Paul," Evans Early American Imprint Series, Evans TCP, https://quod.lib.umich.edu/e/evans/N09814.0001.001?rgn=main;view=fulltext, 22. Accessed January 27, 2020.
18. Moses Paul always maintained his contention that he did not murder Moses Cook, but rather acted in response to aggressive actions Cook had taken toward Paul earlier in the evening.
19. Johnson, "Letter of J–p J–n to Paul."
20. Ibid., Occom, "A Sermon, Preached at the Execution of Moses Paul," 28.
21. Ibid., 29.
22. Ibid.
23. For Occom's request for the labor of an African-American girl, see Samson Occom to Eleazer Wheelock, October 4, 1765, manuscript number 765554.2; and for his displeasure with the lack of Native students, see Samson Occom to Eleazer Wheelock, July 24, 1771 manuscript number 771424; both letters can be found online through *The Occom Circle*, https://collections.dartmouth.edu/occom/html/diplomatic/785554-diplomatic.html, Dartmouth College, Hanover, NH.
24. Other scholars have closely examined Occom's understanding of race. Katy Chiles, for instance, produced a comparative study of Occom's and Phillis Wheatley's conceptions of race. She argued that they both utilized the idea of the malleability of race, particularly its ability to be shaped by the environment, in their constructions of racial understandings. Moreover, for Occom and Wheatley, the ability of the environment to affect the body helps explain the existence of racial difference. See Katy L. Chiles, "On Becoming Colored in Occom and Wheatley's Early America," *Periodical of the American Language Association (PMLA)*, 123, no. 5, Special Topic: Comparative Racialization (October 2008), 1398–1417. More recently, Geoff Hamilton has characterized Occom's racial understanding along lines similar to my own. He has argued that Occom centered relationality as key to Native ability to acquire positive liberty (freedom that originates from the interconnections between people). He refers to the ethics based upon the relationality between people, as well as the relationality between people and nature, as eunomics. He further argued that Occom is an early example of Indigenous writers who from the eighteenth century to the present have drawn on eunomics to pursue self-determination and ultimately resurgence. See chapter 1 of Geoff Hamilton, *A New Continent of Liberty: Eunomia in Native American Literature from Occom to Erdich* (Charlottesville, VA: University of Virginia Press, 2019).
25. This process would mature in the 1830s when the Brothertown Indians would seek and then acquire US citizenship. Ultimately, the Brothertown would develop new and complex identities. The process in which the Brothertown Natives developed identities as both Indigenous peoples and Americans has been well chronicled by Brad Jarvis. See Brad D.E. Jarvis, *The Brothertown Nation of Indians: Landownership and Nationalism in Early America, 1740–1840* (Lincoln, NE: University of Nebraska Press, 2010).

26. This is similar to the same basic point that Silverman makes in *Red Brethren*, in that we both see Brothertown as evidence that Natives had developed their own racial thinking. However, Silverman sees Indian racial thinking as derived from Euro-American precedents, specifically he has argued that Christianity acted as the glue that brought Indians together as a race. I differ from Silverman in that I see ritual kinship as just as important to Natives' racial thinking as was Christianity.

27. Lisa Brooks, *The Common Pot: The Recovery of Native Space in the Northeast* (Minneapolis, MN: University of Minnesota Press, 2008), 68.

28. I am not arguing that land entirely fell by the wayside in acting to link people, communities, and place. Indeed, Brooks finishes the chapter from which the preceding quotation is taken by explaining how Mohegan women continued to use ritual to reaffirm the connection between the Mohegan and their land. I am simply arguing that race became another medium, and for those Natives who left New England to migrate to Oneida land perhaps a more potent medium than land, through which to make and maintain relationships between Native individuals and communities.

2 Servants of God, Masters of Men

Slavery and the Making of a Native–White Alliance, 1816–1859

The Mohegans' weaving of ritual kinship into racial constructs of "Indian," and their consequent use of race as a surrogate medium for "the land," reflected adaptations unique to the specific context of late colonial southern New England. However, the general outlines of their actions were not indicative of a unique strategy. Similarly complex processes linking Native ontological understandings, non-Native institutions, and land unfolded in other settler colonial contexts. The basic pattern in which an Indigenous group planted a seminal Native concept within a non-Native construct was replicated among other Native peoples during the nineteenth century. For the Cherokees and the Choctaws, the institution of slavery (particularly black slaveholding) would house efforts to create and maintain alliances with white missionaries who in the mid-1810s would come to reside within the Cherokee and Choctaw nations. As such, a host of connotations — including reciprocity, gift-giving, and belonging — that were embedded within the Cherokees' and Choctaws' larger conceptualizations of alliance would play out within the concrete practices of slaveholding and slave trading that occurred among and between the Cherokees, Choctaws, and missionaries. And while forged within the medium of slavery, the alliances were nonetheless directly connected to the "land" in important ways. The Cherokees and Choctaws created them in large part because they wanted resident white allies who could help protect diminished and threatened Indigenous land bases. Moreover, in these cases, the relationship between alliance and geography shifted in comparison to earlier time periods. Alliances had often brought together different peoples who generally resided in separate places. Alliances linked people of one area to the people of another. For the Cherokees and Choctaws examined here, alliance still connected distinct groups — Natives and missionaries — but did so *within* the territory of the Indigenous group hosting their missionary allies. In other words, the primary purpose of the alliances was for the defense of the very places upon which the relationships between allies were created and maintained. Despite the more restrained geographical space upon which the alliances developed, and despite slavery's vital domiciling role to the alliances, the fundamental concept brought to bear by the Cherokees and Choctaws concerning what an alliance was and what its purpose was essentially remained the same as it always had been. It was simply a rearticulation of an Indigenous concept that was (re)applied within a settler colonial environment. For the Cherokees and Choctaws, alliance connected them to missionaries through their shared interests both in slavery and in defense of their remaining lands.

***

In 1816 Cyrus Kingsbury wrote to Samuel Worchester to apprise him of his dealings with the Cherokees and Choctaws. Both men worked for the newly formed American Board of Commissioners for Foreign Missions,[1] a missionary organization dedicated to Christian evangelism. Kingsbury had traveled south in the hopes of opening missions to Native tribes. In his letter to Worcester, he reported that he had already approached the Cherokees and informed them that the American Board wished to establish missions and schools. One chief responded in an exceptionally enthusiastic manner exclaiming "that they [the Cherokees] wished to have the school established and hoped they would be of great advantage to the nation."[2] After this generous welcome and a similarly positive reception from the Choctaws, both tribes agreed to Kingsbury's request to create missions within their territories. Over the following months, Kingsbury built on this initial success and opened an American Board mission among the Cherokees in 1816 and another among the Choctaws in 1817. These new "mission stations" usually comprised a church, a school, farms, a staff consisting of four or five missionaries (and sometimes their families), two or three teachers, a doctor, and laborers. In these stations, missionaries regularly preached sermons to Native adults, and taught elementary literacy and mathematics to Cherokee and Choctaw children.

Native slave owners were instrumental in facilitating the founding of these missions. One reason why stems from the fact that they lent their human property to the newly arrived American Board preachers. Cyrus Kingsbury's experience in opening the Cherokee mission illuminates the point. When Kingsbury arrived to the Cherokees, he was given "a negro boy and girl" by a Cherokee slave owner. A week after his arrival, he returned the children due apparently to his initial discomfort with the employ of slave laborers. However, he soon found that he could not manage without the slaves. He returned to the Cherokee family who owned the children and in the youngsters' place acquired two adult slaves, one to tend his garden and the other to clean house. Only by securing these workers would Kingsbury have the time and energy to gather a congregation and begin preaching.[3] Literally from their inception, the Native–white partnerships born in the missions would grow, in part at least, upon the backs of an enslaved black population.

The institution of slavery, in its both black chattel and Native-captive incarnations,[4] served as a vital medium through which the Cherokees and Choctaws maintained alliances with the missionaries. Indigenous ontological conceptualizations of alliance and its concrete connotations loomed large in the context of the Cherokees' and Choctaws' connections to the American Board missionaries. Both Indigenous groups welcomed the missionaries despite the paternalistic, patronizing, and assimilatory motivations behind their presence because they sought allies who could support their interests particularly as they related to land and to relations with the United States. On one level, slavery and the alliances it facilitated provided the grounds upon which the preachers would come to *belong* in the Cherokee and Choctaw nations. The goals of all allied groups would align in their shared interests in slaveholding, making them peoples linked through the practices — slavery — and the objectives — the ongoing protection of slaveholding — they held in common. Thus, the American Board missionaries were welcomed by Cherokees and Choctaws not because they had accepted the Board's "civilization" schemes, but because the Natives saw them as allies.

These allies moreover would be subject to Indigenous understandings of the reciprocity that undergirded all alliances. On the macro level, the alliances the Natives created with the missionaries through the institution of slavery would be leveraged to push missionaries to act on behalf of Cherokee and Choctaw interests in exchange for the missionaries' continued presence among the Cherokee and Choctaw peoples. On another level, Natives used slavery to shape their relations with the preachers in ways that would work to ensure that the power dynamics between them worked in favor of the Natives. Cherokee and Choctaw masters took advantage of their position as slaveholders to augment their power by using their black and Native slaves to diminish the degree to which they were subject to the missionaries' evangelism. Native masters further augmented their power by serving as the preachers' primary suppliers of both black and Native slaves. Again in return, Natives asked that the missionaries act as allies in Native political struggles to retain land. All of this was made possible because the missionaries were dependent on slavery. Not only would they continually earn and re-earn their place among the Cherokees and Choctaws through their involvement in slavery, but the missionaries desperately needed the black slaves Natives initially "loaned" or "rented" to them as they provided essential labor that the missions used to operate. This labor freed the missionaries to preach to their Native hosts. Eventually, the American Board missionaries would become outright owners of slaves, principally because they discovered that slavery facilitated evangelism. In retaining black slaves, missionaries possessed a ready pool of potential converts who could not escape repeated entreaties to accept Christianity; and in the Native captive slaves they would come to hold, they found candidates that could be trained as auxiliary ministers whose purpose was to preach to Natives living on the western frontiers of the Cherokee and Choctaw nations.

The sociopolitical context of the mid-1810s helps explain why the Cherokees and Choctaws warmed to the American Board's initial overtures to open missions. For the Cherokees and Choctaws, the War of 1812 had poignantly revealed that the integrity of Indigenous communities, the ability to maintain possession of their lands, and the viability of tribal sovereignty would increasingly depend on how Natives negotiated relations with the aggressively expanding United States. Some Native leaders advocated for well-worn strategies like voluntary removal or Indigenous nativism that had been used to contend with land-hungry settler societies during the late colonial period. Despite the passionate voices of those who touted the benefits of these strategies, Cherokee and Choctaw leaders increasingly sought to build cooperative relations with particular white Americans whom they believed could be leveraged as useful allies in Indigenous efforts to contend with the ever more powerful United States. Often the formation of such relationships found impetus in the Natives' ostensive collaboration with the various "civilization" plans advocated by American evangelicals. But again, the root explanation for Native openness to these "improvement" schemes lies not in their capitulation to them, but in their hope that they could gain important allies in white reformers, and thereby augment their political power. By 1815 many prominent Cherokee and Choctaw leaders concluded that they could best secure their respective societies through this strategy. This of course proved fortuitous for the eager American Board preachers, but nonetheless, the primary reasons for the missionaries' presence would stem from Indigenous interests that would be pursued through Indigenous understandings of intergroup relations.

Because Natives used slavery as the medium through which they built alliances with the American Board missionaries, their relationships would be complicated by the fact that they would ultimately intersect with the central political problem of the nineteenth century. More specifically, the Native–missionary alliances would significantly affect how the national slavery debate manifested in the Cherokee and Choctaw nations. Because both Natives and missionaries found that their involvement with slavery directly intertwined with their other vital interests — for Natives, land; for missionaries, evangelism — their alliance would work to thwart the expression of antislavery in Indian country. Cherokee and Choctaw elites would leverage their ownership of black slave property to strengthen their claims to land ownership, arguing that as owners of human property they were entitled to remain owners of landed property. They reinforced this position by linking themselves to the greater South and then claiming that their rights as southern slaveholders extended not only to their human but also to their landed property. With Native possession of land so intertwined with their involvement with slavery, they simply would not brook the eruption of antislavery sentiment from their own people or within their nations. This meant, of course, that they would also not permit the missionaries to express any support for antislavery. As the national debate over slavery intensified in the 1830s and 1840s, Native slaveholders pressured the missionaries to suppress any hint of antislavery within the missions or to the Natives those missions served. And because missionary interest in evangelism was so tightly tied to slavery, they readily complied. These particular circumstances surrounding Native slaveholding in the late antebellum period consequently provide one important explanation for why the Cherokees and Choctaws would initially side with the Confederacy when the Civil War erupted — they linked the protection of slavery to their ability to maintain possession of their lands.

The intersection between slavery and colonialism that occurred within the Cherokee and Choctaw nations of the antebellum era produced variants of processes that previously unfolded in other colonial contexts. Slavery, for example, had served in other instances as an important medium for Indigenous negotiation of colonialism. During the colonial era and at times when Natives and Euro-Americans were more or less on an equal power footing, Native peoples often worked with colonizers and used slave systems and slave trades to pursue their interests.[5] The case of the Cherokees and Choctaws demonstrates slavery's centrality to Indigenous efforts to build alliances with colonizers after the establishment of a settler state and after the power balance had shifted decidedly in favor of settlers. In addition, scholars have noted that in the Native nations of the antebellum American South, slavery was vitally important relative to Indigenous "citizenship."[6] In our examination, we see a similar connection between slavery and notions of belonging. For the Cherokees and Choctaws, ownership of black slaves functioned to reinforce Indigenous belonging in the greater South because it connected them to the South's defining social practice. And for the American Board missionaries, their ownership of black slaves linked and aligned them directly with those slaveholding Native elites who hosted them in their communities. The preachers' precarious status as non-Native outsiders was trumped by their involvement in an institution that Native elites had identified as vital to their place in the South. Slavery, in other words, justified the places of the Cherokees and Choctaws within the South, and it supported the presence of the American Board missionaries with the Cherokee and Choctaw nations. Finally, like others have demonstrated, black slavery inside the Cherokee and Choctaw nations worked to reinforce an emergence of anti-black racism among the Cherokees and Choctaws, a racism that increasingly equated blackness with enslavement.[7] In this study, this process is most evident in those efforts the Cherokees and Choctaws undertook to quell the emergence of antislavery sentiment within their respective nations.

Black Slavery and the Opening of the American Board
Cherokee and Choctaw Missions

When the American Board opened its Cherokee and Choctaw missions, both tribes were already thoroughly involved in black slaveholding. They had acquired black slaves in a number of ways. Some Cherokees, such as James Vann, had inherited slaves from white relatives.[8] Tiya Miles has also shown that in the late eighteenth century, the Cherokees still used captive-taking to obtain black slaves.[9] Indeed, captive raiding for black slaves continued in the early nineteenth century. An 1815 article published in the *Daily National Intelligencer* shows that the Cherokees raided the plantations of southern whites for black slaves. The practice seems to have been sufficiently common to elicit attempts to redress it. The article reported that one George Hite of Virginia had petitioned Congress "praying compensation for a number of negroes stolen from his father by the Cherokee Indians."[10] Presumably, Natives also purchased black slaves from white slave traders.

Cherokee and Choctaw entanglement with slavery required the American Board missionaries to define their relationship to the peculiar institution immediately upon arrival in the South. As one missionary put it: "When we came here, the [slavery] question with us had ceased to be a speculative one. It was a practical one. Necessity was laid upon us to learn the desired mode of treating it, for slavery was among the Choctaws."[11] Defining their relationship to slavery was not an easy task as slavery generated controversy among the preachers. Most of the American Board missionaries hailed from New England and many arrived in the South harboring some degree of antislavery sentiment. Yet they soon found that slaves were the only viable source of the labor required to open and run the missions. Though it rattled the sensibilities of some of their brethren, American Board preachers ultimately responded to the presence of slaveholding among the Indians by incorporating slavery into mission life.

The missionaries relied on black slaves because the labor demands of the missions were simply too great to be met solely by the preachers and those who attended them. The intellectual labor — preaching and teaching in the schools — was tackled by missionaries and teachers. But in addition to this work, the missions required continuous house and field labor. People had to till the fields, plant and harvest crops, while still others needed to cook and clean. Missionaries, their spouses, assistants, and a few volunteers from the North attempted to do some of this work, but the reality was that the missions needed to acquire laborers. In this situation, the missions turned to slave labor. A report from the Choctaw mission made this link explicitly clear.

> The early missionaries were called to make it [slavery] a subject of inquiring and prayer. . . . The large boarding school establishments & other multiplied & constant labors, in a hot & sickly climate . . . made the employment of considerable slave labor indispensable.[12]

Natives were the source of this "indispensable" pool of slave labor. Cherokee and Choctaw masters did not simply give slaves to the missions, but rather rented their slaves to the missionaries. So vital in fact were these slaves to the missions that the missionaries and Natives devised ways to make the Indigenous-owned slaves available over long periods. It appears that they initially created agreements that approximate what we today would call a lease — missionaries would rent slaves from Native masters, generally for periods of 6 or 12 months.[13] Between the opening of the missions and the mid-1820s, this system would expand throughout the American Board's southern mission stations, reaching as far as the mission among the Cherokee "Old Settlers" in present-day Arkansas. By this time however, the missionaries were formally "hiring" slaves to labor for them.[14] "Hiring" meant that the missionaries would not only arrange to rent the labor of a slave from his Native (or sometimes a white) master, but that they would also make an agreement with the "hired" slave as to what work he or she would do. Discussing mission slaveholding with the Board's Corresponding Secretary Jeremiah Evarts, Cephas Washburn of the Western Cherokee mission explained in 1826 that "It is known to you that at this mission, as at all others among the southern Indians, we have employed blacks, who are in a state of slavery."[15] Cyrus Kingsbury referenced the same practice engaged in by missionaries stationed among the Choctaws. On April 12, 1826, he sent the American Board a list of laborers hired to work at the mission's central station at Mayhew. It contained 13 workers, four of whom were black slaves. These slaves had been "hired" from both Choctaw slaveholders and white masters who lived adjacent to the Choctaw nation. "Joe a black man . . . [and] his wife" were the property of a white military officer and worked "for $120 a year and their cloths." Two single female slaves also labored for the missionaries. "Fanny, a black woman" was "the cook" and worked "for $8 a month and her clothes." The other was "Hannah, a black woman," who was the property of "an Indian" and worked for "$8/month," washing dishes, setting tables, and milking the cows.[16] The missionaries had turned to black slaves to meet their labor demands. The lack of other available laborers meant that they had but little choice. The missions could remain operational, in other words, only because Cherokee and Choctaw masters provided them with the labor resources they needed.

Black Slavery and Native–Missionary Relations

Their ability to offer the missionaries desperately needed slaves held a host of advantages for the Cherokees and Choctaws. First, as masters, Natives were able to cast their relationship with the missionaries as a partnership rather than as a hierarchical arrangement based on Indigenous subservience. Unwilling to accept the chauvinism embedded in the whole mission enterprise, the Cherokees and Choctaws went out of their way to demonstrate the decisive importance that obtaining their support and cooperation played in the viability of the missions. They would show that the continued operation of the missions depended directly upon Native willingness to supply slave labor. And because the missionaries were indeed so reliant on slaves, the ability of Cherokee and Choctaw masters to offer slave laborers recast and leveled the balance of power between the Natives and missionaries.

Native masters found various ways to strategically use their human property to their advantage, particularly in regard to the power dynamics governing Native–missionary relations. For instance, Indians forced their slaves to attend church, thereby providing the missionaries with a ready and captive congregation to whom they could preach. In the early years of the missions, Native masters, with their slaves in tow, congregated before the missionaries to listen to sermons. Cyrus Kingsbury reported that on a violently stormy Sunday in February of 1818, "9 or 10 blacks, & about as many Cherokees" came to church.[17] By bringing their slaves to church, Native masters demonstrated how vital they were to the mission project. Without their active assistance the mission churches would not have been filled, which would have left the missionaries with far fewer souls to save. Indigenous masters in effect doubled the missionaries' dependence upon them. The missionaries relied on the Cherokees and Choctaws to provide black bodies for labor and black souls for conversion.

Natives leveraged their power as masters in yet another way. They used their slaves as an intermediary source to learn English, rather than learning English through attendance at the mission schools. Instead of seeking language instruction from their American Board guests, Native masters and their relations often learned to read and speak English from the slaves they enrolled in the schools. This is one reason why black attendance at the schools is so conspicuous in mission records. In June 1818 one mission journal recorded that a Cherokee woman was "learning how to read" through her slaves.[18] In August of that same year, it was reported that a "full blood Cherokee youth applying for admission to the school was found to spell correctly in words of 4 or 5 letters." The journal further recorded that "he had been taught solely by black people who had received their instruction in our sunday-school."[19]

The inherent and significant power Natives wielded as masters is readily apparent in this phenomenon of learning English through slaves. Through the control they held as masters, Natives were able to lessen the power imbalance between themselves and missionaries that in part derived from the latter's command of English literacy. By having their slaves educated and then by learning from them, Native masters found a route to English literacy that bypassed the missionaries, which of course meant that Natives were not directly dependent on them for access to education. Just as importantly, it allowed Natives to acquire a skill that the preachers had used to assume a position of social superiority to their Indigenous hosts. Both developments complicated the quotidian interactions between Natives and missionaries by making the social hierarchy of the minister–neophyte relationship less clear-cut. This was to the Natives' advantage as it meant that they had more agency in their dealings with the preachers. If Natives could read the Bible themselves, for example, they could formulate their own interpretations of it instead of having to simply accept whatever meanings the missionaries proffered. More broadly and perhaps more revelatory of the Natives' larger goals, when Indigenous masters and their kin became conversant with the written word, it empowered them in relations with other white Americans. For instance, they would be in a much more advantageous position to use written correspondence in diplomacy or treaty negotiations with state governments and with the US government by virtue of the simple fact that they could read and write English.

Just as Cherokee masters leveraged their black slaves to help them learn English, they also used them to become more well-versed in Christian doctrine. Again, they did so in order to strengthen their position in relation to the missionaries. Only three months after the opening of the Cherokee mission, Cyrus Kingsbury reported that "the blacks are much engaged" in Sabbath school.[20] And in December 1818, the mission's official journal recorded that "the Cherokees in general . . . are very willing their slaves should receive religious instruction."[21] Such willingness on the part of Cherokee masters did not come from any sense that they were obligated to provide their slaves with religious instruction, but rather derived from the desire to use their slaves as a means to deepen their familiarity with Christian theology. By exposing their slaves to Christianity, Cherokee masters deflected and diffused the power the missionaries wielded as religious mentors precisely because they disrupted the preachers' monopoly of knowledge of Christianity. Moreover, by shifting their knowledge source on Christianity from white missionaries to black slaves, the Cherokees gained significant flexibility to negotiate the degree of their involvement with Christianity. They did not have to learn about the religion by only attending the missionaries' sermons, but could do so through their slaves who in essence went to extracurricular church services, like Sunday school, in their masters' stead.

The manner in which Native masters used their slaves in connection to the missions reflects manipulation of a world whose ontological basis remained — for the Indigenous peoples who inhabited it — relational. This conceptual paradigm manifested concretely in Native efforts to place them in more advantageous positions relative to the missionaries via particular uses of their slaves. Through the medium of black slaveholding, Native masters leveraged the master–slave relationship in order to reshape the Native–missionary one. Indigenous black slaveholding was consequently not simply a Native replication of the system that white owners of black slaves practiced in the greater South. Rather, for Native masters, black slaveholding operated as a medium for directly acting upon the interconnected relationships that structured the world. This is made clearer by recognizing how the phenomenon operated through a variety of linked social contexts.

For one, it often manifested at the level of the Native household. Natives brought their families and slaves with them to the mission churches, they learned to read English in their homes through the tutelage of their slaves, and they enhanced their understanding of Christian doctrine through knowledge passed to them in their homes from their slaves who had attended Sunday schools. The personal nature of these exchanges within Native homes suggests the ongoing presence of kin-like relations between Native masters and their black slaves.[22] This is not to state that there always existed defined kinship relations between Native masters and black slaves; but rather that the exchange of knowledge between master and slave occurred on an individual and therefore intimate level that flowed through the Indigenous household. These intimate exchanges, because they were explicitly designed to benefit Indigenous masters in their dealings with missionaries, directly connected to the larger intergroup relationships between Natives and the American Board personnel. And these relationships, by virtue of Native understandings of missionaries as allies who could be leveraged to support Indigenous interests vis-à-vis the settler society, in turn connected directly to Indigenous relationships with the United States. What the cases investigated here therefore show is that Native efforts to garner power, ultimately in relation to an expansive United States, and more immediately in relation to missionaries, flowed through black slaveholding. The Indigenous acquisition of power reaped through the medium of slavery, moreover, was expressed in both a larger inter(national) political context and smaller household and interpersonal contexts that occurred inside Native homes and between Natives and their missionary guests.

Indian Captivity and the Native–Missionary Alliance

Just as black slavery mediated Native–missionary partnerships, so too did another form of slavery: the institution of Indian captivity. And just as both Natives and missionaries used black slavery in service of their interests, likewise did they each exploit captivity for their own ends. Through captive gift-giving, Natives worked to strengthen their missionary alliance so that the preachers would feel a greater weight of obligation to help defend Native lands from appropriation by white Americans, and the missionaries used captivity to once again support their evangelical efforts.

By giving captives as gifts to the missionaries, Natives sought to obligate the American Board missionaries to more readily defend Cherokee and Choctaw lands. Both the Cherokees and Choctaws attached significant social value to captive gift-giving. Traditionally, the act of giving away captives placed the giver and receiver of such gifts into a reciprocal relationship in which each party was obligated to meet the needs of the other when it was in their power to do so.[23] Therefore, the underlying reason that the Natives would give captives was because in accepting them, missionaries placed themselves into a position of obligation to return the favor in some fashion. Natives could cite captive gift-giving as reason why the missionaries should repay them by helping to defend lands. This became particularly important during the 1820s as attempts to take Native lands increased. For example, the Cherokee chief Pathkiller hoped that the missionaries would directly intercede in the Natives' political fight against Georgia's attempts to acquire Cherokee lands. On May 7, 1823 Pathkiller paid a visit to the missionaries and explained that he was "night and day grieved for his children," whom he feared would be forced to remove by the state of Georgia, which would "take this little last [land]" and leave his children destitute. It is more than probable that Pathkiller believed the missionaries had an absolute duty to respond to his request for aid against Georgia's attempts to take land because, in part at least, the preachers had previously accepted the Cherokees' captives.

Though there are not exact numbers on how many captives the Natives provided them, the existing evidence shows that it was not uncommon for the Cherokees to give the missionaries captives. Once offered, the missionaries would accept these captives into their care, give them English names, and then enroll them in the mission schools and churches. Several cases illuminate this practice. In September 1818 the Cherokees captured a 4- or 5-year-old Osage girl[24] and gave her to the missionaries, who then renamed her Lydia Carter. She was later baptized at Brainerd mission station and lived there until her death three years later.[25] In December 1818 another Cherokee man had obtained an Osage captive and subsequently "would leave this boy with us [the missionaries]."[26] In addition, John Ross (eventual Principal Chief of the Cherokee Nation) acquired and then quickly gifted an Osage captive to the American Board missionaries in 1818.[27] And in 1826, missionary and physician Marcus Palmer informed Jeremiah Evarts of the death of yet another Osage captive the missionaries had had in their care.[28]

Besides placing the missionaries in a position in which they would be duty bound to reciprocate the Indians' favors, Natives used captive gift-giving to manage their relationships with the preachers. One way they did so was by giving captives with the intention of smoothing over tensions and restoring "good feelings." For example, in 1817 the important Cherokee leader, Major Ridge, offered the missionaries a captive to redress the misbehavior of his children.[29] Ridge had placed his son and daughter in the mission school at Brainerd station and had subsequently heard that they had acted defiantly toward their teachers. Over a dinner, he asked the missionaries about his children's behavior. "I hear," he stated, "that my children were so bad." He then added, "I have brought a little Loosa [Creek] girl, which I took in the war a prisoner, and design to leave her."[30] From Ridge's point of view, his offer to give the Creek captive to the missionaries was atonement for any offense caused by his children's actions. The girl was meant to heal the Cherokee–missionary relationship by paying for the insult suffered by the teacher.

If Natives had an agenda in supplying captives to missionaries, the preachers had their own reasons for accepting these "gifts." In Indian captivity, the missionaries perceived an opportunity to extend the reach of evangelism. For one, captives represented promising prospects for conversion. After all captives were removed from their families, homes, and cultures, and were consequently less able to resist efforts to alter their beliefs. In addition, captives were often young. The American Board missionaries had long believed that children were more susceptible to conversion as they had not grown as attached to the "customs of their fathers." This logic helps explain why every captive the missionaries mentioned as under their "care" was a child.

Beyond a supply of ready converts, missionaries took in Indian captives because they believed them useful in expanding the reach of evangelism, specifically to other Natives. The zeal of the American Board missionaries did not end with the Cherokees or Choctaws. They looked further afield, planning to infiltrate tribes farther west. Their hope was that Native converts would provide the manpower for this ambitious goal by serving as the vanguard of a growing evangelical project that would reach tribes on the frontier. Ideally these converts would come from those western tribes in which the missionaries hoped one day to establish roots. Their vision was that the captives, whom they had raised and converted, would soon serve as missionaries and interpreters to tribes the American Board had in its sights. In 1826 at the annual meeting of the southern American Board missions, a resolution was drafted that read:

> Resolved that it is desirable that a competent number of Indian youths from the principal unevangelized tribes be procured & placed in circumstances to qualify them to become missionaries or to act as interpreters & teachers of their own language to missionaries & that measures ought, as soon as practicable, to be taken for the accomplishment of this object.[31]

Because the captives they received generally came from those "unevangelized" tribes living on the western borders of the southern tribes among whom the missionaries resided, the captives the Cherokees and Choctaws had taken from nations like the Osage represented the most accessible pool from which to draw the "Indian youths" the preachers wanted. In the captives offered by their Native hosts, missionaries perceived prime candidates who would serve as future agents of the Gospel.

The intersection of Native and missionary interests within the system of Indian captivity ultimately reaffirmed and strengthened their alliances. In fact, it led to extraordinary instances of Native and missionary cooperative action. For example, in 1819 the Cherokees had sold a captive Osage boy to a white slave trader.[32] Missionary William Chamberlin learned that the slave trader had subsequently sold the boy to another white man. Chamberlin became anxious that the boy would fall into "perpetual slavery" and brought his concerns to the influential Cherokee leader, John Ross. Ross pledged that he would reacquire the boy and soon received written permission from President Monroe to enter the United States and — for all intents and purposes — steal the boy. After going to great effort to locate him, Ross and "two assistants" found the boy 250 miles from the mission, where he was lying "entirely naked in the yard before the house" belonging to his new master. They boldly retrieved the boy and after bringing him back to the mission, noted that the boy "appear[ed] delighted with his new situation."[33] After the Cherokees retrieved and returned the boy, the missionaries quickly pointed out that they could now educate and convert him. Chamberlin's concern and the daring raid of three Cherokees worked hand in hand to produce another captive soul for the missionaries to convert.

Natives as Traders of Black Slaves

While Natives had used their ownership of both black and Indigenous slaves to shift the power dynamics between themselves and the missionaries during the early years of the missions, a change in the missionaries' relationship to slavery would reinforce slavery's central role in the Native–missionary alliance. The missionaries would become owners, rather than renters, of black slaves. And with this change, the Cherokees and Choctaws would become the missionaries' primary suppliers of black slaves.

The genesis of the missionaries' shift to slave ownership was ironically the unease some missionaries experienced due to the missions' reliance on black slave labor. The missionaries hailed from New England with some arriving to the South harboring a degree of antislavery sentiment. This caused problems as disagreements arose between missionaries who found themselves caught between their need for labor and the antislavery sympathies of some of their brethren. Discomfort with the use of slaves, for example, led the missionaries to the Choctaws to take the extraordinary step of proposing the closure of the mission schools as a way to reduce labor demands. "The last vote was passed to diminish the schools at the end of the present year, provided we cannot otherwise dispense with slave labor," reported Kingsbury.[34] Despite such efforts to wean themselves from slavery, the missionaries' larger debate over slaveholding would culminate with the decision to purchase slaves. Kingsbury reported that the "unhappy division of sentiment & feeling among ourselves, as to the propriety of hiring slaves" had been removed, and that "[t]he brethren at this station have considered the subject, all approve."[35] The subject they all approved was the purchase of slaves.

The missionaries reasoned that in becoming masters, they would be in a stronger position to help slaves. They could more easily and forcefully proselytize to their slaves, giving them access to religious instruction. Thoughtful slaves could thereby leverage their servility to enhance their odds of obtaining grace. And as an additional bonus, the missionaries could offer slaves a promise that eventually they would enjoy freedom on Earth. Preachers envisioned a gradual emancipation process in which a missionary would purchase a slave by entering into a contract with the slave's current owner. As a condition of purchase, the slave would agree to work for a number of years until he or she had paid the price of his or her purchase, plus interest. In effect, the missionaries viewed the purchase of a slave as a loan to the enslaved person that would be repaid with the enslaved's own labor. When a slave had worked for the requisite years (often around seven) needed to repay his debt, he would be free to leave or to continue to work on the mission as a "hired person." Cyrus Kingsbury reasoned that it would take a slave "6 to 8 years" to repay his or her price, and remarked that this process could be repeated until the missionaries "ultimately became the owners of all the slaves [they] might need to hire."[36] The missionaries would foster what they viewed as symbiotic rather than exploitive master–slave relationships in which the preachers would have access to needed labor and the slaves would be rewarded with religion and freedom.

But as a result of this development, the American Board preachers became more deeply reliant on Native slaveholders. They began to more assertively seek out Indian slaveholders from whom they could make purchases of slaves. As an 1837 report on slaveholding practices in the missions explained:

> The manner of accomplishing it [buying slaves] was briefly and substantially this, The missionary learned that some person holding slaves was willing to part with one: after ascertaining the sum demanded and making a liberal estimate of the annual value of the slave's labor, deducting the necessary expenses, he would go to the slave, acquaint him fully with the labors, treatment & privileges to be expected at the station, and then ask him whether he was willing to labor there a specified number of years, perhaps five or six, at the expiration of that time, if indeed he might become a free man? It was virtually proposing and advancing the money for the slave, with which he might purchase his own freedom.[37]

Because the majority of people "holding slaves" would have indeed been Native slave owners, the Indians became the de facto slave traders to whom the missionaries turned for their supply of slaves.

Even when Native masters had not initially wanted to "part with one" of their slaves, they could often find themselves selling a slave to the missionaries because of the machinations of their slaves. Some slaves perceived a better future for themselves under missionary, rather than Native, masters because of the preachers' promises of emancipation. Slaves holding such feelings would approach a missionary to initiate a sale. For example, Cephas Washburn explained in his journal that he had purchased a slave who had "begged" to be rescued from his "cruel" master. The slave claimed that his Cherokee master was "opposed to religion" and "unwilling" that slaves receive instruction in spiritual matters. This clever slave must have known that his case would win Washburn's sympathy. Washburn was indeed all too willing to take advantage of the situation and buy the slave. After acquiring this slave, Washburn rejoiced that he could bestow upon him both "the rudiments of education" and the ability to "enjoy the means of grace."[38] And according to Cyrus Kingsbury, he too obtained his slaves on account of their desire to leave their Native masters. In 1845 he wrote a letter to David Greene, the then Corresponding Secretary of the American Board, explaining his personal history as a slaveholder. Kingsbury reported that he had become a slaveholder on the insistence of slaves he had initially rented from Native owners. His first slave, Hannah, had "requested that I purchase her, as she did not wish to return to her owner." Likewise, George Freeman, Kingsbury's second slave, "was very desirous that I should place him in a situation to obtain his freedom." The third slave Bartley had "wished to be at a place where he would be comfortably provided for, and where he could enjoy the advantages of religious instruction." According to Kingsbury, the slaves had sought him out because they believed he could give them freedom, religion, or better conditions than did their current Native masters.[39]

By using evangelism to slaves as justification for their decision to become masters, missionaries doubled their reliance on Indigenous slave owners. Not only did missionaries need Natives to supply them with labor in the form of slaves, but now they also relied in yet another way on Native masters to funnel them new souls to convert. In this way and with little effort on their part, slavery placed Natives into an even more advantageous positions vis-à-vis the missionaries. Moreover, now that Natives and missionaries were both masters, their interests in the peculiar institution aligned and intertwined. This would be consequential as Native slaveholders worked to block the emergence of antislavery within their nations.

To Thwart Abolition

The vital utility that both Natives and missionaries found in slavery would produce a significant and far-reaching consequence. Native slaveholders, along with the American Board preachers, would work to stop the emergence of abolitionist[40] sentiment within the Cherokee and Choctaw nations. Their actions help us to better understand why abolitionism did not materialize among two southern constituencies — northern evangelicals residing in the southwest, and non-elite Natives — whom we might consider primed by preexisting beliefs and interests to support abolition. After all, we have already seen on the one hand that during the 1820s some American Board missionaries were deeply troubled by the missions' involvement with black slavery. The missions' progression from renting to purchasing slaves derived in part from attempts to assuage anxieties over slaveholding.[41] On the other hand, the vast majority of Cherokees and Choctaws were not owners of black slaves, and it seems plausible that many might have easily warmed to abolition. They could have perceived abolition as a means to undercut the power of white southern planters who were a significant force behind Removal. Or, they might have wanted to prevent further alignment of Cherokee and Choctaw interests with that of the dominant settler society, which of course had been responsible for the horrors of Removal. But abolition manifested among neither the Natives nor the preachers. The primary reason was because Native slaveholders, who also usually held political power within the Cherokee and Choctaw nations, perceived abolition as potentially injurious to Indigenous capabilities to protect the new western lands that they had come to occupy in the post-Removal era. And missionaries, who feared jeopardizing evangelism by alienating politically powerful Native slaveholders, likewise refused to support antislavery.

The interplay between Native and missionary motivations for their respective anti-antislavery positions surfaced repeatedly throughout the antebellum era. From the mid-1830s until the eve of the Civil War, Native slaveholders would continuously push the missionaries to rebuff repeated attempts by American Board officials in the North to introduce antislavery into the Native nations. For example, in 1836 the American Board made its first substantive move against slavery when it passed a resolution that directed the missionaries to emancipate those slaves in their personal possession. The resolution drew impassioned responses from the preachers who asserted that the adoption of any form of abolition on their part would threaten evangelism by straining missionary relations with Native slaveholders. In a letter to the Board, Cephas Washburn, James Orr, and Aaron Gray explained that missionary slaveholding was vital to maintaining the political support of Native leaders in both the Cherokee and Choctaw nations. They asserted that Native political leaders were on the verge of becoming "bitterly opposed to the Indian missions" due to their fear that the missions would become conduits for northern abolitionism. The preachers warned that "it would not greatly surprise us, if the resolution in question should be the occasion of removing many if not all of the missionaries from the southwestern Indians."[42]

Given the resistance of their own missionaries in the field, the Board backed down, but by the 1840s it made renewed attempts to push abolition upon the Indians. In 1845 the then Board's Corresponding Secretary David Greene penned letters to both the Cherokee and Choctaw missions inquiring about "the prospects as to the abolishment of slavery" and "what impediments [stood] in the way of emancipation."[43] The missionaries' response to Greene bespoke the reality that Native slaveholders remained steadfastly opposed to any missionary involvement with abolition. As Superintendent of the Choctaw mission, Cyrus Kingsbury responded to Greene on behalf of both the Choctaw and Cherokee missions. Making his point as clearly as possible, he wrote that "[a]s missionaries, we cannot interfere directly with the subject of slavery." And reflecting the proslavery position of Native slaveholders, he added: "There can be no prospect of benefiting the slave, in a slave country, without the consent of the owner." He went on to advise that if the missionaries were to make any strides toward the amelioration of the "evils of slavery" within either the Cherokee or the Choctaw nations, they would only do so through collaboration with Native slaveholders.[44]

Not entirely convinced that it could not push the Natives toward abolition, the Board considered resolutions designed to alienate Native slaveholders from the mission churches if they refused to work toward eventual emancipation of their slaves. However, Native slaveholders would weather this assault by again prompting their missionary allies to intercede on their behalf. They warned the missionaries that the resolutions would harm their evangelical efforts. When the missionaries conveyed this message to the Board, it voted down the resolutions explaining that any official action on its part against slavery would destabilize missionary–Native relations and thereby alienate the very people the Board was hoping to convert. Secretary Greene wrote that because "these resolutions, if adopted by the Board, might be used by unfriendly persons, to embarrass the missionaries, and prevent their exerting the salutary influence which they might otherwise exert, in relation to slavery, they were not adopted by the Board."[45] The "unfriendly persons" Greene referenced could have only been Choctaw and Cherokee slaveholders. Yet Greene did not fully relent. He instructed the missionaries

> that you should do whatever you can, as discreet Christian men, and missionaries of the Lord Jesus, to give the Indians correct views on this subject [slavery], and to induce them to take measures as speedily as possible to bring this system of wrong and oppression to an end.[46]

Though given direct instructions, the missionaries simply did not comply with these requests. They would not jeopardize evangelism by espousing abolitionism to Native slaveholders.

During the latter part of the antebellum period, Native slaveholders and missionaries would continue to stand together against the Board's ongoing attempts to push for abolition. For instance, in 1848 the missionaries drafted a letter to the Board and again explained that they could not promote abolition.

> Of late years the subject of slavery has awakened a deep & growing interest in the minds of a large number of our best friends & patrons in our fatherland. . . . [W]e have been often told that a great change has taken place at the North & that we have not kept pace with the change. . . . And we wish that you & all our friends here & elsewhere to be assured that we feel much more pleasure and satisfaction in the hope of doing masters & servants good by preaching the Lord Jesus directly to them, than we can in explaining & enforcing the prominent principles of equal rights. . . . We feel that the Bible contains all that we have need to know or teach. And we prefer to use the plain language of the bible just as it is upon the subject of slavery to any other code of principles or plans of operation.[47]

The missionaries acknowledged that northern attitudes about slavery had greatly changed, and that many northerners thought they were out of touch with the depth of antislavery sentiment felt by many of the Board's supporters. However, they asserted that they were "doing good" for slaves and slaveholders in the most effective manner possible. In the slaveholding Native nations, Native slaveholders constituted a powerful interest that could neither be bullied nor ignored. More to the point, maintaining the goodwill of slaveholders was vital to the evangelism that formed the missionaries' primary objective. They were simply unwilling to risk undermining it for the sake of abolition. "We should be careful how we risk the spiritual interest committed to us by attempting to manage worldly ones," warned the preachers of the Choctaw mission.[48]

And in 1854, the preachers counseled against a Board decision to bring up the subject of abolition with the Choctaw National Council. They explained that Choctaw slaveholders "generally urge no objection against the Board or its missionaries, except as relates to the subject of slavery." They warned that if the Board were to broach the subject of abolition, then Choctaw slaveholders would paint the mission as a politically threatening northern entity.

> But should the [Board] bring the subject before council, in a way that will bring about a discussion on slavery, there is strong ground to apprehend that it would be productive of no good result. It would be represented by those favorable to slavery, as a political movement, gotten up by *northern* people, to establish an Abolition community in the Choctaw nation.[49]

Kingsbury added that "I think the Choctaws generally will have no objection to the continuance of the mission of the board among them provided the slavery question is not agitated."[50] The reality was that the now decades old Native–missionary alliance was inextricably interwoven with slavery, and neither politically potent Native slaveholders nor the missionaries would jeopardize it by entertaining any discussion of antislavery.

In addition to ensuring that the missionaries neither embraced antislavery nor let the Board push for it, Native slaveholders made other more direct efforts to prevent the emergence of antislavery sentiment within the Cherokee and Choctaw nations. The following is one example from the Cherokees and one from the Choctaws that highlight these efforts.

By the late 1820s, the Cherokee were already making attempts to undercut antislavery. We have evidence of this from the pages of the *Cherokee Phoenix*.[51] In 1828 the Phoenix published a didactic poem designed to instill or reinforce acceptance of slavery by its Cherokee readers. The poem entitled "Pity for Poor Africans" asserted that though lamentable due to the severity of suffering it caused blacks, slavery was nonetheless an unavoidable fact of modern life. The poem recognizes black suffering in its opening stanza:

> What I hear of their hardships, their tortures, and groans,
> Is almost enough to draw pity from stones.

However, the rest of the poem then proceeds to develop two arguments that illuminate the futility of antislavery sentiment. The first argument explains that those who benefit from slavery would not be willing to give up what it provides them:

> I pity them greatly-but I must be mum-
> For how could we do without sugar and rum? . . .
> What, give up our desserts, our coffee, tea?

Here the author makes the venal and cynical argument that he must dismiss any qualms he might feel about slavery because he, and others as well, would not be willing, nor should they be asked, to go without the luxuries (sugar, rum, coffee, and tea) produced from slave labor.

The poem's second argument likewise characterized antislavery sentiment as impotent. It was equally cynical, asserting that even if some stood against slavery, there would be several others who would carry on the business of enslavement. Antislavery could never work until all stood against slavery and this, according to this poem's author, would not come to pass. After the poem poses the question of "What, give up our desserts, our coffee and tea?" it continues by answering:

> Besides, if we do, the French, Dutch, and Danes,
> Will heartily thank us, no doubt, for our pains;
> If we do not buy the poor creatures, they will,
> And tortures and groans will be multiplied still.

Antislavery was but a noble fantasy because the scruples of a few would never be matched by everyone involved in slavery. Ongoing black suffering would be the end result of a minority of ethical crusaders acting on their morals. Plus, why should the Cherokees give up their access to luxuries for a lost cause?

> But, while they get riches by purchasing blacks,
> Pray tell me why we may not go snacks?[52]

The cynicism of this argument looms large: the foregoing of self-indulgence on moral grounds alone was silly in a context in which self-sacrifice would not produce concrete results. The message of the poem was clear. It told its Cherokee readers to make their peace with slavery despite any qualms they may have toward it as acting on those feelings was ultimately futile. In this way, the poem served as a powerful instrument working to contain any emerging antislavery sentiment.

Attempts to subvert antislavery also manifested within the Choctaw nation. Cyrus Kingsbury's personal experience with the prominent Choctaw slave-holder, Israel Folsom, illuminates the pressure Choctaw slave owners could exert to ensure that no abolitionist ideas would be expressed in their nation. In 1848 Folsom wrote to Kingsbury explaining that he was leaving the mission church because he feared the church's stance on slavery. "I think on the whole it will be best for me and [my] wife to form a connection with some other church whose sentiments are one with us on slavery."[53] Folsom knew that the missionaries were not founts of antislavery, but his paranoia[54] that they might bend to pressures to raise the question of abolition led him to take preemptory action. His behavior was tactical and calculated. He initially played on Kingsbury's fear of Native abandonment of the church. He then gave Kingsbury a clear way to prevent such an outcome by explaining that he could be dissuaded from this course of action if Kingsbury could prove that he harbored no abolitionist leanings. Folsom asked him if he would "make private and individual efforts to abolish slavery?"[55] To this Kingsbury replied that he would only "teach the Gospel." But this was not what Folsom wanted to hear. Three weeks later Folsom again wrote to Kingsbury, this time directly embedding the difference between himself and the missionary within the broader sectional cleavages over slavery that had solidified in antebellum America. "I am convinced," he wrote, "that there cannot be any prospect of our agreeing on this subject at all." He then added that

> [we so] widely differ in our views on the slavery question, that I do not see how we could all remain in one church. . . . I find that you are more of a northern man and intermeddle yourself too much about the abolition doctrine.[56]

Folsom then once more struck directly at Kingsbury's underlying fear by warning that any hint of church support for abolition would drive the Choctaws from Christianity. "[Y]ou will . . . stop the good work of God, by chilling the hearts of the Choctaw christians, who were just beginning to improve in the christian religion," thundered Folsom.[57]

It is important to point out that while the aforementioned exchange is an example of a Choctaw slaveholder working to squash the potential expression of abolitionism by a white man, Choctaw slaveholders must have taken similar actions to thwart abolitionism from taking hold among their own people. We have indirect evidence of this from missionary records. In 1848 Choctaw mission personnel issued a statement on slavery to the Board. They explained that there was a "but a small portion of the Choctaws interested in slavery . . . but [that] the influence of these few is great in the Councils of the Nation."[58] Choctaw slaveholders must have used that influence to ensure that their non-slaveholding brethren would toe the line on slavery. Ten years later, Cyrus Kingsbury confirmed that the political situation in the Choctaw nation remained much the same. He wrote: "If an unbiased vote could be taken on slavery or no slavery, there would be three to one against it."[59] The implication was that Choctaw slaveholders, though a minority, still wielded sufficient power to ensure that the Choctaw nation assumed a proslavery, anti-abolition position despite the fact that the majority of Choctaws, 75 percent according to Kingsbury, held at least nominally antislavery positions.

The message of the "Pity for Poor Africans" poem and the actions of Israel Folsom raise the question of why some Cherokees and Choctaws, particularly those who held political power, would have assumed an anti-abolition stance. The answer lies beyond the protection of the economic benefits Native slaveholders realized from the peculiar institution. Leaders in both the Cherokee and Choctaw nations linked their involvement with slavery to enhanced ability to stay on their lands. They reasoned that their support for and involvement in black slavery would lead powerful constituencies of white Americans to protect Indigenous land interests. This stratagem proved politic as white Americans in the antebellum period would explicitly tie Native possession of land to Native slaveholding.

We see clear evidence of this dynamic in the emerging debates surrounding Cherokee removal. In the same volume in which the *Cherokee Phoenix* published "Pity for Poor Africans" (and in fact coming immediately after the poem), a paper also published an anti-Removal speech that Congressman John Woods[60] of Ohio had delivered to Congress.[61] This speech directly linked Cherokee hold-ing of black slaves to the argument that they should remain on their lands. At one point, Woods referenced a conversation he had had with Congressman James Meriwether[62] in which the Congressman had cited the salutary benefits of Natives owning black slaves. "'The only way to elevate the Indian, is to give him prop-erty.' He said, 'give an Indian a slave, and he at once becomes a man.'" Woods then built on Meriwether's argument by adding "I say give him property much more valuable — give him the rights of a freeholder and a citizen." Cherokee ownership of slave property was a stepping stone to freehold possession of land. In this instance, Woods argued that the "elevation" of the Cherokees rested on securing their lands, not on removing them from those lands. In another part of the speech, Woods explained:

> Industry and commercial enterprise are extending themselves in every part of the country. Nearly all the merchants in the country are Native Cherokees. Agricultural pursuits engage the chief attention of the people. . . . The census taken this year (1825) shows that there are 13,563 Native citizens; 147 white men and 73 white women are married into the nation; and they have 1277 African slaves. . . . I ask gentlemen, why we should remove them from this situation?

Such arguments that intertwined slaveholding, land ownership, and Native "improvement" were not lost on Cherokee leaders and served to strengthen their resolve to prevent the emergence of antislavery among their people. The Chero-kees' holding of black slaves was one important piece of evidence that proved that they were "civilized" people who had the right to remain on their lands.[63] Cherokee elites would not jeopardize this advantage by brooking the emergence of antislavery among tribal members.

The connection between Native slaveholding and land possession became even more intense in the later antebellum period when slavery debates were reaching a fever pitch. Some white southerners even came to view the Natives as allies against aggressive northerners. Less than a year before the outbreak of the Civil War, the *Arkansas Weekly Gazette* published a letter to the editor that cast the pro-tection of the Cherokees from abolitionists as an act of protection for the greater South.

> But if they think the abolitionizing of eleven hundred Cherokees, the steady progress of aggression Southward, and the increasing (illegible word) of fanaticism, . . . something must and will be set on foot, be it what it may, adequate for the defence of the South.[64]

And a few years earlier, another concerned southerner drew an explicit connec-tion between Native land possession and the Indians' anti-abolitionism. He wrote: "The country of the Cherokees, Creeks and Choctaw is a stronger incentive to quick and vigorous action." The author was referring to the link between efforts to check the spread of abolition and Native possession of their lands. He was arguing that if abolition ever succeeded in spreading into the Native nations of Indian Territory, then their lands must be annexed by Texas, Arkansas, or some other southern state. "The possession [by which the author meant annexation] of this country is advocated only on the contingency of the further inroads and spread of abolitionism. . . . To appropriate it on any other grounds would be wrong and unjustifiable," he wrote. In essence, this author explained that Native possession of land hinged on Indigenous opposition to abolition. If the Indians continued to fight abolition, then not only would they continue to possess their lands, but they would also be accorded the same "rights" as other southerners. The author continued,

> Yet, after all, should the abolitionists enact the miracle of refraining from their foul practices and interference in slavery affairs in the nations, the Indians should be guarded and respected in their rights as if citizens within the jurisdiction of any State of the South.[65]

In other words, Natives would enjoy "citizens' " rights if they proved, through their defense of slavery, that they belonged to the greater South. Finally, to drive home the point he added, "In Georgia, Alabama, Mississippi, and Tennessee, the Indians were Southerners by locality; they became assured as such by practice, for they bought and worked slaves at an early day, and have continued to do so to the present." This meant that white southerners should continue "defending the Indian country against abolition encroachments because of a common feeling for Southern rights."[66] The remarkable calculus developed by this writer — that through their ownership of black slaves Natives had reinforced their rights as southerners and that those rights should be protected by the greater South — was again not lost on Native leaders. This is why Native slaveholders had worked so diligently against antislavery. To protect their lands, Native slaveholders would do all they could to ensure that blacks remained enslaved in the Indigenous nations of Indian Territory.

This in combination with the degree to which Natives and missionaries were successful in containing abolition also explains the fear northern abolitionists expressed relative to the growth of Native slaveholding. By the late 1840s, the American Board, for instance, was receiving numerous memorials from its northern constituency that argued against continued mission slaveholding. In one such memorial, the authors feared that the missionaries had become "propagators of a slaveholding Christianity."[67] To these memorialists, it seemed that the missionaries were teaching Natives that they could embrace God and slavery simultaneously. The effects of such a lesson would be to delude the Indians and to spread the evil institution that was slavery. In the years leading up to the Civil War, abolitionists would continue to lament or fear the presence of slavery among the Indians. For example, Lewis Tappan worried that the Indian nations would spread slavery. Referring to the Choctaw nation, Tappan attacked the American Board because he feared that "a slave state was about to be inaugurated . . . under the auspices of the Missionaries of the American Board."[68] And an 1859 article in the *Christian Inquirer* asked what would become of the Native nations in Indian Territory as the "tide of [white] population is steadily rolling West?" The article explained that the Indians could not be removed again, nor could "Indian States exist" within the United States. The "greatest interest" upon this question though was the fact that the Natives had "adopted the social institutions of the South." To clarify, the article ended ominously with "The Indians are slaveholders."[69] This implied that as the US population moved west in greater numbers, the Native nations of Indian Territory would need to be officially incorporated into the United States as slave states. Obviously, this posed a more than worrisome problem for northerners concerned that the Native nations would only add to the power of the southern slaveocracy. That they were as worried as they were reflected, in part at least, the success Natives and missionaries had achieved in preventing the growth of antislavery within the Native nations.

Conclusion

By the eve of the Civil War, slavery among the southern Native nations had a long and complex history. For our purposes, what is most important is that slavery served as the medium in which Indigenous understandings of alliance would materialize. The rooting of Indigenous conceptualizations of alliance within slavery also however reverberated back to the ultimate source of Indigeneity, the land itself. Natives initially sought the missionaries as partners because they believed they could serve as important political allies who could help them maintain possession of their lands. And during the debate over Removal, the missionaries would work diligently to protect Native land. Indeed, the American Board staunchly opposed Removal and it was Board missionaries who were instrumental in the two famous Supreme Court cases (*Cherokee v. Georgia*, 1831 and *Worcester v. Georgia*, 1832) that would have far-reaching consequences for legal conceptions of Indigenous sovereignty and Native lands.[70] In this way, the alliances functioned as Natives had intended.

This history concerning alliance, slavery, and land would have consequences later as the sectional crisis came to a head. During the antebellum period, Native slaveholders continuously worked to protect slavery and in so doing aligned themselves with the South. Their hope was that by throwing their weight with the slaveocracy, they would protect themselves from further land dispossession. This history in which Natives would fight antislavery, would make sure their missionaries allies do the same, and would cast their lot with the South and its peculiar institution coalesced, and in sum provides an important explanation as to why the Cherokees and Choctaws sided with the Confederacy during the Civil War. The protection of slavery fomented by Natives in their partnerships with missionaries during the early nineteenth century was, in this light, an important antecedent to Cherokee and Choctaw efforts in the late antebellum era to define their national sovereignty in relation to their holding of black slaves.

But there is one more important insight to be gained from this story. This has been a narrative of Native efforts to protect Indigenous land under empire. This goal intersected profoundly with slavery as Natives used their position as slave-holders in a variety of ways to work toward this objective. When we consider this process from a wide perspective that takes into account the different strands of the story thus far told, we can see a significant relationship between black slavery and settler colonialism. That is, the exigencies of colonialism experienced by Native peoples reinforced the enslavement of blacks, at least in the Cherokee and Choctaw nations. This does not refer just to the economic benefits masters reaped from black slavery. Rather, it signifies that the exigencies born from a colonial project that targeted Indigenous people with cultural imperialism and land dispossession ultimately solidified commitments to black slavery on the part of rather unlikely constituencies. Missionaries, in service to their Native allies, and as fanatical devotees to evangelism, would repeatedly and emphatically dedicate themselves both to slaveholding and to shielding slavery from the assaults of abolitionism. And Natives, desperate to retain possession of their lands by proving to white Americans that they were "civilized" precisely because they owned slaves, would similarly devote themselves to the protection of slavery. For black Americans, the end results were the same. The demands that emerged out of a crucible forged from white America's efforts to colonize Natives, and from Indigenous maneuvers to negotiate those efforts, each served as vectors that led a cadre of Native American slaveholders, and their allied white American preachers, to dedicate themselves to the ongoing enslavement of American blacks.

Notes

1. The American Board of Commissioner for Foreign Missions was first formed in 1810.
2. Cyrus Kingsbury to Sam Worcester, October 15, 1816, ABC 18.3.1 v. 3, American Board of Commissioners for Foreign Missions Records, Houghton Library, Harvard University, Cambridge, MA.
3. Journal of Cyrus Kingsbury, January 28, 1817, ABC 18.3.1 v. 2, American Board of Commissioners for Foreign Missions Records, Houghton Library, Harvard University, Cambridge, MA.
4. Historians of the antebellum era have explored the ramifications of slavery on the Cherokee, the Choctaw, or on the black slaves these Natives held. See Circe Strum, *Blood Politics: Race, Culture, and Identity in the Cherokee Nation of Oklahoma* (Berkeley, CA: University of California Press, 2002); Fay Yarbrough, *Race and the Cherokee Nation: Sovereignty in the Nineteenth Century* (Philadelphia, PA: University of Pennsylvania Press, 2007); Barbara Krauthammer, *Black Slaves, Indian Masters: Slavery, Emancipation, and Citizenship in the Native American South* (Chapel Hill, NC: University of North Carolina Press, 2015); and Christina Snyder, *Great Crossings: Indians, Settlers, and Slaves in the Age of Jackson* (Oxford, UK: Oxford University Press, 2017).
5. Brett Rushforth, for instance, has explored how Native and Atlantic slave systems were linked during the colonial era. He has explained that Native peoples in the pays d'en haut used slavery and their particular understandings of slavery's social connotations to build and then shape alliances with the French in New France. The offering of Native slaves by an Indigenous group to the French worked to build alliances with New France, while Natives slave raiding of the French served to demonstrate Native displeasure with French efforts to categorize all Natives peoples together and to build simultaneous alliances with Native groups that were foes to each other. Slavery consequently helped Indigenous peoples exert power and influence within the colonial

context of seventeenth- and eighteenth-century New France. See Brett Rushforth, *Bonds of Alliance: Indigenous and Atlantic Slaveries in New France* (Chapel Hill, NC: University of North Carolina Press, 2014). And Alan Gallay has detailed how a series of Indigenous groups leveraged slavery to their advantage in the colonial American South. He argued that a succession of Natives peoples migrated into the American south over the course of late seventeenth to early eighteenth centuries. Migrant groups like the Westos and Yamasees worked to displace other Natives and then to dominate the lucrative Indian slave trade that had developed after the founding of the Carolina colony. See Alan Gallay, *The Indian Slave Trade: The Rise of the English Empire in the American South, 1670–1717* (New Haven, CT: Yale University Press, 2002).

6. A host of scholars have examined how slavery intersected with understandings of belonging within colonial contexts. Tiya Miles has explored how the Cherokees' holding of black slaves was, in the early decades of the nineteenth century, inflected with notions of kinship. This led some black slaves and their descendants to claim Cherokee citizenship. See Tiya Miles, *Ties That Bind: The Story of an Afro-Cherokee Family in Slavery and Freedom* (Berkeley, CA: University of California Press, 2006). Others have noted that the Cherokees increasingly linked slavery to blackness during the nineteenth century, which led to the exclusion or subordination of black Cherokees within Cherokee society. See Circe Strum, *Blood Politics: Race, Culture, and Identity in the Cherokee Nation of Oklahoma* (Berkeley, CA: University of California Press, 2002); Fay Yarbrough, *Race and the Cherokee Nation: Sovereignty in the Nineteenth Century* (Philadelphia, PA: University of Pennsylvania Press, 2007); Barbara Krauthammer, *Black Slaves, Indian Masters: Slavery, Emancipation, and Citizenship in the Native American South* (Chapel Hill, NC: University of North Carolina Press, 2015).

7. Tiya Miles has noted this process in her study of the Vann family involvement with black slavery. She has argued that as the nineteenth century progressed, the Vann's became more entrenched in the southern plantation complex in which black slave labor produced capital accumulation. As this process gained steam, rival logics concerning Indigenous conceptions of slaves as possible kin increasingly waned. See Tiya Miles, *The House on Diamond Hill: A Cherokee Plantation Story* (Chapel Hill, NC: University of North Carolina Press, 2012). Alan Gallay has argued that the Yamasee War not only more or less ended the Indian slave trade, but just as importantly ushered in a new economic paradigm predicated on the labor of black slaves on cash crop plantations. He saw the end of the Indian slave trade as consequently vital to the beginning of the Old South. See Alan Gallay, *The Indian Slave Trade: The Rise of the English Empire in the American South, 1670–1717* (New Haven, CT: Yale University Press, 2002). And Brett Rushforth has argued that Britain's triumph over France in the French and Indian War (the North American branch of the Seven Years' War) had the important ramification of strengthening the argument in the French Caribbean that blacks were racially fit for slavery. Previous to the War, Native slaves from New France had been traded to French Caribbean colonies, which meant that the racial makeup of French Caribbean slaves was not monolithic. In this context, proslavery ideologues had relied on arguments like the just-war doctrine to defend slavery. These arguments had produced what Rushforth called "counter narratives" to racial justifications for slavery. The result of the War however cut off the supply of Native slaves to the French Caribbean once Britain took over French possession in Canada. This left mostly black slaves in the French Caribbean. In this environment, the logic that blacks were racially fit for slavery and its corollary that Natives were not racially fit for enslavement blossomed. See Rushforth, *Bonds of Alliance*.

8. See Miles, *The House on Diamond Hill*.

9. See Ibid.

10. "House of Representatives," *Daily National Intelligencer*, January 6, 1815, 3, no. 625, 2, Washington, DC, available through Early American Newspapers, America's

Historical Newspapers, https://infoweb-newsbank-com.uri.idm.oclc.org/apps/readex/welcome?p=EANX

11. Missionaries to the Choctaw to the Prudential Committee of the American Board of Commissioners for Foreign Missions, March 31, 1848, Folder 8, Item 53, Cyrus Kingsbury Collection, in the Western History Collection, University of Oklahoma, Norman, OK.

12. "Letter from the Choctaw Mission," March 31, 1848, Folder 8, Item 53, Cyrus Kingsbury Collection, in the Western History Collection, University of Oklahoma, Norman, OK.

13. Unfortunately, I have not found documents that fully explicate the parameters of these exchanges. I only have stories (such as the one already described regarding Kingsbury's initial use of Native-owned black slaves) from which to reconstruct the missionaries' first usages of black slaves.

14. "Hire" is the term that appears in the mission records for this practice. It is clear that the mission would compensate the slave's labor with provisions and cash payments. To whom they gave this compensation, however, is not completely clear. Obviously, compensation that involved food and clothing went directly to the "hired" slave. It appears though that the cash portion of compensation went to the slave's master. This would help explain why masters were willing to temporarily part with their slaves. There are instances, however, in which the documents *could* be interpreted as suggesting that money went directly to the "hired" slave. This is the case, for example, with the reference I make to Fanny who worked for "$8 a month and her clothes."

15. Cephas Washburn to Jeremiah Evarts, October 27, 1828, ABC 18.3.1 v. 6, American Board of Commissioners for Foreign Missions Records, Houghton Library, Harvard University, Cambridge, MA.

16. Cyrus Kingsbury to American Board, April 12, 1826 Folder 8, Item 5, Cyrus Kingsbury Collection, in the Western History Collection, University of Oklahoma, Norman, OK.

17. Journal entry on February 28, 1818 in Joyce B. Phillips and Paul Gary Phillips, eds., *The Brainerd Journal: A Mission to the Cherokees, 1817–1823* (Lincoln, NE: University of Nebraska Press, 1998), 48.

18. Ibid., June 7, 1818, 62–3.

19. Ibid., August 17, 1818, 77.

20. Ibid., April 13, 1817, 33.

21. Ibid., December 27, 1818, 98.

22. Some scholars have concluded that Indigenous notions of kinship could complicate both individual master–slave relationships as well as Native efforts to develop a racial caste system that mirrored that of the United States, and that was designed to align Native and US social practices so as to support Indigenous sovereignty. See Miles, *Ties That Bind*, Introduction, 4.

23. This understanding of captive gift-giving was widespread throughout Indigenous North America during the colonial era. It persisted to some degree into the nineteenth century. See Rushforth, *Bonds of Alliance*.

24. Cherokee Mission Journal, September 28, 1818, ABC 18.3.1 v. 2, American Board of Commissioners for Foreign Missions Records, Houghton Library, Harvard University, Cambridge, MA.

25. Journal of the Arkansas Mission to the Cherokee at Dwight, Alfred Finney and Cephas Washburn, January 8 to May 2, 1821, ABC 18.3.1 v. 1, American Board of Commissioners for Foreign Missions Records, Houghton Library, Harvard University, Cambridge, MA.

26. Phillips and Phillips, *The Brainerd Journal*, 96.

27. Ard Hoyt to Jeremiah Evarts, January 29, 1818, ABCFM 18.3.1 v. 3, American Board of Commissioners for Foreign Missions Records, Houghton Library, Harvard University, Cambridge, MA.

28. Marcus Palmer to Jeremiah Evarts, November 8, 1826, ABC 18.3.1 v. 6, American Board of Commissioners for Foreign Missions Records, Houghton Library, Harvard University, Cambridge, MA.

29. Major Ridge was also known as "The Ridge." He was a leading member of the Treaty Party. He signed the Treaty of New Echota in 1835, and was later killed by the Cherokees, along with Elias Boudinot and Ridge's son John Ridge, for doing so.

30. Cherokee Mission Journal, July 6, 1817, ABC 18.3.1 v. 2, American Board of Commissioners for Foreign Missions Records, Houghton Library, Harvard University, Cambridge, MA.

31. Cephas Washburn to Jeremiah Evarts, November 13, 1826, ABC 18.3.1 v. 6, American Board of Commissioners for Foreign Missions Records, Houghton Library, Harvard University, Cambridge, MA.

32. Indian captives of the Cherokee were subject to sale to white slave traders. Evidence of this practice is found in the Journal of the Cherokee Mission at Brainerd, October 10, 1819, ABCFM 18.3.1 v. 2, American Board of Commissioners for Foreign Missions Records, Houghton Library, Harvard University, Cambridge, MA.

33. Cherokee Mission Journal, August 17, 1819, ABCFM 18.3.1 v. 2, American Board of Commissioners for Foreign Missions Records, Houghton Library, Harvard University, Cambridge, MA.

34. Cephas Washburn to Jeremiah Evarts, October 27, 1828, ABC 18.3.1 v. 6, American Board of Commissioners for Foreign Missions Records, Houghton Library, Harvard University, Cambridge, MA.

35. Ibid.

36. Cyrus Kingsbury to Jeremiah Evarts, October 6, 1825, Folder 6, Item 44, Cyrus Kingsbury Collection, Western History Collection, University of Oklahoma, Norman, OK.

37. "Statement respecting the employment of slaves at the southwestern missions," January 23, 1837, Folder 9, Item 11, Cyrus Kingsbury Collection, in the Western History Collection, University of Oklahoma, Norman, OK.

38. Cephas Washburn to Jeremiah Evarts, October 27, 1828, ABC 18.3.1. v. 6, American Board of Commissioners for Foreign Missions Records, Houghton Library, Harvard University, Cambridge, MA.

39. Cyrus Kingsbury to David Greene, December 25, 1844, Folder 9, Item 8, Cyrus Kingsbury Collection, in the Western History Collection, University of Oklahoma, Norman, OK.

40. I am using the term abolition here because it is the word that was used by the historical actors under examination. It generally refers to antislavery in any form and did not usually denote the form of abolitionism scholars generally define as characterized by immediate emancipation on the grounds that slavery was a moral evil. I will also use the term antislavery and abolition interchangeably.

41. It is also important to note that as Congregationalists and Presbyterians, the missionaries were not immune to the antislavery proclivities of antebellum era perfectionism.

42. Cephas Washburn, James Orr, Aaron Gray to David Greene, May 26, 1836, ABC 18.3.1 v. 9, American Board of Commissioners for Foreign Missions Records, Houghton Library, Harvard University, Cambridge, MA.

43. David Greene to Cyrus Kingsbury, November 1844, Folder 3, Item 6, Cyrus Kingsbury Collection, in the Western History Collection, University of Oklahoma, Norman, OK.

44. Cyrus Kingsbury to David Greene, May 31, 1845, Folder 9, Item 4, Cyrus Kingsbury Collection, in the Western History Collection, University of Oklahoma, Norman, OK.

45. Ibid., David Greene to Cyrus Kingsbury, November 1844, Folder 3, Item 6.

46. Ibid., Cyrus Kingsbury Collection, in the Western History Collection, University of Oklahoma, Norman, OK.

47. "Statement of Choctaw Missionaries," March 31, 1848, Folder 8, Item 53, Cyrus Kingsbury Collection, in the Western History Collection, University of Oklahoma, Norman, OK. Underlining in the original.

48. Ibid.
49. Cyrus Kingsbury to Selah B. Treat, August 14, 1854 Folder 5, Item 34, Cyrus Kingsbury Collection, in the Western History Collection, University of Oklahoma, Norman, OK. My emphasis.
50. Cyrus Kingsbury to Selah B. Treat, January 30, 1855 Folder 5, Item 32, Cyrus Kingsbury Collection, in the Western History Collection, University of Oklahoma, Norman, OK.
51. "Pity for Poor Africans" in the *The Cherokee Phoenix*, Volume 1, #13, p. 4, May 21, 1828. Available online at the Georgia Historical Newspapers website at http://neptune3.galib.uga.edu/ssp/cgi-bin/tei-news-idx.pl?sessionid=7f000001&type=years&id=CHRKPHNX. The specific Cherokee Phoenix volume quoted here is available at http://neptune3.galib.uga.edu/ssp/News/chrkphnx/18280521d.pdf.
52. This and all preceding quotations from "Pity for Poor Africans" can be found in the Cherokee Phoenix, Volume 1, #13, p. 4, May 21, 1828, Georgia Historical Newspapers, available online at http://neptune3.galib.uga.edu/ssp/News/chrkphnx/18280521d.pdf. Though somewhat confusing, I have kept the line as it appears in the original "we may not go snacks." It means that the Natives should have the freedom to go and snack on slave-produced goods like rum and sugar.
53. Israel Folsom to Cyrus Kingsbury, December 20, 1847, Folder 9, Item 10, Cyrus Kingsbury Collection, in the Western History Collection, University of Oklahoma, Norman, OK.
54. The depth of Folsom's fear is apparent because he took these actions even though he knew full well that Kingsbury was at this time an owner of at least one black slave.
55. Cyrus Kingsbury to Israel Folsom, April 8, 1848, Folder 9, Item 10, Cyrus Kingsbury Collection, in the Western History Collection, University of Oklahoma, Norman, OK.
56. Israel Folsom to Cyrus Kingsbury, May 1, 1848, Folder 9, Item 6, Cyrus Kingsbury Collection, in the Western History Collection, University of Oklahoma, Norman, OK.
57. Ibid.
58. "Statement of Choctaw Missionaries," March 31, 1848, Folder 8, Item 53, Cyrus Kingsbury Collection, in the Western History Collection, University of Oklahoma, Norman, OK.
59. Cyrus Kingsbury to Selah B. Treat, October 18, 1858, Folder 5, Item 25, Cyrus Kingsbury Collection, in the Western History Collection, University of Oklahoma, Norman, OK.
60. Congressman John Woods served as a Representative from Ohio for two consecutive terms from March 1825 to March 1829. Woods fought in the War of 1812. Biographical information on John Woods can be found at the Biographical Directory of the United States Congress website at http://bioguide.congress.gov/scripts/biodisplay.pl?index=W000724.
61. "Indian Emigration: Speech of Mr. Woods," *The Cherokee Phoenix*, Volume 1, #13, 4, May 21, 1828. Available online at the Georgia Historical Newspapers website at http://neptune3.galib.uga.edu/ssp/cgi-bin/tei-news-idx.pl?sessionid=7f000001&type=years&id=CHRKPHNX. The specific Cherokee Phoenix volume quoted here is available at http://neptune3.galib.uga.edu/ssp/News/chrkphnx/18280521d.pdf.
62. James Meriwether served as Representative to the US Congress for one term between March 1825 and March 1827. He had fought in the Creek War in 1813, and in 1823 he had served as a Commissioner to the Creek for President Monroe. Meriwether's nephew, James A. Meriwether, also served in Congress. Biographical information for James Meriwether discussed by Woods can be found online at http://bioguide.congress.gov/scripts/biodisplay.pl?index=M000651.
63. Other historians have analyzed the linkages between citizenship and property in modern liberal societies. For an example of such analysis concerning the United States, see Stuart Banner, *American Property: A History of How, Why and What We Own* (Cambridge, MA: Harvard University Press, 2011). For work on the manifestation

of this phenomenon outside of the United States, see Ekaterina Pravilova, *A Public Empire: Property and the Quest for the Common Good in Imperial Russia* (Princeton, NJ: Princeton University Press, 2018).

64. "Mr. Editor; Property; Argument; Satisfactory; Experience; Accomplished," *Arkansas Weekly Gazette* (published as the *Arkansas State Gazette*), June 23, 1860, Early American Newspapers, America's Historical Newspapers, http://infoweb.newsbank.com. Accessed December 17, 2010.

65. "Mr. Editor" in the *Arkansas Weekly Gazette* (published as the *Arkansas State Gazette and Democrat*) June 2, 1860, 2, Early American Newspapers, America's Historical Newspapers, http://infoweb.newsbank.com. Accessed December 17, 2010.

66. Ibid.

67. Cyrus Kingsbury, Alfred Wright, Cyrus Byington, Ebenezer Hotchkins, C.C. Copeland and D.H. Winshib to the Prudential Committee, March 31, 1848, Folder 8, Item 53, Cyrus Kingsbury Collection, in the Western History Collection, University of Oklahoma, Norman, OK.

68. Cyrus Kingsbury to S.B. Treat, October 18, 1858, Folder 5, Item 25, Cyrus Kingsbury Collection, in the Western History Collection, University of Oklahoma, Norman, OK.

69. "Miscellany: The Indian States," *Christian Inquirer*, 13, no. 15, January 8, 1859, 4, American Periodical Series, www.proquest.com. Accessed March 31, 2011.

70. These cases set important precedents, including the idea that Native nations were like "wards to the State" and therefore not fully sovereign. Also, the Worcester case laid the groundwork for the incorporation of Native nations into the American federal system by explaining that Native nations were sovereign in relation to States, but subordinate to the sovereignty of the United States.

3 Educating and Reproducing "the People"

Mission Schools in the Cherokee, Choctaw, and Seneca Nations, 1815–1859

If slavery had served as an important medium in constructing the alliances Natives and missionaries formed, Native leaders among the Cherokees, Choctaws, and Senecas saw the schools missionaries wanted to open as important institutions they could use to serve tribal interests. Missionaries who had traveled to Native nations in the early nineteenth century made education a central focus because they believed that it was a necessary component of their larger evangelical efforts. The American Board, for instance, believed that educating children would yield more conversions because children were less attached than adults to Native cultures and would therefore more readily imbibe Christianity once they were exposed to it. Alfred Finney of the American Board's Dwight mission in Arkansas argued that it was vital for the Cherokees to go to school and learn to read. He explained that by becoming literate, Indians could read the Bible themselves and become inspired through this experience to accept God.[1] Others believed Natives needed "civilization" in order to secure their worldly needs so that they would then be free to focus on meeting their spiritual ones. Schools would teach Natives to create small family farms and by working the land in accordance with American practices, Natives would secure title to their lands and thereby keep their most important and reliable economic resource. The solvency of individual families would in turn reinforce the stability of the larger Native community. Many missionaries believed that only when Natives' basic economic needs were met, could they turn their attention to the daunting goal of spiritual salvation.[2]

Given the ideological links missionaries made between evangelism and education, it is not at all surprising that when they first approached Natives to establish missions, they generally spoke about schools. They often suggested that the schools would raise the social standing of Natives and their communities. In his initial meeting with a group of Cherokee headmen missionary, Ard Hoyt stated that "The missionaries . . . & others in our own country . . . [had an] ardent desire that their red brethren might enjoy the same privileges they did."[3] Another missionary named Moody Hall similarly connected education to Native social empowerment. In 1818 he asked a Cherokee deputation en route to treaty negotiations in Washington, DC, to secure lands for mission schools. He explained:

> You must be sensible that the education of your children demands your
> serious attention; that without something is done for this purpose, you are

lost — you are all lost. . . . We have had the candor to propose to you the following plan, which . . . will greatly promote the best interests of your nation . . . [and] . . . in due time make you an honorable, enlightened, and respectable nation.[4]

Native leaders in turn reacted positively to the promise of schools. The chiefs who received Hoyt, for example, responded to him favorably, explaining that they "were all well pleased" with his words.[5] Indeed, exchanges such as those between Hoyt and the Cherokees occurred repeatedly during the establishment of the American Board missions in the South. In 1818 the Choctaw David Folsom wrote to missionary Elias Cornelius that "the Choctaw are very much anxious to see the school in operation in our nation."[6]

That Natives so eagerly endorsed institutions designed to create radical cultural change within their societies requires explanation. From a sociopolitical perspective, promises such as those given by Hoyt to the Cherokees resonated strongly with Natives who increasingly worried that they were losing the ability to protect their lands and communities. The War of 1812 had made it abundantly clear that tribes up and down the eastern seaboard had, for all intents and purposes, lost the power to use military force against white Americans as a means of stopping encroachment on their lands.[7] With force off the table as a viable option to protect their lands, the missionaries' offers of education appeared more attractive to Indigenous leaders because they offered another potential route to social and political power that Natives could use to protect their lands. Moreover, the care the preachers took to connect the missions to "privileges" and Native social empowerment aligned with Native interests in building partnerships with white Americans who could serve as allies in Native efforts to contend with settler colonialism. From the perspective of many Natives, the language missionaries used to frame the creation of schools seemed to provide a path to power, which Native leaders believed they could wield in service of their needs, and most importantly, in defense of their lands.

However, this logic comprises only one part of the equation. This is not simply a story of Indigenous people employing education for "survival," nor is it only a tale of Natives' desperate attempts at self-directed "assimilation" with attendant hopes of prospering within the socioeconomic and political paradigms of Early National American civilization. Rather, Natives' involvement with formal education, though partly driven by pragmatic needs, was governed by Indigenous understandings of *the people*. People referred to groups of living beings who inhabited a given area, and for most Indigenous North Americans, the human people who resided in an area were often identified with monikers like the "original" people or "first" people. The fundamental purpose of the (human) people was their reproduction on the land through time. This re-creation was achieved through management of relationships and fulfilling of one's obligations to his or her relations within a place. It is in the intersection of this logic with the pragmatic concerns identified earlier that we can more fully understand Indigenous involvement with formal education. Ascribing to pro-education Natives an acceptance of only the dominant society's motives for creating formal education systems within Indigenous nations makes no sense. Natives who embraced education were not participating in cultural apostasy or aiding in the settler society's attempts at cultural genocide. Rather, they saw in education an increased power to regenerate the people. In other words, education would give Indigenous youths the skills to reproduce on their ancestral homelands. These skills included English literacy, which would help them negotiate with white Americans and the aggressive American settler society, as well as trade and artisan skills that would aid their ability to engage with the market, proto-capitalist economy ascendant in American society. These skills however were embedded within the larger paradigm of Indigenous peoples' relation to and inculcation within "the land," as they were instruments to the next generation's (and indeed several future generations') ability to remain on the land. Seen from this perspective, we can understand Indigenous cooperation with the creation of formal education systems as not indicative of a simple defeat or capitulation to the American settler society. They were rather literally drawing on long-standing Indigenous understandings that centered Native purpose as regeneration of the people. Education was a tool to this end; education was not an Indigenous acceptance of their own demise, culturally or in any other way.

This chapter therefore argues that the Cherokees, Choctaws, and Senecas who supported the creation of formal education within their respective nations did so because they believed the incorporation of schools into their societies would ultimately reproduce the people. This was the primary goal. That this goal would be accomplished in part through generations of Natives who had enhanced capabilities to contend with the United States should not lead us to mistake "assimilation" as Indigenous peoples' main objective. Indeed, Native leaders wanted literate tribal members who could use written and spoken English to the benefit of Native communities in everything from simple correspondence, to public protest, to treaty-making. In addition, Native leaders hoped to acquire increased social power for Indigenous communities by pointing to formal education as evidence that Native societies were not "inferior" to the dominant settler society. The promise that schools might yield social empowerment and perhaps even increased recognition by white Americans of Native political rights were also important inducements leading Natives to work with white missionaries in constructing formal education systems. However, the most powerful motivating factor and the conceptual universe within which pro-education Natives operated was the regeneration of Indigenous people on their lands.

This is why Natives, moreover, did not simply leave missionaries to their own devices in running these newly created educational projects. Rather, in the beginning, Natives and missionaries were partners in creating and operating the schools. And once schools opened, Natives were not shy about either shutting them down or calling out problems with the schools, particularly if they were not serving Native interests. As the nineteenth century progressed, Natives would in fact come to exert more power and influence over the schools than did the missionaries. What this required of pro-school Native leaders was that they simultaneously consider and attempt to meet the needs of the various constituencies linked to the schools. Indigenous leaders navigated the demands of those Natives opposed to the schools, those supportive of the schools, students, and the missionaries. In essence, in working toward the realization of creating and operating formal education systems, Natives had to manage the demands and desires of the several groups with whom they had social ties in order to attain their objectives.

The presence of formal education in the Indigenous communities investigated here was highly consequential as it would directly intersect with one of the central questions of nineteenth-century Indigenous history — Removal. The perceptual paradigm in which Natives ensconced education — the ability to reproduce the people on the land through the cultivation of individuals capable of negotiating with white Americans — came to concrete fruition. Educated and literate Natives would have the power to prosecute antiremoval campaigns within the public sphere, as well as directly with US government officials, including presidents and Congress. Without recourse to military power to fight Removal, Natives used words and petitions as weapons, abilities that education had made more possible. Moreover, the parent organizations of their missionary allies would form a second and powerful prong in the public campaigns against Removal. They would arise in fervent opposition to the proposed removals of both southern and northern Native tribes alike. Organizations like the American Board and various Quaker Yearling Meetings would work to marshal sympathetic white Americans in the antiremoval cause. In sum, the schools provided Natives with the ability to wage a sustained nonviolent effort against Removal through the literacy skills and the white allies they gained in the process of creating formal education systems.

Cherokee and Choctaw Objectives for the Schools

The Cherokees and the Choctaws envisioned several ways in which their adoption of formal education would enhance their power to contend with the settler society under which they lived. From a pragmatic standpoint, they viewed knowledge of the English language and familiarity with American culture as vital to their ability to negotiate with the US government. The influential Choctaw chief David Folsom provides a good case in point. The Folsoms were a prominent family that had become wealthy through participation in the burgeoning plantation economy. In 1818 Folsom sent two of his brothers to the American Board's Foreign Mission School in Cornwall, Connecticut. Writing to Reverend Elias Cornelius, he stated: "I give my two brothers up unto you. I hope the great Spirit will give them happiness so as they may be useful to our Nation."[8] What Folsom meant by "useful to our Nation" was that his brothers would be able to use the education received in Connecticut in ways that would benefit the Choctaws in relations with the US and state governments. This hope is clear from the other ways that Folsom threw his weight behind Native education. Seven years after sending his brothers to Cornwall, he helped to broker the 1825 Treaty of Washington, which ceded Choctaw tribal lands in return for an allocation of money earmarked for Choctaw education. This agreement stipulated that in exchange for these lands, the United States would pay $6000 a year in perpetuity for "the sole object of educate our children and for the use of improving our people." In giving his reasons for endorsing the treaty, Folsom stated:

> we have signed a cession of treaty today and I am glad that so much has been done toward the civilization of the Choctaw people. I am so destitute of education and I labor [with] so much difficulty for not having a good learning-for to transact business for the nation. I therefore wish [that the] young aspiring generation may be educated.[9]

From personal experience Folsom had concluded that fluency in English and knowledge of white American society would be useful to Choctaw relations with the United States. His hope was to strengthen the Choctaw position by utilizing education to create a cadre of young Choctaws with the requisite skills to advocate effectively for tribal interests so that the Choctaws would have more power and freedom to remain an Indigenous community.

The Cherokees and Choctaws also saw education as important to their economic stability. This stability centered on maintaining possession of land. Native elites who had begun to embrace the central tenets of American political economy[10] by establishing plantations wanted others to follow their example by working family farms. For instance, the Cherokee Charles Hicks argued that schooling and acceptance of subsistence farming was necessary for the Cherokees persistence as a people. One missionary reported that

> Mr. Hicks says many of the people are very anxious to receive instruction and this anxiety is increased from the conviction that their very existence as a people depends upon it. The experience of the last 20 years in which they have turned their attention more to agriculture and less to hunting he says has convinced them that they can live much more comfortably by tilling their land and raising stock than they can in their old way. They find also that their new way of living tends to increase their population. While they lived in their old way . . . their numbers were constantly diminishing: but since they have provided homes for their women and children, where they can be warm and have enough to eat the whole year, they are increasing like the white people.[11]

Though we rely on a secondhand report of what Hicks actually said, what is clear is that when he made these remarks, white encroachment on Cherokee lands was increasing. Many argued that such lands were "unimproved" and "unused" and were therefore liable to seizure by those who would build upon them. Tribal leaders like Hicks hoped that such arguments would lose their force if the lands in question supported Cherokee farms and homes. He further reasoned that if a formal education system could teach Cherokees to adopt yeoman farming, then Native claims to their lands would be more secure and it would be consequently far more difficult for neighboring whites to seize them. For Hicks, education was directly linked to strengthening the ability of the Cherokees to maintain possession of their land. And because the land and the Cherokees were so intimately interwoven, the ability to maintain lands was in direct relation to the ability of the Cherokees to reproduce themselves. This is why there are several references to the people and to Cherokee population trends in Hicks' remarks.

Other Native leaders made the same case regarding land and the people. Old Glass, a headman of the western Cherokees in Arkansas, specifically connected schooling to land security. In April 1818 he was returning from a visit to Congress and decided to stop at the Brainerd school in the Cherokee nation where he informed the missionaries that land conflicts with whites had led the "Old Settler" Cherokees to migrate to the west. He explained: "the white people crowded upon them so much, that they must go over the Mississippi." However, he concluded that education would now help the Cherokees secure their lands.

> He expressed confidence in the good will of the general government and the good people . . . at the north, who were sending teachers to instruct their red brethren. He said, schools were very good for them, and added "As soon as we get a little settled over the Mississippi we shall want schools there."[12]

Old Glass' calculus here was that education secured the land, which in turn secured the people who lived on it.

Natives also believed that the schools provided a ready venue to strengthen and maintain the beneficial relationships they had with the missionaries. Natives used these relationships in political dealings with the United States, but they also leveraged them when relating to white Americans living on their borders. More specifically, Natives saw the missionaries as key allies who could help mediate conflicts between themselves and white neighbors. Again the Cherokees afford a good example. Writing to the missionary Samuel Worcester, John Ross and the aforementioned Charles Hicks explained:

> when we complain of those bad white neighbors around our frontier, we seek our distress, we are not impressed with a belief that all whitemen are our enemies. We know that great many are our friends and without this fact, we also know that we could not exist.[13]

Though their assertion that the Cherokees might not be able to "exist" was hyperbolic, the ability of white "friends" to protect Cherokee interests represents the underlying message of Ross' and Hicks' letter.[14] They wanted their missionary allies to know that when the Cherokees complained about "bad white neighbors," they were not engaging in simple racialized fulminations, but rather wanted the preachers' help in addressing their concerns. The endeavor to create education systems jointly undertaken by Natives and missionaries bonded them as allies and therefore provided Natives with a group of white Americans who could intervene on their behalf regarding problems with other white Americans.

At base, Cherokee and Choctaw leaders supported the creation of formal education systems in their nations because they believed education would provide a variety of tools to help them remain as distinct Indigenous nations, a goal that was abetted by the schools' abilities to help them contend with an expansionistic United States whose growing white population was eager to seize Indigenous lands. They reached this conclusion by considering their place in relation to several groups, including the US government, missionaries, white neighbors, Native children, and American Board school personnel in New England. It is for this reason that the Cherokees and Choctaws would put in so much work to ensure the schools were created and kept in operation.

Opening the Cherokee and Choctaw Schools

To bring the schools into existence required the Cherokees and Choctaws to work directly in partnership with the American Board missionaries. In 1817 the American Board opened its first school in the Cherokee nation, and in 1818 the organization's first school appeared among the Choctaws. These developments arose from cooperative Native–missionary partnerships in which Natives played a central role. Moreover, the link between education and land possession Natives had drawn was never far from events concerning the schools. For instance, the opening of the first school in the Cherokee nation was facilitated in part by none other than Andrew Jackson. In 1816 Cyrus Kingsbury accompanied General Andrew Jackson to a treaty ratification ceremony commemorating a Cherokee land cession. Jackson, who as President would later preside over Cherokee removal, at this date pursued quite a different policy. He "politely introduced the subject of the schools and urged the importance of Indian education." After Jackson had broached the topic, Kingsbury stepped in and spoke directly to the Cherokee chiefs. "I told them that we would take their children teach them freely, without money. That we would feed as many as we could and furnish some clothes to those who are poor," wrote Kingsbury. This approach was designed to assuage any fear among the Natives that they would be asked to pay for their children's education, and to clearly communicate that the plan for mission schools was not a unilateral demand, but rather represented an opportunity for cooperation. He "further told them that if they wished to have the school that they must let me know it, that I might inform those who sent me." The Cherokees seized upon the opportunity. After Kingsbury spoke, a Cherokee chief "took [him] by the hand very affectionately" and explained that they indeed wanted the school. Under the auspices of a treaty ceremony and the patronage of Jackson, the Cherokees and Kingsbury began negotiations to open an American Board school.[15]

But again, even after they agreed to the schools, the Cherokees and Choctaws did not simply allow the American Board to open them. Rather, they often insisted on drafting official treaties or contracts that granted specific rights and privileges regarding the schools to both Natives and to the missionaries. For example, in 1823 the Choctaw Council entered into an agreement with the Board to create two new schools. The treaty establishing these schools contained three articles. The first granted the missionaries the right to build the schools and the "privilege of establishing mechanical shops, cultivating land, and keeping stock for the benefit of the school." The second article protected Choctaw land rights, and explained that the schools existed for the "sole benefit" of the tribe. It further stipulated that if a school closed, then "the right of soil shall revert to the nation." The third article dealt with finances and laid out a plan in which the Choctaw nation, Choctaw parents, and the Board would share in the costs of supporting Native students.[16] The ability to use contract law to protect tribal interests and land was the exact capability the Choctaws envisioned the schools would prepare their children to do even more effectively in the future. The Choctaws were giving their youth more power to determine the character of Choctaw relations with white Americans. More specifically, they took care to assure that the schools could not be used as tools of land alienation by drafting the contract in ways that protected Choctaw land rights.

As the analysis of the aforementioned treaty suggests, the funding of schools was an important issue especially because the schools, which often supported 25–30 boarding students at a time, were expensive to run. For the most part, Natives and missionaries tackled this problem together by sharing operating costs. The American Board paid the salaries of teachers, assistants, and missionaries, and gave money to support a limited number of pupils. A considerable amount of money came from Natives. In 1820 the Choctaw National Council appropriated the colossal sum of $10,000 for schools. This money was earmarked to feed and clothe students. While Kingsbury hailed this development as "a new era in the history of missions" and gushed that "the fact that the natives have done this freely and unitedly is worth volumes,"[17] it also shows how seriously Choctaw tribal leaders viewed the project to educate their youth, and reveals the depths to which they believed the investment in schooling would empower their people.

The cooperative manner in which missionaries and Natives worked from initial negotiations about schools, to the development of official contracts that governed the schools, to joint funding of the schools were all vital to the opening and sustained operation of the American Board's first schools in the Cherokee and Choctaw nations. The missionaries alone could not have opened the schools, but rather relied upon Native partnerships that addressed the interests of the tribe, the missionaries, and the students, to bring them into being.

Just as Native–missionary cooperation was key to opening the first schools, so too was it in increasing the number of schools during the early 1820s. After the initial school was established at Brainerd in the Cherokee nation, other Cherokee schools opened at Creek Path, Taloney, Fort Armstrong, Wills Town, and Chatooga. In the Choctaw nation, Cyrus Kingsbury opened the first school at Eliot and then left it to the supervision of Cyrus Byington. He then moved to Mayhew in 1819 to open another school for Choctaw youth. By the Removal period, the number of schools had grown substantially in both the Cherokee and Choctaw nations as seven mission schools were in operation among the Cherokees and 13 among the Choctaws.

A collaborative Native–missionary political process governed the opening of new schools. Usually it was the Natives who would initiate this process. Either a headman or a group of local residents would send word to the missionaries that a new school was desired. The missionaries would then inquire about the number of students to be boarded, what land would be used to support the school, and if structures capable of housing the school and the teacher already existed. Once these issues had been addressed and any problems resolved, the missionaries would send a teacher to open the school.

The establishment of the schools at Creek Path in the Cherokee nation illustrates this process. Creek Path was approximately 100 miles southwest of Brainerd station and held both a boys' school and a girls' school. On March 4, 1820, the Cherokee John Brown, along with other local leaders, requested a school. Three days after receiving their request, the missionaries agreed to open the school. Initially they had decided that school would not commence until a teacher from the North could be obtained. However, they changed their minds after considering their previous experience at Taloney, in which the Taloney school had failed to open because the missionaries could not get a schoolhouse built quickly. This course of action had caused disappointment and anger among the Cherokees whose children the school was meant to serve. Fearing that any delay in opening the Creek Path school would cause similar discontent, the missionaries sent Daniel Sabin Butrick, along with Cherokee John Arch, to open the school at Creek Path. Butrick would teach while Arch, by his side, would act as translator. Butrick and Arch left Brainerd for Creek Path on March 11th and two days later they, along with local leaders Captain John Brown and Pathkiller, built a schoolhouse. Captain Brown and Pathkiller had commanded the labor of approximately 50 other Cherokees in order to get the school built. On May 5th, John Arch returned to Brainerd and reported that the school had opened and that it currently held 45 "scholars." In just a month's time, the Cherokees and missionaries had worked jointly to build and open a school. Their partnership continued after the school's opening as Butrick and Arch stayed on together with the former teaching and the latter translating.[18]

Arch's return to Brainerd in May brought news of the opening of the Creek Path boys' school and led directly to initiating work on a school for the district's girls. Arch explained that the Cherokees wanted a girls' school and that if a female teacher could be found, they would immediately construct another schoolhouse. Just as they had done previously, the missionaries reacted quickly to the Natives' request. They considered that a young Cherokee woman named Catherine Brown, who had already spent a couple of years at the Brainerd school, might be competent to serve as instructor. In early May, the missionaries gathered and voted on a resolution on whether or not they would offer the teaching position to Brown. The resolution passed and Brown was confirmed as the new teacher. Upon learning of this decision in late May, the Cherokees fulfilled their promise by building a new schoolhouse. On the last day of that month, Catherine Brown set out from Brainerd for Creek Path. By June 23, missionaries had reported that she had successfully opened the school.[19] Not only had the Cherokees initiated the opening of both of the Creek Path schools, but they were also directly involved in providing instruction as John Arch interpreted in the boys' school and Catherine Brown served as the teacher. The aligning of Native and missionary interests in opening schools produced significant Native–missionary cooperation and served to strengthen their alliance.

By the eve of the Removal era, this would lead to an increase in the number of schools and consequently an exposure of a sizable minority of Choctaw and Cherokee youth to formal education. The Choctaw mission recorded that its 13 schools enrolled 2309 students between the years 1819 and 1831.[20] Given that the Choctaw population numbered roughly 14,000 people, this number of students is significant even when we consider student attrition. Contrary to previous interpretations, it seems clear that the schools reached many young Choctaws.[21] The reach of Cherokee schools was similar. The Cherokees also had a population of roughly 14,000. The two schools at Brainerd enrolled 297 students between 1817 and 1823.[22] Other Cherokee schools often held fewer students than Brainerd. However, considering that Brainerd and many other schools did not close their doors until the late 1830s, just before the Cherokee were removed, it is reasonable to assume that at least a couple of thousand students experienced some form of formal schooling.

Negotiating Opposition to the Mission Schools

Despite initial success in opening schools, by the early 1820s it had become clear that not everyone was pleased with them. Some Natives saw the schools not as serving to reproduce the people, but as working toward their eventual erasure. They particularly worried about the potential loss of Indigenous values and beliefs. Still other Cherokees and Choctaws suspected that the missionaries, like other whites, sought to acquire Native land. These fears stirred discontent with the schools among both the Cherokees and the Choctaws. Such discontent came from political leaders unconvinced of the value of the schools, the common people, and even enrolled students. For example, missionary Isaac Proctor explained that "the child no doubt feels that he cannot be restrained from his vain amusements all that length of time . . . daily attendance has become wearisome, and the restraints painful."[23] Often disapproval of the schools by Native parents led them to either keep children from enrolling, or to remove those who were already attending. Pro-school Native leaders would react to this opposition by working directly with parents, students, teachers, and missionaries to address concerns and keep the schools open.

Tribal leaders usually responded to opposition to the schools by engaging in grassroots campaigns to reinvigorate popular support for education. They reiterated the argument that the schools would serve the interests of the people. In 1820 for instance, Pathkiller had been "telling his people . . . that schools are very good for them, & they must keep their children at school."[24] Seeking to ensure that the Cherokees would produce a class of educated youths capable of effectively dealing with white Americans, the Cherokee Council took the extraordinary step of passing a law that required parents to keep their children in school once they had begun attending. The law also stipulated that a student could not leave school until a teacher had confirmed that he or she had learned a sufficient amount.[25]

Though the passage of this law was important, the grassroots effort targeting parents and students proved to be the most powerful weapon in the hands of the schools' supporters. The opening of the Chatooga school reveals how Cherokee leaders worked to secure local support. Problems first surfaced prior to the school's opening. The headmen of the area had promised that they would build a schoolhouse if the missionaries would open a school. After this agreement was reached, the headmen compelled the local residents to begin construction. However, after the job had begun, missionaries Darius and Milo Hoyt reported that the Cherokees appeared very "dissatisfied" and were unwilling to finish the building. The Hoyts, along with the headmen, completed construction themselves. This proved to be a Pyrrhic victory as no children arrived to school on the day that it opened. The Chatooga headmen frustrated with this development promised the equally frustrated missionaries that children would attend and spent the next few days meeting with parents. There is no record of what was said in these meetings, but the headmens' politicking yielded positive results as a few days later a group of parents had been persuaded to send their children to school. Though the initial attendance was disappointingly low, the Chatooga school remained open until the Removal era.[26]

Cherokee leaders also directly addressed children in efforts to drum up support for schooling. They sought to persuade Cherokee youths that education was vital to the empowerment of their people. In January 1819 two headmen conducted a two-day visit to the Brainerd school. On the second day of their visit, they addressed the students and explained that as they grew up "they would do much good to their people."[27] A similar scene played out three years later when the local headman in the Wills Town district asked permission to speak at the school. The headman explained to the pupils that he had learned English only with difficulty and that the children's ability to attend school was a "privilege." He then urged the students to "learn as fast as they could every day — that they could be a great advantage to them and to their people."[28]

In addition to the political efforts of tribal chieftains who targeted Native parents and their children, Native parents who had already lent their support to schooling worked directly with missionaries to keep unenthusiastic children enrolled. The student Horace Loomis is a case in point. Loomis was an older Cherokee boy who had gone absent without permission. When he returned to school the following day and was asked why he had left, Loomis responded that he had "felt uneasy." Whatever the source of those feelings, both the missionaries and the boy's parents worked to keep him in school. The day after his return, "Mr. Hoyt conversed with the lad alone" and told him to ask God to give him "rest and peace." When on the following day Loomis was still unhappy, the missionaries "sent for his father." Upon his arrival nearly two weeks later, the father reported through an interpreter that "he had given his son a long talk, & thought he would no more be so foolish, but would hereafter be obedient & stay out his time [at the school] contentedly." Loomis returned to school, reportedly with a better attitude.[29]

Though we have no record of the conversation between Loomis and his father, we can infer from the missionaries' records that the father, like other Cherokees, perceived education as vital to sustaining the Cherokee nation. The missionaries recorded that Loomis' father had stated that "he had always been glad of the coming of the missionaries" and that "people all over the nation are seeing more & more clearly the great good of having such teachers."[30] Explaining what the father meant by this, the missionaries wrote: "Many [Cherokees] consider it an honor to have been among the first to discuss the national advantage of these institutions [the schools]" and that they see it as "a mark of a weak mind not now to see" the advantage accrued to the nation through education.[31] The larger sociopolitical advantages of Native education persuaded some to support the schools regardless of the personal discomfort Native children might experience.

Finally, Native leaders worked directly with missionaries and teachers to keep students in schools. This is evident from the way Natives addressed a problem surrounding disparities between Native and white disciplinary methods. Anger over white teachers who had used corporal punishment drove some Natives to remove their children from school. On one occasion Cherokee grandparents removed their two granddaughters from the Brainerd school having "expressed great dissatisfaction that one of the girls had been whip[p]ed."[32] Similarly at Mayhew in the Choctaw nation, an uncle removed his nephew because he "was much displeased that his nephew was reproved and threatened with punishment (whipping)."[33]

To address these problems in the Choctaw nation, the Choctaw chief Mushulatubbee formulated an agreement with the missionaries and teachers that permitted limited use of corporal punishment. Mushulatubbee informed Cyrus Kingsbury "that it would do to whip the small scholars, but not the large ones."[34] In another case an uncle pulled three boys from the Mayhew school after one of the children had provided his parents with "false reports" about the school. He subsequently returned and reenrolled them in the school. The boys had most likely complained about school discipline methods as their uncle found it necessary to have a long talk with the missionaries "relative to the government of the school." The uncle, Captain Mishanhaniah, explained that he "wished them to continue at school and be obedient." However, he also "did not wish his nephews to be punished," but rather if "they were disobedient we must send for him and he would give them a talk." The missionaries responded by explaining the "rules of schools among white people and the importance of government." They consented to "first make use of persuasion" and promised that "punishment would not be resorted to unless other means failed." This seemed to appease Mishanhaniah as he reportedly "assented and said he was willing the teacher should govern as he thought best." Ultimately Mishanhaniah accepted that his nephews would be, at least potentially, subject to corporal punishment. On the other hand, Mishanhaniah's complaints made it clear to school authorities that they needed to constrain themselves from freely using their own disciplinary methods.[35]

While Native leaders managed to keep opposition to the schools in check during the early 1820s, by the middle of the decade opposition had significantly increased. Two factors drove the escalating opposition to the schools. First, Natives became increasingly suspicious about the missionaries' intentions relative to the schools. Many claimed that missionaries used the schools to enrich themselves by using Indigenous lands to support the schools and by compelling Native students to work in the fields. The missionaries at Brainerd reported that "while so many white people are grasping for their land it is no wonder if the poor misinformed Cherokees sometimes suspect that missionaries . . . have the same object in view."[36] Choctaw chief Mushulatubbee reported that much "bad talk" was heard among his "warriors" who say "that Capt Folsom has been selling land to the Missionaries and that the missionaries will ruin the nation."[37] Two Choctaw headmen named Cole and McCurtain also voiced distrust of the missionaries, characterizing them as "liars and cheats." They fulminated against the schools and claimed that during "the balance of the day they [the students] were driven in the field in the same manner that negroes were on the plantations in the southern States."[38] Similar complaints about student field labor compelled teacher Joel Wood to explicitly state to Native parents how much time Choctaw students spent doing field work.[39] Though the missionaries were in fact not interested in procuring Native lands, those Natives concerned about the schools found an effective weapon in the claim of supposed land theft.

The other significant reason for the rising discontent with the schools was ironically Native concern that not enough children were receiving an education. School supporters feared that the schools would not produce a sufficient number of adults who would have the requisite skills to negotiate the demands of the American settler society, and thereby be unable to strengthen the Cherokees and Choctaws in their dealings with the United States. This fear is most evident from the anger caused when mission schools failed to open as planned. As already discussed, the delayed opening of the Taloney school in the Cherokee nation caused discontentment with the missionaries. A similar attitude manifested among the Choctaws. Cyrus Kingsbury reported that

> the natives . . . are beginning to say that we have not fulfilled our promises. And some have even gone so far as to say, that if we do not get a school into operation by such a time, we must quit the county.[40]

Problems also arose when missionaries failed to accept new students into a school. On one occasion the refusal to accept new scholars actually forced a school closure. When teachers at Bethany in the Choctaw nation explained that they simply could not board more students due to lack of space, many local Choctaws became agitated. "Much dissatisfaction had been manifested almost from the first, because we would not board more scholars,"[41] reported Kingsbury.

In addition, some Natives worried that the schools did not adequately teach children to speak English. One missionary reported that a Choctaw man had complained that "instead of learning the Choctaws to talk English we ourselves [the missionaries] were learning to talk Choctaw."[42] The aforementioned Coles and McCurtain also lamented that the children did not spend enough time learning English. They argued that students did not have enough time to practice speaking, reading, and listening to English because they "were allowed only two hours in a day for story,"[43] by which they meant the reading and speaking of English.

Waning confidence in the schools placed Native leaders and their missionaries allies on the political defensive and forced them to explicitly address concerns of those people opposed to the schools. In 1823 Mushulatubbee visited the Mayhew station to address some troubling "reports in circulation." He averred that the "best way to keep friendship was to state . . . [the grievances] frankly," and then relayed the concern "that the missionaries had become merchants," presumably meaning that the missionaries were selling food grown in school garden plots. He also described reports about teachers taking clothes from the students. "When the scholars leave the school to go home, they are stript and their clothes taken from them." Finally, the chief argued that students worked too much in the fields. The missionaries personally rebutted these charges by asserting that they derived no personal financial benefits from the schools. They explained that any money generated by selling the produce grown on school lands was "not kept on their own accounts, but for the benefit of the school[s] solely." They argued that such profits were reinvested in student clothing and school supplies.[44]

The missionaries' personal responses to Mushulatubbee were not sufficient to contain the growing momentum against the schools, which led them to follow up on Mushulatubbee's efforts to quell concerns. Four days after Mushulatubbee's visit to Mayhew, Cyrus Kingsbury answered Choctaw complaints directly within the public forum of a council that had been called to inquire into "wicked reports which have been put in circulation relative to the Missionaries, the Chief and Capt. Folsom." Kingsbury made explicit answer to the charges against himself and others regarding the selling of produce and the insufficient time teaching English to Choctaw students, and then he reaffirmed the importance of maintaining an ongoing collaborative partnership with the Choctaws. Kingsbury's subsequent report on this council to the ABCFM reveals the tenuous situation in which the missionaries found themselves. He informed Board Secretary Jeremiah Evarts that the missionaries had to be careful and could give "no just occasion of offence," otherwise the "progress of light and truth" would be impeded.[45] Kingsbury well understood that the widening political cleavages between those Choctaws who supported and those who opposed the schools needed to be mended if the schools and the mission itself were to continue.

The Choctaws were not alone in their escalating opposition to the mission schools; similar complaints arose among the Cherokees. By 1824 missionary William Chamberlin had reported to Jeremiah Evarts that opposition to the schools was increasing and that some prior supporters had now reversed their position. In fact, many Cherokees were preparing to argue in open council for closure of the schools. Chamberlin explained that now even "Pathkiller and the Speaker are violently opposed" to the mission and the schools. He was very much worried that "as they have great influence among common people, and the unenlightened chiefs, it is very probable that there will be a very powerful opposition to mission in the next council." But Chamberlin also reported that opposition was not yet universal, and explained that the missionaries still had allies among influential Cherokees who had already taken the initiative to deflect the political power of those inclined against the schools. "At the last council in the summer some of the chiefs were calculating to deliver speeches against the missionaries, but Major Ridge took the advantage of them and delivered a very long and animated speech in favour of the mission."[46] Ridge was an example of the efforts pro-school Native leaders took to simultaneously manage the demands of Natives wary of the schools with the precarious position of their missionary allies.

Indeed, in the face of growing opposition to the schools, a cadre of important Native leaders reaffirmed their continued support for education. Major Ridge, Charles Hicks, and others continued to link the schools and the mission to increased Indigenous power. One missionary, for example, declared that "Mr. Hicks is unshaken in his confidence in the Amer. [Board] Com. and more than ever convinced of the utility of their mission among his people. This I believe is the case with all the enlightened chiefs"[47] Hicks was not the only Cherokee leader to support the mission. In 1825 Isaac Proctor wrote: "I am happy to find that missionaries are becoming more and more highly esteemed by the chiefs and head men of this nation,"[48] largely due to efforts by supportive leaders like Hicks.

Regardless of the actions of pro-school Native leaders, a sizable degree of Native opposition to the schools remained until the end of the decade when a stunning reversal of opinion occurred at the beginning of 1829. Both the Cherokees and the Choctaws began to conspicuously sing the praises of the mission schools. Moreover, student attendance shot up, so much so that many would-be students were refused admission. From Brainerd, John Elsworth gleefully reported that among the Natives "all were gratified so far as I can learn, and there is no doubt but the schools are regarded with much more interest by the people than formerly."[49] That same year Cyrus Kingsbury summarized Choctaw attitudes toward the schools by writing

> there never has been a time since we came to this nation when instruction was so much sought for and attended with such encouraging fruits as at the present. . . . The schools are becoming important in the estimation of many of the natives. Applications for admission at this place have become so numerous that we have an opportunity of selecting the most promising.[50]

Kingsbury was not viewing Choctaw attitudes through rose-colored glasses because many were indeed effusively praising the schools. For instance, a group of Choctaw parents whose children attended the school at Elliot drafted a letter expressing their gratitude to the mission and their "approbation" for the school. They wrote:

> The improvement of the children in every instance has fully equaled our expectations and in many instances altogether surpassed our most sanguine hopes and we do hereby express our warmest thanks to the teachers and patrons of the school for the interest they have manifested in behalf of ourselves and our children.[51]

The imminent threat of Removal was the root cause of the quick and dramatic increase in Cherokee and Choctaw support for the schools. Andrew Jackson had strongly supported Removal in his presidential campaign and with his victory in the 1828 election, Removal became a real possibility. As will be discussed in the next chapter, Natives responded to the threat of Removal through a public sphere campaign built on petitions and memorials in which they laid out their reasons for opposing Removal and the horrors it would entail if carried out. The ability to write persuasive rhetoric was of course central to these efforts, and therefore the education that young Natives had received in the preceding decades proved absolutely crucial to Native defense in the face of an existential threat. In other words, the 1830s witnessed pro-school Native leaders doubling down on their commitment to formal education because the political change in the United States made the calculus Natives had drawn between schooling, land, and the ability of the people to reproduce exponentially more important.

Formal Education in the Removal and Post-Removal Eras

But this commitment was not only based on the utility of Indigenous literacy in the fight against Removal. Rather, Native leaders saw education as key to the persistence of their people. Regardless of the outcome of the Removal debate, Indigenous leaders knew that their societies would have the best chance to survive if those societies were prepared to coexist with, navigate, and compete with the world that the dominant settler state had built. For many Native leaders this meant that their societies had to, at least partially, align with dominant economic and land use practices, as well as with modern sociopolitical structures. This is why in the late 1820s, the Cherokees, for instance, had created a written constitution and the Cherokee Syllabary. From the perspective of many Native leaders, formal education was foundational to the ability of Indigenous societies to make and remake themselves in ways that would give them the best odds of persistence, and some degree of self-determination, in a world dominated by an oppressive settler state. This idea resonates clearly in an 1834 letter from a group of Cherokee chiefs to a Seneca Delegation in Washington, DC. The Cherokees wrote:

> We are sensible that it is by education the mind is cultivated and enlightened. . . . And that in wisdom & Superior Knowledge, the force of power exists. Let us therefore encourage schools and the education of our children and the adoption of the habits of civilized life — for the superiority of the white people over the Indian mainly consists only in their cultivation and acquirements, of the arts and sciences.[52]

In the world of 1830s America, it was clear to these Cherokees that ability of Natives to contend on a more equal footing with "white people" resided in part at least in Indigenous education. Consequently, Native leaders worked not merely to educate their children, but to make formal education an important institution in Indigenous societies so that Natives could exist as distinct peoples within the settler colonial world in which they lived.

It is therefore no wonder that during the immediate pre-Removal years, the Cherokees worked to keep the American Board mission schools open in the Cherokee nation. Indeed, their efforts led to the opening of additional schools. But even more important than the opening of more schools was the fact that the schools now mostly employed Cherokees, rather than white, instructors. For example, at one point two young Cherokee men, one named Jesse and the other called Run About, had several schools in operation under their guidance.[53] This turn to the use of Native teachers reflected the degree to which these schools had now become Indigenous schools rather than mission institutions.

Even though both the Cherokees and the Choctaws exercised far more influence over formal education during the years prior to Removal, both nations also ensured that the alliances they had built with American Board missionaries and the formal education systems they had developed remained intact. In fact, when it became clear that the Cherokees and the Choctaws would be removed, both tribes requested that the missionaries move west with them. They also made it clear that they wanted them to help them reestablish schools in their new lands beyond the Mississippi. The Cherokees John Ridge and Elias Boudinot, only a few months prior to the signing of the Treaty of New Echota, asked the white schoolteacher Sophia Sawyer to move west with the Cherokees.[54] And in 1837 as the tribe was preparing to emigrate, Ridge informed Board Secretary David Greene that the Cherokees expected a host of missionaries, including William Chamberlin and D.S. Butrick, to move beyond the Mississippi with them.[55] Choctaw leaders such as David Folsom, Greenwood Leflore, and Mushulatubbee — all of whom had been supporters of formal education — also all worked to ensure that new schools would open in the west. Subsequent to the signing of the Treaty of Dancing Rabbit Creek (the treaty that provided for Choctaw removal to west), they requested that missionaries Cyrus Kingsbury and Cyrus Byington move with the tribe in order to help open new schools.[56] Furthermore, as signatories to the Treaty they had demanded that the agreement contain a provision for the funding of new schools.[57] In the midst of their subjection to the debilitating effects of America's Removal policy, Natives did not abandon, but rather intensified, efforts to solidify the presence of formal education within their societies.

These efforts continued after Removal as both the Choctaws and Cherokees took decisive steps to construct new schools in Indian Territory. In 1842 the Choctaws "established an elaborate system of schools," including the all-male schools of Spencer Academy, Fort Coffee Academy, and Nanawaiya Academy. The tribe also constructed four schools for Choctaw girls: Koonsha Female Seminary, Chuwala Female Seminary, Wheelock Female Seminary, and Ayanubbee Female Seminary. These schools were established by the Choctaw Council but run initially by the American Board missionaries.[58] The Cherokees likewise set up new schools. On September 26, 1839, the Cherokee National Council passed an act "for the promotion of education, by the establishment of schools."[59] This included a system of 11 lower schools and two national Seminary Schools in which one seminary served males and the other educated females.[60]

These developments stemmed in great part from the efforts of Cherokee and Choctaw leaders who had direct experience as students in mission schools in the pre-Removal period. Their experiences with formal education had served them well as they had put their skills to use as tribal leaders who managed relations with white Americans and the United States. So, while only a minority of Cherokees and Choctaws had attended the mission schools prior to Removal, many of those former students who had had now risen to positions of political power. It was these former students turned tribal leaders who had direct knowledge of the power and potential of formal education, and who during the Removal and post-Removal eras supported schooling in the west. For example, Peter Pitchlynn, the influential Choctaw chief who had been educated at the Choctaw Academy, explained in 1848: "My heart is ever turned towards the schools of my country, for on them I build all my hopes of the prosperity of the Choctaws."[61] In addition to Peter Pitchlynn, other Choctaw leaders such as Israel Folsom supported education. Folsom had attended the Mayhew mission school and the Board's Foreign Mission School in Cornwall, Connecticut. In the post-Removal period, he explicitly explained the importance of female education:

> If we have our girls educated, civilized, Christianized, enlightened . . . they will put a stamp in society & character & weight to our nation, & their off-springs will be considered civilized as soon as they are born — O, what advantage.[62]

Important Cherokee leaders of the era had also been students in their youth. John Ridge and Elias Boudinot had each attended the Brainerd mission school, and each had also enrolled in the Board's School in Cornwall, Connecticut. Finally, Boudinot's uncle Stand Watie, also a former mission school student, became an influential political figure who advocated for education and continued Cherokee integration into the plantation economy of the South.

But it was not just former students who supported formal education in the Removal and post-Removal eras. Others also ensured that education would continue to be a part of Indigenous communities. In 1818 David Folsom had supported the establishment of the Choctaw mission, and in 1830 he pushed to include the education provision in the Treaty of Dancing Rabbit Creek. And Cherokee John Ross had been an ardent early supporter of the American Board schools. As Principal Chief, he used his position to push for the establishment of new schools in the post-Removal era. Like many others he linked tribal empowerment specifically to the ability of the Cherokees to make formal education a foundational institution in Cherokee society.[63] After Ross and the Cherokees arrived in the west, he submitted a proposal for schools to the National Council. He stated that "the establishment of Schools, and a printing press for the dissemination of knowledge, & such other subjects of general interest as would conduce to the improvement and happiness of the people, are respectfully referred for your consideration"[64] His statement evinced his belief both in the power of knowledge and in the power to be gained by Indigenous participation in a public sphere in which knowledge and ideas were distributed and debated through the written word.

Seneca–Quaker Collaboration and Schooling

Just like their southern counterparts, the linkages between education and enhanced ability of Native societies to reproduce themselves within a settler colonial context were drawn by Natives in the North. The experience of the Allegheny Senecas in adopting formal education followed a trajectory similar to that of the Cherokees and Choctaws. Like the Cherokees and Choctaws, those Senecas who supported schooling worked closely and cooperatively with missionaries (in this case Quakers from the Philadelphia Yearly Meeting) in order to open and run schools. And similar to the Cherokees and Choctaws, the Senecas saw education as beneficial to their national interests because educated Senecas would be better equipped to negotiate with the United States, with the state government of New York, and with private interests such as the Ogden Land Company, all of which would strengthen their ability to stay on their lands and reproduce their communities. The Senecas' expectations about land were also directly connected to their willingness to work with the Quakers to open schools as they saw the Quakers as allies who could be called upon to help protect Seneca lands. Finally, Seneca supporters of schooling believed that Seneca youths would gain skills that would allow them to effectively navigate and use the larger American economy for their benefit. The greatest divergence between the Senecas' relationship with schooling and those of the southern Native nations was the degree of opposition the schools faced. The Allegheny Senecas were bitterly divided over schooling. There was strong opposition from certain political leaders and pervasive apathy for formal education among the "warriors" or common rank of Senecas. This opposition persisted until Jackson's election and resulted in the opening of far fewer schools among the Senecas than among either the Cherokees or Choctaws. Ultimately, the arguments over whether or not to open schools and how to manage those that did operate demonstrate that the process undertaken by the Senecas to incorporate formal education into their community was similar to those pursued by the Cherokees and Choctaws. To realize the creation of a formal education system, Seneca supporters of schooling had to simultaneously negotiate the demands of various constituents to whom they were connected, including Senecas who opposed the schools, Quaker missionaries, and students.

***

A year after the end of the War of 1812, a Quaker missionary named Joseph Elkinton traveled to New York to proselytize to the Senecas. Elkinton was born in New Jersey in 1794 and died in Philadelphia in 1868. He was trained as a silversmith but "found that calling unsuitable for him as a Quaker," which apparently led him to missionary work as a young adult. In 1817 he would open a school among the Senecas on the Allegheny Reservation. While running the school Elkinton also educated himself by learning the Seneca language. He would live among the Senecas until 1832.[65]

Elkinton's arrival and his desire to open a school brought to the forefront strong disagreements among the Senecas as to the best way to pursue relations with white Americans. Many distrusted Elkinton because they generally distrusted white Americans. By the mid-1810s, the Senecas had experienced two decades of intense pressure from white Americans concerning their lands. The creation of Seneca reservations after the American Revolution was just the beginning of ongoing attempts from settlers, the state of New York, and the Ogden Land Company to take lands that the Senecas still possessed.[66] The Senecas' struggles to defend their lands from encroaching whites had not surprisingly led many Natives to equate white people with land dispossession. For many members of the Pagan Party (one of the dominant Seneca political parties), the Quakers were no exception, and they feared that the Friends had an ulterior motive in running a school. They were deeply afraid that the Quakers would seek payment in the form of land for educating Seneca children. Elkinton reported:

> Tunis said they thought the different communications given them by friends stating that no charge would ever be brought against them for these things [schooling, tools, etc] were of little account, as every few years white people made different laws, & he thought the Quakers were cheats.[67]

Elkinton's characterization of Tunis Halftown's perspective was representative of the views of many Senecas — white people cheated Natives out of land regardless of statements and promises to the contrary.

Other Senecas however approached relations with the Quakers from an entirely different perspective. Rather than equating white Americans primarily with land dispossession, Christian Party (the other dominant Seneca political party) leaders like James Robinson, John Pierce, and Blue Eyes saw the Friends as potential allies. They desired to create and leverage a Seneca–Quaker alliance in service of Seneca interests in ways similar to what the Cherokees and Choctaws had done through their relations with American Board missionaries. For example, they believed that Quakers could provide the Senecas with the language skills, English literacy, and cultural knowledge needed to negotiate with white Americans and the United States. As the Chiefs Wandongotha and Sunaweeyah explained to the Friends:

> Brothers since our first acquaintance with you many that were then children have grown up to maturity on whome the concerns of the Nation must shortly devolve and on this class we hope the fruit of your labours will be better seen.[68]

Some Senecas of this opinion even took extra measures to ensure that the young would be better equipped to serve the Senecas into the future by sending their children to live with Quaker families in Philadelphia. In 1822 the Seneca James Robinson asked the Quakers to take in both his son (for a second time) and another Seneca youth because he believed that "We are much in want of an interpreter that we may be able to transact our business."[69] Robinson hoped the two Seneca boys would learn enough English to negotiate treaties and other business that required English literacy.

In direct opposition to those who feared the presence of the Friends, those Senecas who sought alliance with them did so precisely because they thought that the Friends could provide instrumental help in the fight to save Seneca lands. In 1825, for example, the Senecas asked the Quakers for intelligence on the US government's intentions relative to Seneca lands. "Brothers," they wrote, "you know the movements of government in regard to Indians more particularly than we hear of at Buffalo & we desire that you would continue to inform us thereof . . . that thereby we may be instructed."[70] For many Seneca leaders, the Quakers represented a source of succor rather than a threat.

Therefore, the potential ramifications of Elkinton's arrival and his desire to open a school differed depending upon the ideological perch from which one viewed it. Because of this, the school was a flashpoint for a clash of Seneca factions. On the one hand, opponents of the school embraced a perspective in which white people represented dangerous outsiders who sought to take Seneca lands. From this vantage point, the school was a potential instrument of dispossession. On the other hand, supporters of the school fell back on an older ontological tradition that had served the Senecas throughout the colonial period: one in which outsiders (particularly white Americans) could become connected to the Senecas through alliance, enmeshed in ritual kinship relations (this is why the Senecas and the Quakers referred to each other as "brothers"), and made subject to the obligations of reciprocity. Those Senecas who held this perspective would support the school because they saw it as part of an exchange for aid that took the form of Quaker help in Seneca political struggles to maintain their lands.

Those Senecas who were predisposed to alliance with the Friends initially carried the day. Upon Elkinton's arrival, they warmly welcomed him and then took the opportunity to strengthen ties with the Philadelphia Friends by writing to the Philadelphia Yearly Meeting Indian Committee. In one of their missives, they articulated their desire to have Quakers among them affirming "We are glad you, our old Counsellors continue to regard and advise us." They then reported that they were working on opening a school. "We shall endeavor in a few days to open the way for a school," they wrote.[71]

Elkinton held the Senecas to their word and over the next year worked with Seneca leaders such as Blue Eyes, James Robinson, and John Pierce to open a school. By the summer of 1817 Elkinton and his fellow Quaker missionary Jonathan Thomas had convinced the Senecas to build a schoolhouse. However, those Senecas wary of the Quakers would not be ignored, and their influence remained strong.

This influence would prove to be a continual hindrance to the school during the years immediately following Elkinton's arrival. Shortly after construction of the school had begun, Seneca workers simply refused to continue the build. Elkinton and Thomas reported that "The Indians raised roof and plastered a house in the town 18 by 20 feet square, [but] they could not be prevailed upon to finish the house." Elkinton and Thomas consequently paid one Seneca worker to install the windows and doors of the school and then put the finishing touches on the house themselves. By early December, the school opened its doors to Seneca pupils.[72] However, it proved to be somewhat of a disappointment as few Seneca children attended it. Moreover, those who did enroll usually stayed on only from the late fall to the end of winter. By April of 1820 — after three years of struggling to operate — Elkinton reported to the Quaker Indian Committee that "15 to 23 scholars" attended the school "pretty regularly."[73] But by the beginning of summer the school was virtually empty causing Elkinton to decide to close it for the season and then reopen in Fall.

Elkinton's plan to reopen the school in the fall of 1820 caused a minor crisis as those Senecas hostile to it refused to let it open. By November the school was still closed due to stringent Seneca opposition. The opposition in fact became so strong that Elkinton feared for his safety if he tried to reopen the school. While riding home one day he was approached by Tunis Halftown, who questioned him regarding when he planned to reopen the school and how long it would remain in operation. Halftown then explained that many Senecas were "much opposed" to the school and were determined to "break up the school at Allegheny." Jonathan Thomas meanwhile had become so alarmed at Seneca displeasure with the school that he suggested that the Quakers call a council with the purpose of obtaining a pledge from the chiefs to protect Elkinton. Thomas worried that those opposed to the school would "either insult or injure" Elkinton on his way to and from school.

The depth of the opposition required that pro-school Senecas work directly with Elkinton to address it. They asked Elkinton to suggest that the Senecas hold a Council on the question of the school. However, other Christian Party leaders, though supportive of the school, refused because many of the Pagan Party chiefs who opposed to the school had gone hunting. Undeterred by this setback, John Pierce decided to call the Council. In an attempt to preempt the need for the Council, Blacksnake and Tunis Halftown, both of whom opposed the school, visited Elkinton to persuade him to give up teaching. They informed him that a new Council would be of no avail as the people were too divided over the school. Nonetheless, at the request of James Robinson and John Pierce, the Council was held and it was decided over strong opposition to commence with the school. This decision was reached only because the opposition was sufficiently mollified by a proposal that the Friends would put in writing their promise not to demand land in repayment for teaching Seneca children. Days before the school reopened, James Robinson explained that "for the satisfaction of some of our people's minds," he needed "the parchment that has been promised."[74]

The school reopened on November 27, 1820, but not without continued problems. As Jonathan Thomas had feared, Elkinton was subjected to intimidation. The chief Blue Eyes informed Elkinton that one Seneca whose house Elkinton passed on the way to school intended to "get a hickory and give me a whipping," while another Seneca threatened to smash the canoe Elkinton used to cross the river on his way to the schoolhouse. And true to the threat, one day after school Elkinton returned to the river to find his canoe "considerably broken." Despite these problems, Elkinton kept the school open with the ongoing support of the Christian Party chiefs. He continued to teach while Seneca supporters such as Pierce and Robinson formed a committee to oversee the school. On the day of the school's reopening, the committee came to school and encouraged the children to learn.[75] Yet the intensity and depth of Seneca disagreements over Elkinton's school led it to experience an alternating series of openings and closings. The opposition was simply too strong and emotionally heated to keep the school running for long lengths of time. As school supporters reported: "It has been a time of great commotion with these people, those opposed to improvements have succeeded in getting the school discontinued."[76]

To quell this commotion, pro-school Seneca leaders proposed a novel idea for the school. Rather than operate the school on Seneca land, they suggested that the Quakers open a school on farm land at Tunesassa — an area that abutted the Allegheny Reservation but that was already owned and occupied by the Quakers. We "wish to know," wrote pro-school Seneca chiefs, "whether friends are willing a school house should be built on their land at Tunesassa."[77] This plan had a host of benefits. Foremost among these was that due to the fact that the school was on land already owned by the Friends, the presence of the school would not act as a potential mechanism to transfer ownership of the land upon which it sat from Seneca to Quaker hands. And just as importantly, the Senecas would, from the school's inception, be partners with the Quakers in creating and running it. This would mean that the Senecas were not just receiving a benefit from the Quakers — a benefit for which the Friends could potentially demand repayment in the form of land. Rather, they would be equal contributors to the school. In fact, it was decided that the Senecas and the Quakers would work jointly to build the school. This plan sufficiently addressed the concerns of wary Senecas, and in early March of 1821 the Quakers also accepted it. To add more reassurance, the Friends reiterated in writing their pledge to not to ask for land in exchange for teaching. At the end of March, they delivered the written pledge to the Senecas[78] and shortly thereafter construction on the new schoolhouse began.

The Christian Party chiefs continued to collaborate closely with the Friends in order to open and maintain the Tunesassa school. By August 1821 they had made great strides in building the new schoolhouse.[79] And despite continued opposition from some Seneca leaders like Cornplanter and Blacksnake, by January 1822 the schoolhouse was ready to open.[80] Once the school opened in early 1822, Christian Party chiefs continued to support it by hiring a Seneca woman to come and work at the school. She cleaned and cared for the children who boarded at the school, alleviating the Friends from doing this work and thereby further assuaging worries that the Friends would demand payment for services rendered. "The chiefs about 3 weeks since have concluded to hire one of their women to attend to cooking & washing for the school children,"[81] reported Elkinton.

The effect of direct Seneca involvement with the Tunesassa school was to keep it in operation for the next five years. However, the school remained small, serving between 25 and 30 students at any given time. Eventually it broke into two and housed one school for boys and another for girls. By January 1827 the Quaker missionaries reported somewhat mixed news on school attendance. "The schools under our care at Tunesassa continue to be attended by the children — the one for boys not as large as would be desirable — the girls pretty full."[82]

Even though the school served small numbers of students, the Senecas maintained it because they saw it as serving to prepare the next generation of Seneca leaders. "We wish you to continue your labours amongst us & instruct our children as they are the persons who will shortly have to take the reins of government,"[83] they explained to the Quaker Indian Committee in Philadelphia. And just as importantly, Seneca–Quaker cooperation around the school strengthened their alliance and provided opportunity for the Senecas to leverage the Friends in protection of Seneca lands. Throughout the 1820s, the Senecas repeatedly asked them for advice and information concerning land.[84] The school would remain open and functioning until the end of 1828, when it would briefly close. The cause of this closure was a suggestion by a contingent of Philadelphia Yearly Meeting Indian Committee members who were visiting Allegheny. Upon seeing the small number of students, they suggested to the Senecas that the Natives entirely take over operations of the school. Their move offended the Senecas who perceived it as the Friends shirking their obligation as allies.[85] The incident resulted in the school's complete closure by the end of the 1828 spring term. It would remain closed for the fall term of 1828.

By the beginning of 1829 however, the Tunesassa school would enter into a new phase and reopen. Its prospects would brighten precisely because the Senecas decided to take up the Friends' suggestion and run the school themselves. Elkinton aided this change by recommending a Seneca to take over as teacher. He approached the Seneca Robert Pierce and asked him if he would be willing that his son James Pierce teach at Tunesassa. Robert Pierce proposed this possibility to the Seneca Council and in early February they agreed to employ James at Tunesassa for a period of two months. Moreover, they decided that students would pay for their schooling (either $1 or 50c per month). The school consequently reopened on February 4th with seven girls and 12 boys.[86] It would close for the summer two months later but then reopen in November 1829. By the fall, the Seneca Council was more keen to keep the school running and decreed that it would be in operation for at least five months. Other Seneca leaders would maintain this momentum. For example, in December 1829 Maris Pierce wrote: "The importance of having a school in our limits is great."[87] By late December, the Council threw more support to the school by establishing opening and closing dates and school hours, and by setting up a committee of Senecas that was to visit the school weekly and provide reports.[88] After running for a few months, more and more Senecas began to support the Tunesassa school. Reporting on a Council held on March 1, 1830, Elkinton recorded that "one of the chiefs of the nation was present (whose son attended school) and he spoke of having it discontinued, but the minds of others present did not appear to be prepared thereto."[89]

As was the case with the Cherokees and Choctaws, the election of President Jackson and the renewed threat to Native lands was one reason Seneca interest in the Tunesassa school revived. Jackson's pro-Removal position had led even members of the Pagan Party to consider supporting the school. Elkinton recorded that Blacksnake had admitted that he had been "backward" in his views toward schooling and was now "disposed to encourage a school" as were "some of his party."[90] Between late 1829 and the first months of 1830, declining opposition and increasing support for the Tunesassa school would ensure that formal education remained in operation at Allegheny. However, and importantly, the Senecas themselves would run it. And as with the southern Native nations, increased Seneca support for formal education was not just a reaction to reinvigorated threats of Removal, but rather reflected a coalescence around the idea that to persist, the Senecas would need to find ways to be best prepared to coexist with an increasingly threatening settler state.

By the antebellum era, Seneca desire to promote formal education was clearly on an upswing as other groups of Senecas also concluded that their continued persistence depended on their ability to navigate and interact with the settler society. A group of chiefs from the Cattaraugus Senecas reported that "our people are now more in favor of education than they have been in years that are past, some appearing quite anxious to have their children educated." One reason for the increased enthusiasm was the recognition that education would provide skills that would be economically beneficial to Seneca individuals. Indeed, when the Cattaraugus Senecas asked the Quakers to open a school on their reservation, they explained that the Natives chose the Quakers because their instruction "is well calculated to benefit our children" because it included "various branches of industry."[91]

Schools ultimately became more prevalent in Seneca country during the 1840s and 1850s. More Native men and women became teachers to Seneca youths, relegating the Friends, who had previously been the main source of school teachers, to the roles of advisor or administrator. For example, Ebenezer Worth reported that one school was "taught by Edward Pierce, a Native." Nor was Worth insecure in Pierce's abilities as a teacher. "I do not know that I could have been better suited in any white man I could have got."[92] Seneca women also assumed the role of teacher. In 1858 Joseph Elkinton reported that Cynthia Pierce, a relative of Edward Pierce, was the teacher of the "state school." Elkinton commented: "it is very pleasant to find instances of the Natives being engaged teaching their own people."[93] Once white intermediaries were banished to the margins, the schools became thoroughly Native institutions with Indigenous individuals occupying the roles of teacher and of student. What this created was a new element of Seneca experience in which part of what it meant to be Seneca involved attending formal schools with other Seneca youths under the guidance of a Seneca teacher. The realization of this eventuality resulted, in great part, because those Senecas who had imagined formal education taking root among them believed that schooling would help reproduce their community amidst growing settler threats.

Conclusion

Between the close of the War of 1812 and the passage in May 1830 of the Indian Removal Act, the Cherokees, Choctaws, and Senecas engaged in similar processes that aimed to create formal education systems within their nations. Indigenous leaders supportive of establishing formal education systems in their communities negotiated and leveraged their relationships with a variety of groups to realize their goals. They simultaneously addressed demands of their missionary allies, of Native groups opposed to schooling, and in many cases, of Native students and parents, in order to open schools and keep them in operation. In so doing, they took a non-Indigenous institution — formal education — and used it to serve Native interests. Indigenous supporters of education saw opportunities for Native youths to acquire skills that would help Native nations in political negotiations with white Americans and with the United States. In this way, and through the alliances Natives reinforced in working with missionary partners on the schools, Natives sought to strengthen their position to protect their lands and to ensure that their communities persisted. Those Natives who opposed the schools initially checked the degree to which formal education would spread within each Native nation examined here. Yet such opposition would ultimately prove far less significant as experiments with schooling created important foundations for utilizing formal education as a means for Native nations to continue to regenerate themselves as Indigenous peoples under settler colonialism. By the Removal period, that role would expand and formal education would become an important institution among the Cherokees, Choctaws, and Senecas.

The utility of formal education would become clear with the Removal crisis as Natives would wage anti-Removal campaigns using words, rhetoric, and logic. The literacy skills that Natives had acquired in the early part of the nineteenth century was in other words highly consequential as it provided Native writers with the abilities to prosecute sustained, public antiremoval movements in which they saliently delineated the inequities of Removal, and cogently laid out their reasons for opposition to it. The calculus they had drawn between education, land, and the people proved prescient.

Notes

1. Aflred Finney to Jeremiah Evarts, July 11, 1825, ABCFM 18.3.1 v. 6, American Board of Commissioners for Foreign Missions Records, Houghton Library, Harvard University, Cambridge, MA.
2. The links between evangelism and education were not new in the nineteenth century, but rather had a long history dating back to the early colonial era. In the middle of the seventeenth century, for example, the Puritan missionary John Eliot created his well-known "praying towns" in Massachusetts. They comprised English-speaking Natives who had adopted Christianity. Some religious leaders in the Bay Colony saw these settlements as models of the potential education held for Native improvement. Between Eliot's experiment and the opening of missions in the early nineteenth century, others tried their hand at Indian education. For instance, in the middle of the eighteenth century, Eleazar Wheelock, a Congregationalist minister from Connecticut, founded his Indian School with the specific intention of promoting Christianization. He envisioned a cadre of Native preachers, who having come to God would serve as ministers to other Indians. The Mohegans, Joseph Johnson, and the more famous Samson Occom, were among his most successful pupils as both learned English, became ordained ministers, and spent many years preaching to various Native peoples. For an autobiographical account of Samson Occom, see Samson Occom, "A Short Narrative of My Life," in Bernd Peyer, ed., *The Elders Wrote: An Anthology of Early Prose by North American Indians, 1768–1831* (Berlin, Germany: Dietrich Reimer, 1982). For Joseph Johnson,

see Laura Murray, ed., *To Do Good to My Indian Brethren: The Writings of Joseph Johnson 1751–1776* (Amherst, MA: University of Massachusetts Press, 1998).

3. Joyce B. Phillips and Paul Gary Phillips, eds., *The Brainerd Journal: A Mission to the Cherokees, 1817–1823* (Lincoln, NE: University of Nebraska Press, 1998), November 2, 1818, 88–90.

4. Moody Hall to Cherokee Deputation, December 4, 1818, ABC 18.3.1 v. 3, American Board of Commissioners for Foreign Missions Records, Houghton Library, Harvard University, Cambridge, MA.

5. Phillips and Phillips, *The Brainerd Journal*, November 2, 1818, 89–90.

6. David Folsom to Elias Cornelius, October 9, 1818, Jay L. Hargett Papers, Western History Collection, University of Oklahoma, Norman, OK.

7. On the Creek War, see Claudio Saunt, *A New Order of Things: Property, Power, and the Transformation of the Creek Indians, 1733–1816* (New York: Cambridge University Press, 1999). Like southern nations, many northern Natives also perceived force as an unworkable strategy for their protection. The defeat of the Shawnee brothers Tecumseh and Tenskwatawa in 1815 spelled a virtual end to Native military power in the northern section of trans-Appalachian west. On the end of Native military power east of the Mississippi, see Daniel Richter, *Facing East From Indian Country: A Native History of Early America* (Cambridge, MA: Harvard University Press, 2001), and Francois Furstenberg, "The Significance of the Trans-Appalachian Frontier in Atlantic History," *The American Historical Review*, 113, no. 3 (Chicago, June 2008), 647–77.

8. David Folsom to Elias Cornelius, October 9, 1818, Jay L. Hargett Papers, Western History Collection, University of Oklahoma, Norman, OK.

9. David Folsom to Jeremiah Evarts, January 19, 1825, Folder 6, Number 15, Cyrus Kingsbury Collection, in the Western History Collection, University of Oklahoma, Norman, OK.

10. For an examination of this transformation among the Creek, see Saunt, *A New Order of Things*.

11. Phillips and Phillips, *The Brainerd Journal*, July 15, 1818, 73–5.

12. Ibid., April 16, 1818, 53.

13. John Ross and Charles Hicks to Samuel Worcester, March 6, 1819, ABCFM 18.3.1 v. 3, American Board of Commissioners for Foreign Missions Records, Houghton Library, Harvard University, Cambridge, MA.

14. Hicks and Ross to Worcester, March 6, 1819, in Phillips and Phillips, *The Brainerd Journal*.

15. Cyrus Kingsbury to Samuel Worcester, October 15, 1816, ABCFM 18.3.1 v. 3, American Board of Commissioners for Foreign Missions Records, Houghton Library, Harvard University, Cambridge, MA.

16. Cyrus Kingsbury to Jeremiah Evarts, July 18, 1823, Folder 7, Number 4, Cyrus Kingsbury Collection, in the Western History Collection, University of Oklahoma, Norman, OK.

17. Cyrus Kingsbury to Samuel Worcester, December 20, 1820, Folder 10, Item 2, Cyrus Kingsbury Collection, in the Western History Collection, University of Oklahoma, Norman, OK.

18. Phillips and Phillips, *The Brainerd Journal*, see entries for March 3, 7, 8, and 11, 1820 and see entry for April 13, 1820.

19. Ibid., see entries for May 4, 8, 24, and 31, 1820, and entry for June 23, 1820.

20. Peter Pitchlynn Papers, June 1832, Folder 113a, Call number 3026.328, Gilcrease Museum, Tulsa, OK.

21. Clara Sue Kidwell has argued that among the Choctaws, "education had little or no impact." See Clara Sue Kidwell, *Choctaws and Missionaries in Mississippi, 1818–1918* (Norman, OK: University of Oklahoma Press, 1995), 68.

22. On the number of students enrolled at Brainerd, see Phillips and Phillips, eds., *The Brainerd Journal*, tables 4 & 5, pages 406–23.

23. Isaac Proctor to Jeremiah Evarts, Annual Report of the Hightower School, July 30, 1825, ABCFM 18.3.1 v. 4, American Board of Commissioners for Foreign Missions Records, Houghton Library, Harvard University, Cambridge, MA.
24. Phillips and Phillips, *The Brainerd Journal*, March 24, 1820, 160.
25. Ibid., November 1, 1820, 195. For the text of this law, see Scholarly Resources, Inc., *The Constitutions and Laws of the American Indian Tribes*, Volume 5 (Wilmington, DE: Rowman and Littlefield Publishers, 1973), 13–14.
26. Phillips and Phillips, *The Brainerd Journal*, May 13, 1820, 173.
27. Ibid., January 2, 1819, 100–1.
28. Ibid., July 19, 1822, 289.
29. Ibid., see entries for July 18–19, 1822 and for August 3, 1822.
30. Ibid.
31. Ibid, August 3, 1822, 294–5.
32. Phillips and Phillips, *The Brainerd Journal*, May 29, 1819, 117.
33. Mayhew Journal, May 31, 1823, Folder 9, Item 21, Cyrus Kingsbury Collection, in the Western History Collection, University of Oklahoma, Norman, OK.
34. Mayhew Journal, May 8, 1823, Folder 9, Item 21, Cyrus Kingsbury Collection, in the Western History Collection, University of Oklahoma, Norman, OK.
35. Ibid., June 8, 1823.
36. Ibid., December 11, 1822, 321–2.
37. Mayhew Journal, April 12, 1823, Folder 9, Item 21, Cyrus Kingsbury Collection, in the Western History Collection, University of Oklahoma, Norman, OK.
38. Extract of a letter dated July 9, 1825, from Holcomb contained in Cyrus Kingsbury to Jeremiah Evarts, August 8, 1825 Folder 6, Number 47, Cyrus Kingsbury Collection, in the Western History Collection, University of Oklahoma, Norman, OK.
39. Joel Wood to Cyrus Kingsbury, April 12, 1822, Folder 9, Item 27, Cyrus Kingsbury Collection, in the Western History Collection, University of Oklahoma, Norman, OK.
40. Cyrus Kingsbury to the American Board, July 16, 1821, Folder 10, Item 4, Cyrus Kingsbury Collection, in the Western History Collection, University of Oklahoma, Norman, OK.
41. Cyrus Kingsbury to Jeremiah Evarts, February 10, 1825, Folder 6, Item 53, Cyrus Kingsbury Collection, in the Western History Collection, University of Oklahoma, Norman, OK.
42. Mayhew Journal, June 25, 1824, Folder 9, Item 21, Cyrus Kingsbury Collection, in the Western History Collection, University of Oklahoma, Norman, OK.
43. Extract of a letter from Hocomb, August 8, 1825, Folder 6, Item 47, Cyrus Kingsbury Collection, in the Western History Collection, University of Oklahoma, Norman, OK.
44. Mayhew Journal, May 6, 1823, Folder 9, Item 21, Cyrus Kingsbury Collection, in the Western History Collection, University of Oklahoma, Norman, OK.
45. Cyrus Kingsbury to Jeremiah Evarts, May 10, 1823, Folder 9, Item 19, Cyrus Kingsbury Collection, in the Western History Collection, University of Oklahoma, Norman, OK.
46. William Chamberlin to Jeremiah Evarts, September 11, 1824, ABCFM 18.3.1 v. 4, American Board of Commissioners for Foreign Missions Records, Houghton Library, Harvard University, Cambridge, MA.
47. Ibid.
48. Isaac Proctor to Jeremiah Evarts, Annual Report, July 30, 1825, ABCFM 18.3.1 v. 4, American Board of Commissioners for Foreign Missions Records, Houghton Library, Harvard University, Cambridge, MA.
49. John Elsworth to Jeremiah Evarts, August 8, 1829, ABCFM 18.3.1 v. 4, American Board of Commissioners for Foreign Missions Records, Houghton Library, Harvard University, Cambridge, MA.
50. Cyrus Kingsbury to the American Board, April 9, 1829, Folder 9, Item 2, Cyrus Kingsbury Collection, in the Western History Collection, University of Oklahoma, Norman, OK.

51. Letter of Choctaw Parents, June 27, 1829, Cyrus Kingsbury Collection, in the Western History Collection, University of Oklahoma, Norman, OK.

52. John Ross, Richard Taylor, Daniel McCoy, Hair Conrad, John Timson to Seneca Delegation, April 14, 1834, in Gary E. Moulton, *The Papers of Chief John Ross, Vol. 1, 1807–1839* (Norman, OK: University of Oklahoma Press, 1985), 285.

53. Elizur Butler to David Greene, April 28, 1836, ABC 18.3.1 v. 7, American Board of Commissioners for Foreign Missions Records, Houghton Library, Harvard University, Cambridge, MA.

54. Sophia Sawyer to David Greene, April 17, 1835, ABC 18.3.1 v. 8, American Board of Commissioners for Foreign Missions Records, Houghton Library, Harvard University, Cambridge, MA.

55. John Ridge to David Greene, February 20, 1837, ABC 18.3.1 v. 8, American Board of Commissioners for Foreign Missions Records, Houghton Library, Harvard University, Cambridge, MA.

56. Kidwell, *Choctaws and Missionaries in Mississippi, 1818–1918*, 160.

57. Ibid.

58. Clara Sue Kidwell, *The Choctaws in Oklahoma* (Norman, OK: University of Oklahoma Press, 2007), 9.

59 *The Constitutions and Laws of the American Indian Tribes*, Vol. 5, "Laws of the Cherokee Nation: Adopted by the Council at Various Periods, Printed for the Benefit of the Nation, 1852," Scholarly Resources Inc. (Wilmington, DE, 1973), 30.

60. Phillips and Phillips, *The Brainerd Journal*, 401.

61. Peter Pitchlynn to Thomas McKenney, December 13, 1848, Jay L. Hargett Papers, University of Oklahoma, Norman, OK.

62. Israel Folsom to Peter Pitchlynn, n.d., Box 1, Folder 76, Peter Perkins Pitchlynn Collection, Western History Collection, University of Oklahoma, Norman, OK. Quoted in Kidwell, *The Choctaws in Oklahoma*, 10.

63. See Devon Mihesuah, *Cultivating the Rosebuds: The Education of Women at the Cherokee Female Seminary, 1851–1909* (Urbana, IL: University of Illinois Press, 1993). Mihesuah has argued that Cherokee leaders hoped the Seminaries would show others the tribe's "modernity."

64. John Ross to the Cherokee National Council, September 12, 1839, in Moulton, *The Papers of Chief John Ross, Vol. 1, 1807–1839*, 760.

65. For biographical information on Joseph Elkinton, see "Elkinton, Joseph, 1794–1868," in the Dictionary of Quaker Biography, Quaker Collection, Special Collections, Haverford College, Philadelphia, PA. Also see Elkinton's obituary in *The Friend*, 41, no. 27 (February 29, 1868), Quaker Collection, Special Collections, Haverford College, Philadelphia, PA.

66. For the dispossession of the Haudenosaunees in the early nineteenth century, see Laurence Hauptman, *A Conspiracy of Interests: Iroquois Dispossession and the Rise of New York State* (Syracuse, NY: Syracuse University Press, 2001).

67. Joseph Elkinton to Holliday Jackson, December 3, 1820, Correspondence of PYMIC, AA41, Box 2, Folder 3, #98, Special Collections, Quaker Collection, Haverford College, Philadelphia, PA.

68. Wandongothta or Chief Warrior and Sunaweeyah or Snow to PYMIC, June 28, 1824, AA41, Box 1, #151, Correspondence of PYMIC, Special Collections, Quaker Collection, Haverford College, Philadelphia, PA.

69. Joseph Elkinton to Thomas Wistar, transcribed speech of Blue Eyes, Robinson, John Peirce, George Silverheels, and Big John to PYMIC, March 29, 1822, AA41, Box 2, Folder 3, #112, Records of PYMIC, Special Collections, Quaker Collection, Haverford College, Philadelphia, PA.

70. Blue Eyes, James Robinson, Long John, John Pierce to PYMIC, March 13, 1825, AA41, Box 2, Folder 3, #159, Records of PYMIC, Special Collections, Quaker Collection, Haverford College, Philadelphia, PA.

71. Joseph Elkinton's transcription of Seneca speech, September 18, 1816, AA41, Box 2, Folder 3, #6, Records of PYMIC, Quaker Collection, Special Collections, Haverford College, Philadelphia, PA.

72. Jonathan Thomas and J. Elkinton to Isaac W. Morris, December 17, 1817, Correspondence of PYMIC, AA41, Box 2, #30, Special Collections, Quaker Collection, Haverford College, Philadelphia, PA.

73. Joseph Elkinton to the Committee on Indian Concerns, April 13, 1820, Correspondence of PYMIC, AA41, Box 2, Folder 3, #89, Special Collections, Quaker Collection, Haverford College, Philadelphia, PA.

74. Joseph Elkinton to Holliday Jackson, December 3, 1820, Correspondence of PYMIC, AA41, Box 2, Folder 3, #98, Special Collections, Quaker Collection, Haverford College, Philadelphia, PA.

75. Ibid.

76. Joseph Elkinton to PYMIC, translation of Seneca words, March 5, 1821, AA41 Box 2, Folder 3, #103, Records of PYMIC, Special Collections, Quaker Collection, Haverford College, Philadelphia, PA.

77. Ibid.

78. Joseph Elkinton to Thomas Wistar, March 27, 1821, AA41, Box 2, Folder 3, #104, Records of PYMIC, Special Collections, Quaker Collection, Haverford College, Philadelphia, PA.

79. Joseph Elkinton to Thomas Wistar, August 20, 1821, AA41, Box 2, Folder 3, #126, Records of PYMIC, Special Collections, Quaker Collection, Haverford College, Philadelphia, PA.

80. Joseph Elkinton to PYMIC, January 2, 1822, AA41, Box 2, Folder 3, #113, Records of PYMIC, Special Collections, Quaker Collection, Haverford College, Philadelphia, PA.

81. Joseph Elkinton and Robert Scotton to Thomas Wistar, July 27, 1822, AA41, Box 2, Folder 3, #130, Records of PYMIC, Special Collections, Quaker Collection, Haverford College, Philadelphia, PA.

82. Robert Scotton, Joseph Walton, Joseph Elkinton, Abigail Walton, and Mary Nutt to PYMIC, January 4, 1827, AA41, Box, Folder 3, #167, Records of PYMIC, Special Collections, Quaker Collection, Haverford College, Philadelphia, PA.

83. Joseph Elkinton to PYMIC, translation of speech by Seneca chiefs, September 14, 1823, AA41, Box 2, Folder 3, #147, Records of PYMIC, Special Collections, Quaker Collection, Haverford College, Philadelphia, PA.

84. See, for example, Wandongothta or Chief Warrior and Sunaweeyah or Snow to PYMIC, June 28, 1824, AA41, Box 1, #151, PYMIC Correspondence, Special Collections, Quaker Collection, Haverford College, Philadelphia, PA; and Blue Eyes, James Robinson, Long John, and John Peirce to PYMIC, March 13, 1825, AA41, Box 2, Folder 3, #159, Records of PYMIC, Special Collections, Quaker Collection, Haverford College, Philadelphia, PA.

85. Journal of Joseph Elkinton, 1815–1864, entry for March 8, 1828, AB 39, Records of PYMIC, Special Collections, Quaker Collection, Haverford College, Philadelphia, PA.

86. Ibid., entry for February 5, 1829.

87. Ibid., entry for December 18, 1829.

88. Ibid., entries for December 21 and 23, 1829.

89. Ibid., entry for March 1, 1830.

90. Journal of Joseph Elkinton, 1815–1864, entry for November 13, 1828, AB 39, Records of PYMIC, Special Collections, Quaker Collection, Haverford College, Philadelphia, PA.

91. Young Chief, Joseph Snow, and Isaac Warrior to Philadelphia Yearly Meeting Indian Committee, July 1, 1852, Indian Records Vols. 1–10, AB 31, 1850–1861, Records of PYMIC, Quaker Collection, Special Collections, Haverford College, Philadelphia, PA.

92. Ebenezer Worth to Philadelphia Yearly Meeting Indian Committee, February 1, 1845, Indian Records Vols. 1–10, AB 30, 1841–1850, Records of PYMIC, Quaker Collection, Special Collections, Haverford College, Philadelphia, PA.
93. Journal entry on October 17, 1858, Journal of Joseph Elkinton, 1815–1864, AB 39, Records of PYMIC, Quaker Collection, Special Collections, Haverford College, Philadelphia, PA.

4   The Campaigns Against Removal, 1829–1842

The Removal question became the nation's central political controversy of the late 1820s. Conflict began in earnest during the winter of 1829 when Congress began to debate the Indian Removal bill — a proposed law that would facilitate the migration of eastern Native nations by allowing the President to exchange lands west of the Mississippi River for the tribes' existing lands in the East. Andrew Jackson, who had to a considerable extent predicated a large portion of his presidential campaign on the promise that he would enforce Removal, thrust the debate more clearly onto the national scene. His assumption of office followed shortly by the introduction into Congress of the Indian Removal bill stoked fears that Removal might become a reality. In response to this threat, a coalition consisting primarily of Cherokee leaders, American Board officials, and northern evangelicals organized and prosecuted a vigorous antiremoval campaign. As contention over the Indian Removal bill filled the halls of Congress, antiremovalists undertook concerted action to persuade Congressmen to vote against the bill. Tribal leaders sent both houses of Congress detailed antiremoval petitions explicating their reasons for opposing the bill, while northern churches drafted antiremoval memorials that were signed by congregants and other local citizens before they too were sent to Washington. By the late spring of 1830, over 1400 memorials from Natives and white Americans had reached Congress. In addition to their focus on US government officials, antiremovalists also laid their cause before the American public by publishing a flurry of newspaper articles outlining their case against Removal.

While the antiremoval campaign of 1829–1830 focused most conspicuously on preventing Cherokee removal, another equally heated political effort against Removal would erupt in 1838 as a coalition of Native and white Americans would work to prevent the removal of the Senecas from western New York. The controversy began with charges of fraud in the proceedings surrounding the signing of the 1838 Treaty of Buffalo Creek — an agreement concocted by agents of the Ogden Land Company, which claimed proprietary rights to Seneca lands. This controversy pitted the Senecas and their Quaker allies against the Ogden Land Company and officials of the US government. And as with the Removal debate of 1829, this campaign featured petitions to Congress and to the President, as well as efforts to sway the American public to support the Senecas and their rights to stay on their lands. The campaign against Seneca removal would endure into the early 1840s and ultimately would prove more successful than antiremoval efforts undertaken on behalf of the southern Native nations.

The efforts antiremovalists undertook along with the charged emotions they displayed during the national antiremoval campaigns beg the question of motivation. Why did they so desperately want to prevent Removal? While the rationale that engendered a visceral opposition among Natives to emigration is clear — they did not want to be forced from their homes — it is not so immediately apparent why Removal proved so troubling to a number of white Americans. To explain white opposition to Removal, we must consider both religious and secular factors. On one level, white opposition to Removal derived from the fear that it posed a serious threat to evangelical efforts to Native Americans. Religious leaders, missionaries, and common churchgoers worried that Removal would deprive Natives of the economic means to support themselves by driving them from their farms and lands. In addition, they worried that Removal would prove to be a debilitating and traumatic event that would create severe emotional distress. This combination would inevitably lead Natives to lose focus on their efforts to convert to Christianity. Removal, therefore, disrupted what many white Americans perceived as a divine directive to spread the Christian faith to those who had not yet heard "the good news." On another level, white antiremovalists were profoundly troubled by the secular ramifications of Removal and in particular fretted over its impact on America's national character. During the Jacksonian period, the United States was still in the process of determining its collective identity. Antiremovalists believed that if the United States sanctioned Removal, it would define America as an avaricious nation whose society was callous and inhumane. The policy would officially condone the greed of settlers clamoring for Native lands and would signal a conscious decision by the nation's political leaders to turn away from what white antiremovalists saw as a paternalistic duty to protect and "improve" the Indians. Natives would be subjected to a cruel fate in which they were simultaneously exploited and abandoned. The fear of what Removal would do to the nation's character, along with the possibility that it would thwart Native evangelism, worked in tandem to drive particular white Americans to unite with Natives in fervent opposition to the policy.

As Native and white antiremovalists would find common cause in the drive to stop Removal, they would likewise work together to develop a powerful strategy to press their case. They cast Removal as an immoral and illegal policy that violated Native rights. Moreover, they asserted that instead of "savages" who must be separated by force from the United States, Natives were "civilized" peoples possessed of rights that could be exercised within American legal, social, economic, and political arenas. This rhetoric was central to both the antiremoval campaign of 1829–1830 involving the Cherokees and the 1838–1842 case concerning the Senecas.

The Removal debate however ran deeper than the obvious dispute over land and who would occupy it. Removal was a referendum on who could participate in early nineteenth-century American civilization. More specifically, Removal reflected an ideological debate over what peoples could pursue the liberal promises of self-interest and self-actualization, and which groups could take advantage of Enlightenment beliefs like the ability to improve community through the harnessing of human agency. Essentially, pro-removalists argued that Natives were not to participate in any of these central national concerns of early US civilization; while antiremovalists, with their repeated invocation of Native rights, argued for the opposite. All involved recognized that Removal as a policy was designed to displace Natives from participation in the core ideological and social concerns of the early United States just as powerfully as it sought to extirpate Natives from their lands.

For the Indigenous historical actors, however, such concerns boiled down to connection. Would Natives remain in relationship to American civilization or not? And if so, what would those relationships look like? Native antiremovalists essentially argued that they had been linked to the United States and that they would continue to be so. Their understanding of this connection though did not take the settler logic of whether or not Indigenous peoples could or would engage with the liberal promises of American civilization. And though Native antiremovalists would argue passionately for "rights," the base upon which they made these claims rested on and was embedded within Native conceptualizations. More specifically, Native antiremovalists understood their relationships to the United States as ones in which agreements and treaties had brought Native peoples and white Americans together as allied partners in which they had mutual and ongoing obligations to each other. At the heart of these relationships lay Indigenous understandings of *reciprocity*. Allies bound by agreements (treaties) were to keep alive those agreements by meeting the needs of each. From the perspectives of Indigenous antiremovalists, the decades preceding the Removal controversy had showed that Natives had taken seriously the needs of the settler society. Native peoples' willingness to engage with Christianity, family farming, private land ownership, and formal education systems were proof that Natives had worked to accommodate, at least to a degree, the interests the United States had articulated relative to Natives. In return, they demanded simply that the United States not literally cast them aside. In the context of the Removal debate, this demand manifested in assertions and arguments prosecuted by Indigenous peoples through the public sphere. These arguments generally claimed that Natives were possessed of a variety of natural, legal, and civic rights. It might appear then that Natives made their case by drawing on principles inherent to liberalism, democracy, and the Enlightenment. While this was the language that they employed, the larger context within which they spoke or wrote remained based upon Indigenous conceptions of reciprocity. In other words, the reason Natives had "rights" was not because they were to be possessed abstractly or objectively as a priori constructs that existed apart from human relations, but rather they held them explicitly because Natives and white Americans had constructed real relationships that had placed them in positions of ongoing responsibility to each other. These relationships (alliances) gave birth to the mutual obligations (understood by white Americans as rights) and it was through these continuing relationships that Natives would not be and should not be subject to Removal. The protestations of Native antiremovalists were in this regard reminders to Americans and to the United States of their obligations to their Native partners. Even though Native antiremovalists cited their rights and made their case through the public sphere, these were the media, not the fundamental driving principles behind their arguments against Removal. The fulfillment of reciprocal obligation was the basic concept Indigenous peoples brought to bear on the Removal debate. This is why they continuously cited what Natives had done on behalf of white Americans (treaties, land cessions, engagement with cultural change) when they argued that the United States should not proceed with Removal. The antiremoval campaigns waged by Natives should not be read as futile attempts to ask for "rights" that were "earned" through Indigenous "assimilation." Rather, Native antiremovalists based their position upon the principle that they and their white American partners occupied stations in which they were mutually obligated to each other. They would transplant this concept key into a different domain — the public sphere[1] — so as to protect their presence within and upon the lands to which they were a part.

Antecedents of Antiremoval Rhetoric and Thought

The origins of the arguments that antiremovalists employed in the campaigns of the late 1820s through the early 1840s had antecedents that dated back to earlier in the century when Natives had forged partnerships with religious groups and agreements with the American government. Such connections were the base on which rhetorical and conceptual foundations of the antiremoval movement were laid. Following the turn of the nineteenth century, for example, many Native leaders had already begun citing Indigenous cultural changes as evidence of actions Natives had done on behalf of white Americans and thus a reason why white Americans should in return help protect Native lands. The Seneca James Robinson, for instance, explained that he and others

> were afraid to oppose the views of the President & have nothing to do with improvements because they believed their situation would be very critical & dangerous if they should do so: for to the President they looked for safety, respecting the holding of their lands.[2]

By "improvements" Robinson meant Christianization, formal education, and family farming; and as his words clearly show, he thought that Seneca incorporation of these cultural institutions was directly connected to the Senecas' ability to leverage the President's protection of Native lands. Other Senecas followed Robinson's example. In one typical instance, Seneca leaders combined a request for a political favor from the Philadelphia Quakers with a reminder that the Friends had promised assistance if Natives embraced cultural change. "Brothers," wrote the Senecas, "you have often told us if we would live soberly, be industrious and learn the good ways of the white people, it would be a lasting benefit to our Nation, and also encourage you in assisting us."[3] The Cherokees utilized the same strategy as the Senecas had by repeatedly attempting to persuade the President to secure their lands by citing progress in "civilization." In 1824 Cherokee leaders wrote to President Monroe and asked him to intercede on their behalf regarding land disputes with the state of Georgia. Their request began with a status report on their "progress" in becoming "civilized." "Your magnanimous and benevolent exertions have not been in vain, as respects the Cherokees; education, agriculture, manufacture, and the mechanic arts have been introduced among them, and are now progressing." They followed this account with a request for the President to protect their land rights:

> The Cherokee Nation have now come to a decisive and unalterable conclusion not to cede away any more lands. . . . [T]herefore it is an incumbent duty on the nation to preserve unimpaired the *rights* of posterity to the lands of their Ancestors. . . . Father. We would now beg your interposition with Congress in behalf of your red children the Cherokees, so that provision may be made by Law to authorize an adjustment between the United States and the State of Georgia, so that the former may be released from the existing compact [of 1802].[4]

From the Cherokees' perspective, their adoption of certain American cultural practices was an important gesture that had nurtured the kinship relationship between the Cherokees and the United States. In return, these actions had entitled them to claim the President's (their father's) aid and to call on him to guard their land rights. Moreover, even before Removal exploded on the national political scene, the Cherokees were already attaching conceptions of "rights" and "law" directly to the political relationship they had with the United States.

One reason Natives made direct and explicit connections between cultural change within Indigenous communities and land rights was because many white Americans had drawn the same link, generally characterizing it as an explicit quid pro quo agreement. This of course reinforced the reciprocal character that Indigenous peoples had placed on their relations with white Americans. As their documents reveal, some Quakers seemed to mimic Native understandings of reciprocity when they cited Indigenous cultural change as the most powerful way for Natives to secure rights. In 1819 the Indian Committee of the New York Yearly Meeting reported:

> It was concluded that it would be proper to recommend the committee to memorialize our legislature to adopt some general and liberal plan, that would effectually secure the protection of those rights to which they [the Indians] are justly entitled, and to instruct them in school learning, the useful arts and agriculture.[5]

Well before 1829 both Natives and their white partners had already created a precedent in which Americans protected Indigenous rights in return for Native engagement with cultural changes that would more closely connect Native nations to American civilization.

Beyond tying cultural change to the protection of land rights, Natives likewise argued that the preservation of their lands was necessary to their continued ability to pursue the cultural changes white Americans desired. In other words, Natives could not continue to meet American needs if Americans did not meet Native demands that their lands not be alienated. Such arguments were precursors to those that Native antiremovalists would make in the 1830s and 1840s against Removal. The Cherokees and the Senecas, for example, both asserted that alienation of land would impede their "progress" in the acquisition of "civilization." In one case the Cherokees responded to a demand for land by stating that they were "proud to acknowledge that their people are improving fast in agricultural pursuits" and that "[t]hey think it would be impolitic in the Nation to bind themselves in a smaller compass of country than they now occupy."[6] The Senecas offered the same basic argument when in 1818 a Council address to the President argued:

> Father, We have confidence in you; you cannot see your red children with their little bones driven off of their land . . . leaving the sepulchers of their fathers, their farms, their farming tools and cattle, dying by families on the road through hardship and privation. Exchanging all their advances in civilization, and all its comforts, for the hardship of the chases, without house or friend.[7]

This was an articulation of how the reciprocal and interdependent connections linking land possession, cultural changes, and the relationships between the Senecas and the United States had manifested in a concrete and real way. Ongoing Seneca possession of their lands and continued cultural transformations rested upon the foundation of a healthy relationship between the Senecas and the United States. A major disturbance — like dispossession — to one of these elements would produce disruptive reverberations to the others.

During the antiremoval campaigns, Natives would also repeatedly make the point that Removal was unjust. This strategy, which relied upon emphasizing the shameful actions of ignoring duties to partners, also had direct roots in earlier antecedents. In 1816 the Cherokees protested an attempt by the US government to use the 1814 Fort Jackson Treaty to acquire a tract of land by writing it was not "agreeable to justice," and that it contravened the Cherokees' "legal right."[8] The Cherokees had also previously argued that the United States had a fiduciary (read reciprocal) duty to abide by its treaty obligations and to recognize those Cherokee treaty rights that provided secure title to their lands. In a letter to Secretary John C. Calhoun, they explained that they were "Confiding in the good faith of the United States to respect their treaty stipulations with the Cherokee Nation," so that the Cherokees might "retain their present title to their lands."[9]

All the arguments Natives made about cultural changes, land, and rights were essentially linked by Indigenous attempts to maintain a literal geographic place for themselves within the orbit of American civilization through citations of the reciprocal obligations to which they and their American partners were subject. Natives therefore used the relationships they had established with missionary and religious groups, presidents, and Congress to voice their opinions in service of their social and political objectives. So while direct Native participation in American politics reached new heights during the antiremoval campaigns, it had been developing in earnest in the decade or two prior to the Removal question rising to the political center stage.

The Birth of the National Antiremoval Movement of 1829

The summer of 1829 witnessed the birth of a vigorous, national antiremoval movement that was inflected with long simmering tensions over social change. The event that triggered the movement was the election of Andrew Jackson to the presidency. Jackson had campaigned on the promise that he would support Removal. His victory in 1828 changed the political dynamics surrounding Removal in large part because Jackson broke with the Indian policy that presidents since Washington had followed. Prior to Jackson, presidents had used treaties to wrest lands from Natives but generally had stopped short of using outright force through employ of the regular American military. At the same time, they had continued to support Jefferson's policy of Indian assimilation by calling upon Natives to take up farming and weave themselves into the larger fabric of American society. The rationale behind this approach lay in the belief that Indian assimilation would free up "surplus" lands. Those lands could in turn be sold to white Americans, including land speculators and would-be yeomen. Jackson however immediately showed his willingness to coerce Natives to remove by employing forceful political arguments that centered on advising "them to emigrate beyond the Mississippi."[10]

Jackson's support for Removal though flew in the face of the goals of northern religious reformers. Rather than encouraging the spread of religion and morality, Removal did the opposite. In addition to disrupting white efforts to convert Natives to Christianity, Removal challenged evangelicals' belief that religious activism would resolve social and political tensions. Instead of Native integration into Christian brotherhood and American society, Removal rested on the premises of racial separation, Indigenous expulsion from the United States, and white economic advancement. As such, Removal represented the antithesis to the reformers' vision of social democracy. Adding to these fears was the belief that Removal dealt devastating blows both to law and to a shared sense of social morality. In a free society, the viability of law was critical as it acted as the last and most definitive line of social protection against those individuals whose own sense of social duty or moral value were not strong enough to keep them from antisocial or criminal behavior. The nineteenth century witnessed a change in which social elites sought to replace localized legal systems with a state-centered system of law based on the protection of individual rights.[11] Antiremovalists sought to marshal this new focus on rights in defense of Natives by claiming that the law, particularly as it was established through treaties, protected Native lands. To their consternation, Removal undercut the force and value of law and the rights it was supposed to uphold by making a mockery of past treaties that had guaranteed Indigenous possession of their lands "forever." The policy also promoted decadence in social morals by justifying white exploitation of Natives. It legitimized white efforts to acquire Native lands by force, and cast the consequences Natives would suffer as secondary to the economic benefits that would fall to white Americans. Removal consequently assaulted two of the most basic constructs of social stability: law and the duty of the constituent groups of a society to treat each other humanely. This assault threatened to transform the United States into a different and less humane nation; one that would be guided by greed and corrupt individualism.

Jackson's election and the changes in Indian policy he articulated intensified all of these fears. In turning away from assimilation and toward Removal, the United States under Jackson became an enemy, rather than a friend, to Natives because it would leave Indigenous communities defenseless against the states and vulnerable to encroaching settlers. The eruption in 1829 of staunch antiremoval sentiment was therefore the result of two intersecting factors connected to Jackson's assumption of the Presidency: the abandonment of US protection of Native peoples, and the government's official sanction of a cruel policy that many reformers feared would transform America into a less humane nation. Natives well understood this context and used their relationships to white religious reformers to work with them to launch national antiremoval campaigns.

The Constituency and Strategy of the Antiremoval Movement of 1829

The introduction of the Indian Removal Bill in Congress in fall of 1829 set in motion a heated national political debate over Indian emigration. To prevent the United States from forcing Natives west, a number of groups joined forces to prosecute a political campaign against Removal. The most significant Native antiremovalists included Cherokee leaders such as Principal Chief John Ross, The Ridge, Charles Hicks, and Elias Boudinot, editor of the *Cherokee Phoenix*. White antiremovalists were comprised mostly of northern evangelical preachers, protestant missionaries, and Quakers from both the Orthodox and Hicksite branches. The American Board of Commissioners for Foreign Missions was instrumental in the antiremoval movement, as were members of northern evangelical congregations. The Board and evangelicals became heavily involved in antiremoval when in 1829 northern churches launched an antiremoval petition campaign through which hundreds of petitions were sent to Congress. Important New England politicians like Massachusetts Governor Edward Everett also embraced antiremoval. And in Congress the most vocal antiremovalist was Senator Theodore Freylingheusen of Vermont. Others like Representative Bates of Massachusetts also vigorously opposed removal on the floor of Congress.

The actual number of people who considered themselves antiremovalists is hard to determine. Tribal leaders repeatedly asserted that the vast majority of their people opposed Removal. There were approximately 60,000 Natives in the most populous southern nations, and in the North there were probably an additional 5000 people, principally among the Haudenosaunee tribes, who had a direct and immediate stake in stopping Removal.[12]

It is harder to determine the number of white antiremovalists. Both branches of the Quakers were opposed to Removal, but the various Quaker Indian Committees who spoke out against it did not necessarily speak for all of the Friends they represented. However, judging from the amount of antiremoval memorials written and published by several Quaker Yearly Meetings, it is safe to assume that thousands of Quakers opposed the policy. For instance, the Ohio Yearly Meeting, which published a memorial that expressed vehement opposition to Removal, technically spoke for all of its 6238 Orthodox and 2846 Hicksite members.[13] Even if we assume that only half of these Friends were against Removal, it would still mean that several thousand Ohio Quakers would number among the ranks of white antiremovalists. Quakers from the Philadelphia area numbered 2926 Orthodox and 1461 Hicksite members.[14] Their respective Yearly Meetings also drafted antiremoval petitions. In addition to those of Ohio and Pennsylvania, yearly meetings from New England, New York, New Jersey, and Indiana wrote antiremoval memorials. Their members would have represented thousands opposed to the policy. Other religious sects also contributed to the groundswell of antiremovalists. Scholar Alisse Portnoy has identified over 1400 antiremoval memorials written by northern evangelicals.[15] These memorials were signed in the name of churches, church districts, and often entire towns. Consequently, they (theoretically at least) spoke for thousands of individuals. Though we cannot know with certainty the actual numbers of white antiremovalists, what is clear is that the issue touched a nerve and was deemed serious enough to lead to the production of antiremoval literature that pervaded the public sphere and that spoke in the name of thousands of white Americans.

The two people most directly responsible though for the coherent formation of the national antiremoval movement of 1829 were John Ross, Principal Chief of the Cherokees, and Jeremiah Evarts, the Corresponding Secretary of the American Board of Commissioners for Foreign Missions. Together they devised the movement's basic strategy. First, Natives would lobby against Removal through the public sphere; second, both Native and white antiremovalists would attempt to win the support of the white American public by revealing the immorality of Removal; third, antiremovalists would show that Natives had become "civilized" and that in return they were entitled to rights that protected them from forced emigration.

This plan seems to have been based upon efforts Cherokee leaders had been making for a number of years. Throughout the 1820s, tribal leaders like John Ross, Pathkiller, George Lowrey, Charles Hicks, and others had pinned much hope that they would retain their lands on a strategy in which Native cultural adaptation would be leveraged to place sympathetic white Americans into a position in which they would repay Indigenous people with rights that would prevent them from suffering land dispossession. In 1824 Cherokee leaders explained:

> we do thank God, sincerely, and our benevolent White Brothers . . . who . . . came into our help, with letters and the lights of civilization & Christianity. . . . [T]he chase is abandoned, and churches are rising, and the Great Spirit is felt in his influence upon our hearts and our gratitude and our little ones are learning to read his blessed word. . . . [O]ur cause is with God and goodmen, and there we are willing to leave it.[16]

By 1829 Jeremiah Evarts had appropriated their strategy. In a letter to missionary Cephas Wasburn, he explained that convincing Americans of Cherokee "civilization" was vital to Cherokee interests and the protection of their lands. He discussed the evils that would result from Removal and then told Washburn to continue "vigorous efforts to instruct & evangelize them." Evarts then explained that "These efforts, if anything will turn the attention of the public to their case & awaken that sympathy in their behalf which will not suffer their rights to be disregarded."[17] In this explicit articulation of antiremoval strategy, Evarts explained his hope that awareness of the Cherokees' progress in adopting "civilized life" would move white Americans to protect Native rights, and consequently, the ability of Indigenous peoples to remain on their lands.

Having developed a foundational strategy against Removal, antiremovalists disseminated their ideas through a well-organized political campaign. When the Removal Bill was introduced into Congress, antiremovalists responded with a strong counteroffensive that distributed their arguments through a variety of media. First, Natives wrote memorials to Congress pleading their case. Second, northern preachers delivered sermons that excoriated Removal and cited its evils. At the same time, Natives and white Americans drafted a host of antiremoval articles and published them in periodicals such as *The Cherokee Phoenix, Niles' Weekly Register*, and the *National Intelligencer*. Notable among these were a series of essays by Jeremiah Evarts, entitled "The William Penn Essays," which appeared in the *National Intelligencer* between August and December of 1829, and which developed detailed and explicit arguments against Removal. This vast literature articulated a variety of reasons why Americans should oppose the policy. At the most profound level, though, antiremoval literature shared the basic premise that Removal was an immoral policy because it legitimized the naked abuse of power. To combat this abuse, antiremovalists based their position on the idea that Natives had "rights" that derived from the long-standing relationships they had with white Americans and the United States.

Antiremoval, Morality, Law, and Native Rights

Antiremovalists hoped that their focus on the moral issues of Removal would sway public opinion to their side. Native and white antiremovalists consequently illuminated a variety of ways that Removal would either cause suffering and pain, or legitimize unjust and unethical behavior. For example, Native antiremovalists like Cherokee leaders John Ross and George Lowery wrote:

> A crisis seems to be fast approaching when the final destiny of our nation must be sealed. . . . The United States must soon determine the issue — we can only look with confidence to the good faith and magnanimity of the General Government, . . . whose obligation are solemnly pledged to give justice and protection.[18]

The "obligation" they referenced referred concretely to the treaty stipulations to which the United States had agreed, but metaphorically to the duties to its Native partners to which it was bound. The treaties conveyed rights underwritten by human relationships. For their part, white antiremovalists used similar language but contextualized the situation of a potential removal as more of an existential crisis based on miscarriages of justice. In an antiremoval memorial written to the Georgia State Senate, Robert Campbell, "a resident of Savannah," stated "Your memorialist feels it to be his duty . . . to approach your honourable body . . . against a measure fraught with so much impolicy, injustice, and disgrace."[19] Again, the reason antiremovalists used such language was because they hoped that their campaign would move American political leaders to just action. *The Friend* in April of 1830 stated:

> What may yet come of the multiplied declarations indicative of public feeling on this deeply affecting and momentous subject, we are not able to perceive, but have reason to believe that at least a powerful sensation has been produced in the minds of our rulers at Washington.[20]

Native antiremovalists brought particular attention to the human suffering that Removal would engender. Just a month and a half before the passage of the Indian Removal Act, John Ross predicted what would happen to the Cherokees if they were to be removed. "If the U. States . . . should ever compel them to make a general removal . . . Wretchedness, dispersion and extinction must inevitably await them."[21] Others focused more on the psychological ramifications of the policy. They argued that forced Removal would create great emotional suffering. "To the land of which we are now in possession we are attached — it is our fathers' gift — it contains their ashes — it is the land of our nativity, and the land of our intellectual birth,"[22] wrote a group of Cherokee memorialists. Uprooting the nation from its ancestral land disrupted attachments to the Cherokees' place, history, and culture; and as such represented an existential threat to the entire nation. Unlike white antiremovalists, Natives focused their concerns about Removal mainly on its impact on people, not on freestanding notions of "justice." The reason is because from their perspective, Removal was an act embedded in relationality. In this case, it signaled a deep rupture between erstwhile partners that would result in severe human suffering caused by the failure of one partner to another.

Native antiremovalists moreover continued to set these partnerships within a reciprocal framework. They explained on the one hand that Removal would disrupt Native ability to meet the interests that the United States had traditionally articulated it held relative to its relations with Natives — namely, that it would disrupt Native evangelism and "civilization." Yet on the other hand, this disruption would reverberate among Natives themselves and cause suffering. Coerced dispossession would endanger future progress Natives would make in conversion and cultural transformation, an objective white Americans and the United States had often claimed they desired, while it would simultaneously lead to death in both the secular and spiritual realms for Natives. According to a Cherokee memorial of 1830, their

> existence and future happiness are at stake — divest them of their liberty and country, and you sink them in degradation, and put a check, if not a final stop, to their present progress in the arts of civilized life, and in the knowledge of Christian religion.[23]

Other Natives made similar claims. A writer from Wilstown, Cherokee nation calling himself "A Cherokee Farmer" asserted: "This posture of affairs is adverse to the progress of religion and other improvements, in the nation."[24] Native antiremovalists were not really so concerned with the sincere conversion of individual Natives, but rather knew that the language of promoting Native evangelism resonated with a white audience. They therefore carefully articulated the premise that Natives should not be subject to forced relocation precisely because they had already begun the work, either as individuals or as communities, of the "self-improvement" that American civilization was supposed to underwrite. Hence, a letter signed simply "Journal of Humanity" explained that Natives routinely objected to Removal because of its adverse effects on Native evangelism. "Remove us from our cultivated lands and we shall again roam the desert. Separate us from the place where we have learned heavenly wisdom, and our children will live and die ignorant of the blessing of Christianity."[25] The goal here was to realign Native and white interests by pointing out how Removal would erode both. It would "separate us from the place where we have learned heavenly wisdom." The land, in other words, encapsulated both the Cherokees' ties to their homelands and their engagement with Christianity. This was because it held the relationships that continuously reinvigorated ties to place, and in this case, also to Christianity. The partnerships between Cherokees and white Americans lived on and within the land of the Cherokee nation. Therefore, the tearing of the Cherokees from their lands would also rip them from their ongoing relationships with people like Christian missionaries and with Christianity itself. By making this point, Native antiremovalists worked to refocus attention on the linkages that connected Native and white partners, asserting that Removal would be a mutually harmful policy, though of course it would be far worse for Natives.

Native antiremovalists also linked their arguments to law and treaties. As John Ross wrote: "the permanent security of our territorial boundary and our right to exercise sovereign jurisdiction over the country embraced by the same have been very unjustly called in question. And are infringed upon by the State of Georgia."[26] The underlying idea of this strategy was to show that the United States was legally as well as duty bound to meet its obligations to its Indigenous partners. The treaty was the most easily accessible instrument through which Natives could reify their understandings of the reciprocal nature of their relations with the United States. First and foremost, they pointed out that the United States had entered into a series of treaties in which agreements had been made that stipulated that the United States would forever protect Native lands from coerced alienation in exchange for land cessions. For instance, in a memorial to the American public, the Cherokees asserted that treaties unambiguously and contractually pledged the United States to protect their lands. According to the Cherokees, "in acknowledgment for the protection of the United States and the consideration of guaranteeing to our nation forever the security of our lands, etc, the Cherokee nation ceded by treaty a large tract of country to the United States."[27] The Cherokees asserted that the duty of the United States was clear: America must protect the Cherokees' remaining lands. Moreover, this duty was all the more sacrosanct as it was born from a solemn relationship enshrined in a legal instrument, the treaty, which was rooted both in the deepest principles of Native understandings of relationality and in the American law:

> Our treaties of *relationship* are based upon the principles of the federal consti-
> tution, and so long as peace and good faith are maintained, no power, save that
> of the Cherokee nation and the United States jointly, can legally change them.[28]

The arguments Native antiremovalists articulated were designed not only to illuminate the more than dubious legality of Removal, but also to show that the issue
of treaty rights had broader implications both for Americans' trustworthiness and
for the legitimacy of the US government. Natives drew these implications from
conceptions they and white Americans shared about treaties. Treaties sanctified
the idea that there existed duties and obligations between signatories that reached
beyond simply what each group had promised to the other. If the United States rup-
tured the relationships with Natives that it had established through treaties, then no
trust could be placed in its people or government. Both would be seen as frauds that
did not live up to their promises or ideals. John Ross and George Lowrey wrote:

> If the . . . United States shall withdraw their solemn pledges of protection,
> utterly disregard their plighted faith, and wrest from us our land — then, . . .
> we may justly say, there is . . . no confidence left in the United States.[29]

White antiremovalists worked in parallel with their Native compatriots and
made similar arguments. Jeremiah Evarts, for instance, called into question what
faith could be placed in Americans and the US government should they disregard
treaty obligations. "Are the people of the United States unwilling to give a fair,
candid, and natural construction to a treaty thus made?" he asked.[30] The Philadelphia Orthodox Quakers made explicit claims that treaties protected Native land
title under the auspices of US law. In an antiremoval memorial they sent to Congress, they pointed out that

> From the testimony of a series of treaties under the sanction of the first five
> presidents . . . your memorialists conceive that they have conclusively dem-
> onstrated that the United States of America have guaranteed in the most
> solemn manner to the Cherokee nation, in the first place — the entire title —
> undisturbed possession — and complete enjoyment of all their lands.

Given this legal recognition of Cherokee title, the United States could not carry
out Removal without "undermining the faith of the United States pledged to the
Cherokees."[31] In addition to the legal rights to their lands provided by previous
agreements, white antiremovalists contended that Natives possessed natural rights
to their lands given Natives' historical occupation of their lands:

> It must certainly be admitted by all that the descendents of the aboriginal
> inhabitants of this country are entitled, by immemorial inheritance, to a home

and a resting place upon the land of their fathers, that *their* title to the soil by priority of occupation and constant possession, is paramount to that of every other claimant.[32]

Others made similar arguments. "They [the Cherokee] have a perfect right to their country, the right of peaceable, continued, immemorial occupancy," claimed Evarts. Moreover, this right was not diminished by the claims of others.[33]

Treaties established still other rights. Most important in relation to the Removal debate was the question of who had power to alienate Native lands. Native antiremovalists argued that treaties codified in law that Indigenous lands could be sold or exchanged only if Natives gave their consent. John Ross explained that the Cherokee people by and large believed that treaties guaranteed this right:

> The Cherokees generally are fully sensible of their acknowledged rights . . . and they can never believe that that Genl. Washington and his predecessors in the execution of Treaties with them for upwards of forty years had been influenced by motives of policy to deceive them. . . . . [T]hey have resolved never to exchange this country for any other west of the Mississippi.

Claiming they had the right to decide whether or not to sell their lands, Ross argued that the Cherokees would move west only if the United States would "commit a breach of faith and forcibly compel them" to go.[34] Ross' words are telling. Removal was not simply about expulsion from a geographic space, but also about a concerted attempt to exclude Natives from the power, protections, and sanctity of agreements and contracts. It was about an abrogation of relationality and reciprocity.

Finally, Native antiremovalists argued that Natives possessed unique political rights that derived from the unique relationships that they had made with the United States. For example, they had the political right to call on the President's direct assistance in protection of their lands and communities. This right derived from the historical relationship between the United States and particular Native nations. In the case of the Cherokees, there existed a long-standing ritual kin relationship in which the President acted as the "father" to his Cherokee "children." "The various tribes of Indians emphatically call the President, *Father*, and to him, they as children look for protection and preservation," wrote the Cherokees.[35] As explained in Chapter 1, ritual kin relationships embodied Native notions about reciprocity, which held that each party in a relationship was to give according to their means to the other. With the Cherokees and the United States, the President's primary duty was to provide protection and guidance. The obligation applied to political needs, which meant that the Natives could demand that he intercede on behalf of their political interests.

The Cherokees consequently called on the President to prevent Removal once Georgia and other states took more drastic steps to dispossess the southern nations. They asked President Adams in 1825 to settle the Compact of 1802 so that Georgia could no longer threaten them with Removal:

> For the peace and tranquility of our nation we do sincerely hope that measures may be adopted by the United States & the State of Georgia so as to close their compact without teasing the Cherokees any more for their lands.[36]

When President Jackson assumed office and it became clear that he would not intercede to stop Removal, the Cherokees called on the Congress to take the President's place as the ritual father who would protect their interests. "Between the compulsive measures of Georgia and our destruction we ask the interposition of your authority, and a remembrance of the bond of perpetual peace pledged for our safety,"[37] stated a Cherokee memorial sent to Congress. The historical and "perpetual bond" between the Cherokees and the United States gave the Cherokees the political right to call on the Congress to intercede on their behalf.

In sum, antiremovalists, both Native and white, worked in tandem to argue that Natives possessed a variety of rights that protected them from Removal. Such exertions lay bare the expression of the Native conceptualization of relationships as power. The bonds they had established with religious reformers were leveraged by Natives in a time of existential crisis. Natives had no recourse to force or military power to defend themselves against Removal. They worked with white allies to articulate through the American public sphere, a variety of arguments that exposed the immorality and illegality of Removal. At their foundations, these arguments made the case that only through the severing of the obligations between Natives and white Americans could Removal proceed. These obligations were conflated with rights, which in turn drew force from the historic and present relationships between Natives and the United States. In the context of the Removal debate, the clearest indicator of Indigenous understandings of the reciprocal nature of these relationships had to do with the apparent willingness showed by Natives to engage with schemes for their "civilization."

Cultural Adaptation and the Validation of Rights

Antiremovalists viewed Native cultural adaptation as an alternative to Removal. Instead of dispossession, white antiremovalists hoped "Indians" would become "civilized" and merge into American society. Natives did not so much envision themselves becoming assimilated, but rather saw cultural change as a means for Natives to acquire power through the creation of relationships that could be used to leverage economic, social, and political advantages. In this strategy, Natives expressed a long-standing belief that the power of relationality lay in the reciprocal obligations upon which relationships were constructed. In their national political fight against Removal, Native and white antiremovalists alike highlighted cultural changes within Indigenous communities because they believed doing so would significantly strengthen the case against Removal. One important reason why such a path appeared attractive stemmed from the link white Americans drew between Native cultural change and Native rights. As already explained, Native antiremovalists exploited this link to argue that the relationships between Natives and white Americans required that in exchange for Native participation with cultural changes sought by Americans, the United States in return must respect the "rights" Natives held to remain on their lands.

White antiremovalists chauvinistically supported their antiremoval position by claiming that Indian "assimilation" was viable because Natives possessed an inherent capacity to become "civilized." They argued that it was America's moral duty to see to it that Indian improvement was realized. "Let us save them now, or we never shall. For, is it not clear as the sunbeam, sir, that a removal will aggravate their woes?"[38] thundered Senator Frelinghuysen. Other white antiremovalists claimed that Natives would benefit by remaining on their lands because it would allow them to continue to adopt a "civilized" life under the paternalistic guidance of white "benevolence." A memorial from the Quakers of the New England Yearly Meeting stated:

> Your memorialists are encouraged to hope, that if these interesting natives are permitted to remain in their present location . . . that the influences of the customs and manners of civilized life, with which they are immediately or more remotely surrounded . . . will prepare them for a participation in the rights and duties of citizenship in common with other civilized people.[39]

Native antiremovalists of course recognized the paternalism and chauvinism of their white counterparts, yet they made the pragmatic decision to lend support to arguments that cultural adaptations had legitimized their claim to "rights." However, they did so in a way that consistently tied together Native land, cultural change, and rights into a web of interconnected parts that were underwritten by the relationships between Natives, white Americans, and the United States. A memorial from the Cherokees to Congress is emblematic of this point. In writing to Congress, the Cherokees R. Taylor, John Ridge, and W.S. Coodey declared "we cannot better express the rights of our nation than they are developed on the face of the document we herewith submit." This document was a physical manifestation of both the relationship between the United States and the Cherokees and a reminder of the reciprocal nature of that relationship. It highlighted the "rights" Natives were owed by the actions they had taken for their American partners. The Cherokees proceeded to enumerate the indicators that white Americans saw as signs of "civilization":

> The schools where our children learn to read the word of God, the churches where our people now sing to his praise, and where they are taught that "of one blood he created all the nations of the earth," the fields they have cleared, and the orchards they have planted; the houses they built, are all dear to the Cherokees, and there they expect to live and to die, on the lands inherited from their fathers.[40]

In this instance the Cherokees used the Biblical reference "of one blood" to highlight the kinship underpinning their relationship with the United States. Their argument though was indeed much more sophisticated. With these few lines, the Cherokees created a matrix of kinship, relationality, reciprocity, rights, cultural change, and articulation of their uninterrupted and deep being of and attachment to their lands. This was the Native antiremoval movement in all its force. Through the media of borrowed instruments (the memorial and the public sphere), the Cherokees invoked the reciprocal duties by which the American government was bound to safeguard Native lands, precisely because those Natives had worked to meet American interests by their engagement with cultural transformations. This, and not a desperate reaction to the threat of Removal, was what was at play for the Cherokees. In other words, the pragmatism of cooperation with demands for cultural change was subsumed within, and given force by, the Cherokees' inculcation of it within a relational world defined by deep reciprocity.

The Boudinot–Gold Marriage and the Signing of the Treaty of New Echota

The antiremoval movement of 1829–1830 failed in its ultimate objective. In a series of close votes, Congress passed the Indian Removal Act in May 1830. In the House, the vote was extremely tight as the bill only passed by five votes.[41]

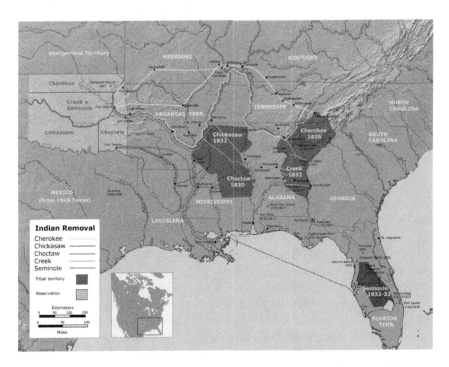

Figure 4.1 Map Depicting Southern Tribes' Locations Before and After Removal

Source: Courtesy of Demis, www.demis.nl and Wilcomb E. Washburn (Hrsg.), *Handbook of North American Indians, Vol. 4: History of Indian-White Relations.* Smithsonian Institution Press, Washington D.C. 1988. ISBN 0-16004-583-5.

In 1835 ten delegates representing the Cherokee nation signed the Treaty of New Echota. This treaty paved the way for the infamous Cherokee removals of 1838 and 1839 in which the Cherokee people would be forced to march from their homes in the American South to Indian Territory in what is today the state of Oklahoma. Cherokee citizens remained generally opposed to the Treaty both before and after it was signed. However, there existed an important division among Cherokee elites over whether or not to support the Treaty. The majority of Cherokee leaders were opposed to the Treaty, and even after it was signed in late 1835 contention remained as many Cherokee leaders refused to accept its validity. Cherokee Principal Chief John Ross and erstwhile editor of the *Cherokee Phoenix* Elias Boudinot became embroiled in a public argument over the question of the Treaty and Removal. Ross argued that he would continue to oppose the Treaty and fight Removal despite the fact that the Treaty had been signed, while Boudinot asserted that he had signed the Treaty because Removal represented the Cherokees' last best hope for ethnic and tribal survival. Boudinot would ultimately pay for his decision with his life. He was stabbed to death in 1839 near his new home in Indian Territory by a group of Cherokee men who were angered over his signing of the Treaty of New Echota.

Boudinot's story provides insight into the connection between the Removal debate and Cherokee understandings of relationships and reciprocity. This insight in turn sheds light on why a group of Cherokees would make the monumental decision to sign a document that in effect sanctioned the ethnic cleansing of the Cherokees from the South. At its core, the answer lies in the failure of white Americans to comprehend or accept the reciprocal nature upon which the Cherokees understood their relations both with the United States and with white Americans.

It is clear from his writings that Boudinot did not want to leave the Cherokee homeland. In *Cherokee Phoenix* he wrote: "In regard to the controversy with Georgia, and the present policy of the General Government, in removing, and concentrating the Indians . . . in our opinion, if carried into effect, will prove pernicious to us."[42] He wrote these words at the end of 1828, yet only a few years later he would come to the opposite conclusion on the question of Removal. Experiences earlier in Boudinot's life can help us explain this vacillation and Boudinot's ultimate decision to sign the Treaty of New Echota.

In 1822 Boudinot traveled from his Cherokee home to Cornwall, Connecticut, where he became a student at the American Board's Foreign Mission School. The school was dedicated to educating and evangelizing Natives with the ultimate goal that these Indigenous pupils would go on to spread Christianity to other Native peoples. While in Cornwall, Boudinot met and fell in love with a young white woman named Harriet Ruggles Gold. He and Gold announced in 1825 that they were engaged to be married. Boudinot's marriage later in March 1826 was one of two marriages between white women and prominent Cherokee men who attended the Foreign Mission School. Boudinot's cousin, John Ridge, had become engaged to a white woman named Sarah Northrup. Ridge and Northrup married in 1824, two years before Elias and Harriet wed. After their time at the school, Ridge and Boudinot would follow parallel paths as the two became the principal leaders of the Treaty Party of Cherokees who advocated for and signed the Treaty of New Echota.

The Ridge–Northrup wedding caused consternation among white Americans in Connecticut and in New England broadly. A year after the Ridge–Northrup wedding, one newspaper summarized the public response by writing that "Most of the papers spoke of it in terms of decided disapprobation."[43] But it was the announcement in 1825 of the engagement between Elias Boudinot and the young Harriett Gold, coming on the heels of the 1824 Ridge–Northrup marriage, that set off an even stronger and more intense storm of protest. The worry was that the two marriages could potentially normalize Native–white unions, which would undercut the racial hierarchy of early nineteenth century America.

The racism underlying the vitriolic response to Boudinot's engagement to Harriet was expressed in a several newspapers in New England. For example, Isaiah Bruce, editor of the Litchfield, Connecticut, newspaper, the *American Eagle*, wrote that the engagement was an "affliction, mortification, and disgrace of the relatives of the young woman . . . who has thus made herself a squaw, and connected her race to a race of Indians."[44]

Perhaps even more damaging to the young Boudinot's psyche was the racism that emanated not from strangers but from the Gold family, Boudinot's soon to be in-laws. Though some of Harriet's family supported the marriage and even defended the couple publicly, others turned on Harriet. Harriet explained that among the "respectable young people" of Cornwall was her brother Stephen, who participated in burning her in effigy. Harriet wrote: "Payne carried the corpses & Brother Stephen set fire to the barrel of Tar or rather the funeral pile — the flames rose high & the smoke ascended."[45] Other members of Harriet's family also openly opposed her marriage. Her brother-in-law Daniel Brinsmade declared: "I have not words to express my indignation at the whole proceeding — the whole family are to be sacrificed to gratify if I may so express it the animal feeling of one — of its members — and lo!"[46] Within Harriet's family, her impending marriage to a Native man was met with the ritual execution of the pair, and the explanation that the driving force behind Harriet's actions was "animalistic" lust. From these perspectives, Harriet's decision to marry Boudinot was tantamount to a choice to debase and dehumanize herself.

While Brinsmade worried that Harriet's transgressions might bring opprobrium upon the family, others of the Gold family argued that the marriage would have broader and more pernicious results. Harriet's brother-in-law Herman Vaill worried that it could injure missionary work to the Indians and counseled Harriet to "give up all present intentions, & all thoughts, of becoming united in marriage with an Indian." He explained that the union would "greatly injure the cause of Christ, both in its relation to the Mission School, & to the interests of missions from our churches to the heathen."[47] He reasoned that Harriet's marriage would only confirm fears that the Foreign Mission school was promoting interracial marriage, and that consequently the Christian community would withdraw its financial and political support for missionary work. "[I]f confidence . . . be so withdrawn by Christians . . . it will naturally follow that their confidence . . . will be diminished as it respects other branches of missionary operations."[48] Vaill's letter linked missionary work to a social vision of racial segregation, rather than one of racial integration that would become incarnate with the proposed marriage. He explained that missions were designed not to assimilate Natives into American society, but rather to create separate communities of Indian believers.

> The object of it [the mission] was to civilize, & to Christianize the heathen; to prepare them to become ... the sober, chaste, kind husbands of wives from *among their own people*; & to qualify them to become the enlightened, converted, & obedient subjects of the kingdom of Christ.[49]

In other words, what Boudinot would have learned from members of Harriet's family was that Natives and whites were to remain separate regardless of shared religion, or for that matter, any shared cultural values or practices. Natives could never intermix through any form of social equality with white Americans regardless of how much they heeded white America's calls to become "civilized."

If disillusioned by the response of Harriet's family, Boudinot must have also found disappointment in the actions of his white mentors. When the couple announced their plans to marry, the directors of the Foreign Mission School publicly denounced the lovers as "criminals." They published an article in a local newspaper in which they explained that they were "bound, to say, that we share the unequivocal disapprobation of *such connexions*," and that "we regard the conduct of those who have been engaged in, or accessory to this transaction, as criminal."[50] And even though Jeremiah Evarts was initially dismayed by the school's actions and concerned by the town's fervent opposition to the marriage — he wrote, "I am extremely distressed to learn of the violent opposition made at Cornwall to the marriage of Boudinot and Col. Gould's daughter"[51] — he too would cave to the public outcry over Boudinot's marriage. Evarts wound up sanctioning the closing of the Foreign Mission School, explaining that he had no choice "but to recommend that the school discontinue."

Such reactions, along with the town of Cornwall's continued opprobrium in the wake of Elias and Harriet's wedding, must have been disheartening and disillusioning for Boudinot and his vision of Native–white relationships. Indeed, the situation in Connecticut was untenable and prompted Elias and Harriet to leave Cornwall after their wedding and live among the Cherokees. Boudinot had learned through first-hand experience that his conversion to Christianity would not override the racial divide that white Americans had drawn between themselves and Natives. He responded to this disappointment by literally removing himself and his new bride from New England to Cherokee country.

It comes then as little surprise that he would reenact that same basic response ten years later when the Cherokee nation was faced with impending removal. John Ross and his supporters opposed Removal, in part, because they clung to the hope that the Cherokee nation would still be protected by the United States. Ross wrote: "when we reflect upon the honor magnanimity, and binding obligations of the General Government ... we cannot but hope and believe that justice will yet be extended to our nation."[52] But Boudinot was unconvinced by the underlying logic of this position. His earlier experience in marrying Harriet had clearly shown him that considerations of what was just or not would not trump racial division. White Americans would not meet their obligations to their Native partners if those obligations interfered with the settler society's dominant racial logic or with economic opportunity. Thus, Ross was like a false prophet leading his flock blindly to destruction through adherence to a specious belief. Boudinot explained that Ross should have leveled with the Cherokees and explained that there was by 1835 no way to save the Cherokee homeland. Boudinot wrote that Ross should have said:

> "I have done what I could to have our nation reinstated — I have failed. There is now no other alternative, for the salvation of the Cherokees, but to make a treaty, and to treat is to sell the land." But what was his reply? He told them that they may rest assured that he was their friend. . . . Poor consolation to a perishing people![53]

For Boudinot then, the only answer for the future of the Cherokee people was clear. Just as he had sought physical separation from white Americans after his marriage to Harriet as the only path for a viable future for his family, so too with his Cherokee family. The only answer left to the Cherokees was physical, geographic separation from white America. The epidemic of racism in white America left no other option open. His experience in getting engaged to Harriet had proven this to him in 1825, and by the early 1830s, though he had initially opposed Removal, he had come to the conclusion that Removal was the only viable option due to what he saw as a powerful racialized divide between Natives and white America. In 1832 he wrote:

> That it is our decided opinion, founded upon the melancholy experience of the Cherokees within the last two years, and upon facts which history has furnished us in regard to other Indian nations, that our people cannot exist amidst a white population.[54]

That racist ideology would prevent coexistence in the same geographic space between Natives and whites was, according to Boudinot, simply an obvious and unavoidable reality. This conclusion, proven by his earlier personal experience, goes a long way to explaining why he signed the Treaty of New Echota.

The Treaty of New Echota and the policy of Indian Removal sought geographical and physical separation between the white Americans and Natives. Boudinot saw segregation (in the form of Cherokee removal) as a path, indeed the only path, to the perpetuation of the Cherokees and the maintenance of their ethnic integrity. Writing to John Ross, Boudinot explained:

> In another country, and under other circumstances, there is a *better* prospect. Removal, then, is the only remedy — the only *practicable* remedy. By it there *may be* finally a renovation — our people *may* rise from their very ashes to

become prosperous and happy. . . . I would say to my countrymen, you among the rest, fly from the moral pestilence that will finally destroy our nation. . . . Subject the Cherokees to the laws of the States in their present condition? It matters not how favorable those laws may be, instead of remedying the evil you would only rivet the chains and fasten the manacles of their servitude and degradation. The final destiny of our race, under such circumstances, is too revolting to think of. Its course *must* be downward, until it finally becomes extinct.[55]

The "moral pestilence" Boudinot feared was the drinking, poverty, and prostitution he witnessed among his people. "See the spread of intemperance and the wretchedness and misery it has already occasioned!" he wrote. Boudinot continued, "we are making a rapid tendency to a general immorality and debasement. What more evidence do we need . . . than the slow but sure insulation of the lower vices into our female population?"[56] Boudinot saw the impetus of this moral decline as grounded in the proximity of the Cherokees to the United States. This proximity combined with virulent racism explained for Boudinot the present condition of the Cherokees, and helps us understand why he saw Removal as "the only remedy." The alternative context that the Cherokees had attempted to create had failed. They had attempted to build a relationship with the United States and with white Americans that was based on mutual obligation to each other. Boudinot was living example of this effort as he had gone north to become "Christianized" in an effort to help the Cherokees meet the needs of the white Americans to which they were connected. When Boudinot attempted to reify this connection in the flesh through his marriage to Harriet, he was met with sustained public vitriol. White Americans would not meet their obligations to their Native partners, or repay Natives for having met theirs. This is why Boudinot, Ridge, and others saw no other choice but to separate physically from the United States. The relationship had failed at its core because demands of reciprocity were abandoned by the white American public.

Yet even in this situation Boudinot did not advocate for complete cession of relations with the United States. He explained to Ross that "an independent existence, [was for the Cherokees] impracticable, and perhaps not desirable."[57] In other words, by the 1830s it was clear that even if they moved west, the Cherokees could not completely extricate themselves from their connections to the United States. Therefore, Boudinot argued for a realignment of the relationship between the Cherokees and the United States. Instead of a relationship predicated on overlap and integration of Cherokee and American societies and peoples, Boudinot sought a relationship in which the United States acted to guarantee the security of the Cherokees' western lands. The Treaty of New Echota accomplished this through Article V, which provided for secure and perpetual Cherokee title to the new lands. In the same letter to Ross already quoted, Boudinot countered Ross' argument that the Treaty would permit the United States to take the Cherokees' western lands. Boudinot wrote:

According to the provisions of the Treaty, a patent is to be given by the President of the United States for all the Cherokee lands West, agreeably to those provisions of the act of May 28, 1830 — that act secures those lands to the Cherokees by a guarantee as strong as the United States can make.[58]

Removal, as Boudinot understood it, consequently boiled down to a choice over the type of relationship between the Cherokees and the United States. As he explained:

> You must either go out of the limits of the United States . . . or you must pursue a contrary course — instead of *receding, approach* this great people by a modified connexion: a connexion that will somewhat identify your interest with theirs, and theirs with yours.[59]

In the end, Boudinot would return to relationality and reciprocity, only it would be of a nature less profound than he had envisioned in his younger years.

The Political Fight Against the Treaty of Buffalo Creek

The passage of the Removal bill into law in 1830 did not end the antiremoval movement. During the 1830s, many continued to fight the policy. In fact, just months before the Cherokees would finally succumb to Removal and begin the terrible walk along the Trail of Tears to Indian Territory, the Senecas became embroiled in their own campaign against a compulsory removal from their lands in New York. Though efforts to remove the Senecas were shaped by a particular set of circumstances, they and their Quaker allies would marshal the same basic arguments and the same fundamental strategy against Removal that the Cherokees and their white allies had employed almost a decade earlier.

The fight over the Buffalo Creek Treaty, as it was soon called, began in earnest in January 1838. Complicating matters was the fact that the Senecas were split on the question of Removal. Unlike the Cherokees, there was a significant group of Seneca leaders (though in the minority) who supported emigration. Those for and against Removal aligned with the two major political parties of the Seneca nation: the Christian Party and the Pagan Party. These parties had long vied for influence and power, and it was no different in regard to the Removal controversy. Simply stated, the Christian Party was more favorable to deeper engagement with American civilization, including ongoing adoption of Christianity, family farming, formal education, and the use of the English language; while the nativist Pagan Party supported policies that either moved away from acceptance of white American sociocultural institutions or that more strongly protected ancestral cultural values and practices. We will examine the Christian Party and how it leveraged alliances with white Americans in efforts to protect Seneca lands. Just as had occurred with the Removal controversy surrounding tribes in the southern United States, the effort to remove the Senecas would lead the Natives to fight vigorously to remain on their lands. Most importantly, antiremoval Senecas understood that reciprocity lay at the foundation of their efforts to stop Removal, and they embedded this concept into their antiremoval campaign.

***

On January 15, 1838, the Seneca Council house at Buffalo Creek was tense and chaotic. The Natives had called a council to discuss a Removal treaty recently proposed by US Indian Commissioner Ransom H. Gillet. The treaty stipulated that the Senecas, along with the other Haudenosaunee nations, would enter into a land exchange agreement with the United States. In 1831 the United States had made a treaty with the Menomonees, which involved the sale by the Indians of a tract of land near Green Bay, Wisconsin. The US government then gave this land to the Haudenosaunees in order to induce them to emigrate westward. However, only a small percentage of the Haudenosaunees had removed. The new treaty stipulated that the Haudenosaunees would exchange their remaining Wisconsin lands for a large tract in what is today Kansas.[60] The Ogden Land Company of New York also had a major stake in the outcome of this treaty, which is why its agents were present at the treaty council. The Ogden Company held preemption rights[61] to Seneca land and wanted the Indians removed to the Kansas site. The Company could then take ownership of the Senecas' New York lands, survey them, and sell off smaller plots at a great profit.

Despite the fact that both US and Ogden agents had made sustained efforts to convince the Senecas to accept the land exchange agreement, most Senecas remained set against it. The majority of Seneca headmen who offered their opinions in open council argued against the Treaty, articulating a variety of reasons why the Senecas should not go west. During these proceedings, officials of the Ogden Company tried to persuade individual Senecas to support the Treaty "by offering them sums of money and other advantages" or "by intimidation." However, the Senecas voted on the Treaty and it failed by a large margin. In response, Commissioner Gillet quickly asked the Natives to close the council. What happened next is not entirely clear. But from all accounts we know that Gillet reopened the council "at a tavern" where he and the Ogden agents pressured some of the Seneca chiefs to sign the Treaty. They used threats, bribes, and other "artifices" to persuade them to finally agree to it.[62]

Once the Treaty of Buffalo Creek was signed in January 1838, antiremoval Senecas mobilized in concert with their Quaker allies. They planned to jointly lobby the most powerful arms of the American government. The first order of business was to send delegations to Washington, DC, to protest the Treaty. Maris Pierce, John Kennedy, Israel Jimerson, and James Robinson represented the Senecas in this endeavor.[63] Maris Pierce and James Robinson each had extensive experience with white Americans: Pierce had attended a Quaker grammar school and later went on to Dartmouth College,[64] while Robinson had sent his son to live with Quakers in order to be trained as an apprentice cobbler. The Quaker delegation comprised Sam Bettle, Thomas Evans, Joseph Elkinton, and Enoch Lewis. Of these, Elkinton had the most experience with the Senecas. Though a silversmith and soap maker by trade, Elkinton had from 1816 until 1832 lived at the Allegheny Reservation where he had learned to speak the Seneca language fluently while he oversaw the Native school at Tunesassa.[65] Though he had left the Senecas in 1832, he remained a member of the Philadelphia Yearly Meeting Indian Committee until shortly before his death in 1868.[66] Both the Seneca and the Quaker delegations planned to meet with members of Congress and with the President in order to argue that the Treaty was obtained fraudulently, and to assert that most Senecas opposed both the Treaty and Removal.

When the delegations arrived in mid-January 1838, they scheduled an appointment to meet with President Van Buren and Secretary of War Joel Poinsett. Once the President arrived, the Senecas and Quakers jointly addressed him. Joseph Elkinton translated as "James Robinson . . . spoke in the Indian language." Robinson explained that the Senecas were opposed to the treaty and added they were "attached to their homes" and did not want to be "compelled to move." Van Buren replied that the treaty "should be fully & impartially investigated and justice should be done them." The Quakers felt compelled to add that the treaty had been procured through fraud and mismanagement and to that end produced evidence in the form of a letter (written by Gillet) obtained from a New York Congressman. The letter revealed that Commissioner Gillet had deliberately withheld the Senecas' annuity (due to them from an earlier treaty) in an attempt to blackmail them into signing the Treaty. Gillet's letter explained that annuity distributions were suspended pending "negotiations with the New York Indians."[67] Nor was Gillet alone in such actions. For instance, the Natives explained that Ogden Company agents had claimed that if the Senecas failed to sign the Treaty, the President would stop payment of their annuities.[68] In other words, the Buffalo Creek Treaty was a twofold abrogation of the essence of treaties in that it was obtained through an exercise of force that itself drew its power from the US representative acting in exactly the opposite fashion of what had been agreed to in a previous treaty.

After their meeting with President Van Buren, the joint delegations pressed their case directly with Congress. They consulted members of the Senate, including most of the "the members of the Committee on Indians Affairs"[69] before meeting with Senator Ambrose Sevier, the Committee's chairman. During this meeting, the Quakers moved "for the printing" of several antiremoval memorials that the Senecas and Quakers had drafted and now wished to distribute to members of the Committee. Sevier consented, which gave the Quakers the confidence to ask Senator James Buchanan, the future President, to copy and distribute the memorials to the entire Senate. Senator Buchanan likewise complied with their request. Nor did the delegations stop there. They also sought an audience in the House of Representatives as the Quaker delegation asked John Sargeant to copy and distribute the memorials, which he "cheerfully" agreed to do.[70] Meanwhile, the Seneca delegation distributed to Congress anti-Treaty memorials that had been signed by hundreds of their own people.[71]

The several memorials Congressmen now had before them built the case that the Buffalo Treaty was fraudulent. Many opened with a claim that the Senecas did not desire to emigrate. "The great mass of our people are opposed to emigration and are determined not to leave their reservations,"[72] read one Seneca document. This laid the groundwork for the contention that the Natives had not agreed to the Treaty under normal political procedures because the chiefs never consented to it in open council. Moreover, the Senecas pointed out that those who had signed the Treaty were not authorized to do so. "Those persons who are stated to have signed said alledged Treaty, are not chiefs, never having been duly appointed by the nation . . . and therefore are not competent to act for the nation."[73] From the Senecas' perspective, the illegitimate status of the signatories meant that the Treaty itself was invalid as it did not represent the will of the Seneca people as expressed through their legitimate leaders.

The Senecas strengthened the case they made to government officials by leveraging their white neighbors in New York for help. They used these neighbors to substantiate the relentless pressure applied upon them to support the Treaty. In concert with their Quaker allies, they had asked several citizens of Chattaqua County, New York, to draft a petition against the Buffalo Creek Treaty. Because so many Chattaqua County citizens agreed to sign the petition, it is most probable that the Senecas reminded them that they (the Senecas) had been good neighbors and that in return they now needed help. The signatories included important officers such as the sheriff, officers of the court, the district attorney, 14 other attorneys, and all 20 members of the grand jury. Eighty-nine other white citizens signed the document. The petitioners explained that they were not against Removal as a general policy. "We admit the benefits that would result to the white population from their [the Seneca] removal, & concede to the proper authorities the right to adopt such measure." This notwithstanding, the citizens of Chattaqua were nonetheless upset because the Indian Commissioners had used pressure and subterfuge to coerce the Senecas to sign the Treaty. As they put it: "we have been desirous that our Indian neighbors might judge it for their interest to emigrate; but no motives of interest can induce us to approve of that result, if effected by deception, fraud, or violence." The petition then confirmed that the Senecas had rejected the Treaty in Council and it detailed the "iniquitous" methods the Indian Commissioners used after the council to obtain Seneca signatures, including "intoxication" and "large rewards." The petitioners continued that they wanted the government to act "in good faith" and "protect the rights of the feeble."[74]

In arguing against Removal, the Senecas, like the Cherokees before them, invoked the underlying reciprocity attached to Native cultural transformation. Again, the notion was that in exchange for changes in cultural practices that would align Seneca communities with American civilization, those communities would not be subject to forced dispossession. Thus, the Senecas noted that "the moral condition of our people has been visibly improving beyond our expectation" and therefore "there is . . . no sufficient reason for the whole nation to be removed."[75] They specifically asserted that the Senecas had "improved" by adopting family farming, Christianity, education, and the English language. These changes, they further argued, reinforced the Senecas' connections to their lands in profound ways. The Senecas had in fact evoked these connections even before the Buffalo Creek Treaty was signed. In carefully crafted language they declared that "we don't want to sell out and leave our old homesteads . . . for a great many reasons. That a great many of our hunters have turned into farmers long ago."[76] After the Treaty was signed, the Senecas made the same point more boldly:

> We have resolved to adhere to our present locations. . . . We have acquired knowledge of the arts of civilization and of agriculture. . . . We have now many amongst us who have built large barns and who have good wagons and other useful implements of agriculture; We have also built school and council houses and convenient churches; We have several sawmills and a grain mill amongst us.[77]

The Senecas hoped to convince officials of the US government that they were obligated to respect Seneca land rights specifically in exchange for the changes the Senecas had made.

The Quakers likewise argued that Seneca cultural changes had validated Seneca claims to their lands. They explained that the Senecas should remain in New York because "many of them are living on well enclosed farms, stocked with horses, cattle, hogs, . . . and have erected and occupy substantial houses, respectably furnished and kept in decent order."[78] Citing cultural transformation as an argument against Seneca removal came easily to the Quakers who had long regarded it as the Senecas' best opportunity for collective defense. In 1819 the Indian Committee of the New York Yearly Meeting had devised a plan to "effectually secure the protection" of Seneca "rights" by "instruct[ing] them in school learning, the useful arts and agriculture."[79] By 1838 their fear was not simply that the Buffalo Creek Treaty would lead to forcible removal of the Senecas, but worse, that it would disrupt the "progress" the Natives had already made:

> The remnants of these once populous tribes have, within a few years, made great progress in the arts of civilized life: and the time was looked to . . . when all of them would . . . turn their attention exclusively to agriculture & the mechanic arts. It is therefore with deep concern and regret your memorialists learn, that a part of the Six Nations . . . have been induced . . . to remove west.[80]

Underlying the Quakers' argument was the assumption that Seneca cultural and economic practices had entitled them to live free from fear of forced dispossession. They in essence echoed the claim that the Senecas had made.

In making such claims, both the Senecas and the Quakers also explicitly argued that the Natives possessed political rights that the United States was obligated to protect due to the treaties that they had made with the United States. In an address to President Van Buren, the Senecas employed the language of kinship and reciprocity when they explained that

> his red children have in latter years made rapid advances in Civilization, morality, And religion . . . and that it is heart rendering to think that amidst

the improvements that are making among us that the individual Chiefs should dispose of the rights . . . of the nation.[81]

From their point of view, the Buffalo Creek Treaty laid bare all the legal and moral implications of a transgression of reciprocity. Consequently, the battle over the Buffalo Creek Treaty was not a simple skirmish over a nefarious agreement reached through fraud and bribery, but rather a larger struggle over whether or not the Senecas would receive the fair and ethical treatment that was due to them. It was for this reason that the Senecas characterized their stand against the treaty as a fight to "guard our rights."[82] Protection of those rights derived from the obligations inherent in the existing relationship and treaty agreements between the Senecas and the United States.

Finally, the Senecas fought Removal by inverting its logic. Supporters of Removal had argued that by separating from white populations, Natives would be more secure as no settlers would try to acquire their lands. On the contrary, the Senecas insisted that their well-being lay in continued proximity to white Americans. Writing to the President, they explained: "we are now surrounded on every side by the white people. We love them and suffer no inconvenience from them, but on the contrary We desire from them great and permanent assistance." This was an argument calculated on the logic of reciprocity. If the United States would not force the Senecas from their homes in New York, they would continue to live with white Americans and even accept "assistance" from them, which could have only meant continuing to play along with American "civilization" schemes. Despite its apparent acceptance of the chauvinistic logic that white Americans applied to "Indians," the Senecas' argument was nonetheless an expression of a vision of American civilization in which the landscape was composed of interconnected groups. "We believe we can continue at home and be at peace with our neighbors," the Senecas concluded.[83] This was their alternative to Removal.

Opponents of the Buffalo Creek Treaty would soon reap the benefits of all their efforts to undermine the treaty. Even though Ogden Company representatives, Indian subagent James Stryker, and a small delegation of pro-Removal Senecas all descended on Washington to plead their case at roughly the same time as the Quaker and Seneca antiremoval delegations had, the pro-removalists fell short in their efforts.[84] After debating the issue, the Senate refused to ratify the Treaty. Testimony and evidence provided by the Senecas and the Quakers convinced the majority that fraud, deception, and intimidation had indeed marred the treaty proceedings. According to Senator Ambrose Sevier, the Senate found the Treaty "so *essentially defective*" that it could not "recommend its ratification." Instead on June 11, 1838, the Senate amended the Treaty with a resolution that required the Indian Commissioner to resubmit it to each of the six Iroquois nations. Each nation would then vote separately on the Treaty. An Indian Commissioner was to fully explain the Treaty to each nation in "open council" and each tribe would need to give its "free and voluntary assent." In addition, the Treaty would only bind those bands in each Haudenosaunee nation that wanted to emigrate. Those who wanted to remain on their existing reservations in the east could do so.[85]

In accordance with the Senate's resolution, Commissioner Gillet, on August 17, 1838, called a council to discuss the new treaty. Many Seneca headmen did not attend the council, leading many of the Natives present to ask Gillet to close it. Gillet agreed to this request and closed the council late in the day on 17th. He had planned to reopen the meeting on August 20, but when he returned to the council house to do so he found that it had been "burnt down." This was more than an inauspicious sign. The destruction of the council house signaled the depth of Seneca antipathy to Removal. Gillet, however, remained undeterred and had a new house erected. He then reopened the council in late August.[86]

The new council lasted seven weeks and again was the scene of intense politicking as US commissioners engaged in repeated attempts to persuade the Senecas to adopt the treaty. And as had occurred the preceding January, the council ended in disappointment for the US commissioners. According to reports, only 16 or 17 of the approximately 90 Seneca chiefs signed the amended Treaty.[87] And they signed only after succumbing to intense pressure from the commissioners. Witnessing the commissioners' arm-twisting tactics, a group of chiefs thought it prudent to sign a remonstrance against the Treaty. Gillet turned down their request that he witness the signing of this document. Nonetheless, 60 chiefs, along with "General [Henry] Dearborn, the Commissioner on behalf of the State of Massachusetts," signed the remonstrance.[88]

The Senecas' remonstrance was the opening salvo in a renewed political fight that would erupt in January 1839 over the second Buffalo Creek Treaty. As had occurred before, those opposed to the Treaty sent delegations to Washington in order to prevent its ratification. And in another repeat of the events of 1838, the Senecas and Quakers allied in the fight against ratification. The members of their respective delegations were essentially the same men who had journeyed to Washington the previous summer. The Senecas instructed Israel Jimerson, Maris Pierce, and Seneca White to present their papers to the President, and the Quakers once again sent Bettle, Elkinton, and Evans to speak with the President and the Secretary of War.[89] While opponents of the Treaty presented their arguments, the amended Treaty was making its way through the ratification process. On April 4, 1840, the Senate ratified the amended Buffalo Creek Treaty.[90] Although the Senate finally proclaimed the Treaty, the political struggle continued. The President had to decide whether to use force to remove the Senecas or delay enforcing the Treaty. Government action was stalled by his indecision and by Congress's failure to follow the necessary procedures to enact the Treaty. Meanwhile, Senecas opposed to emigration took advantage of this delay and for the next two years continued to make public arguments against the Treaty. They also forcibly prevented surveyors from parceling out land on the Cattaraugus Reservation, and they considered bringing a lawsuit against the United States.[91] For their part, the Quakers maintained efforts to stop the Treaty by sending new memorials and petitions to Congress and the President.

A compromise reached in the spring of 1842 finally settled the dispute over the Buffalo Creek Treaty. The Philadelphia Hicksite Quakers opened negotiations with the Ogden Land Company with the goal of saving as much Seneca land as possible. The Hicksites correctly assumed that the Ogden Company would be in the mood to compromise. For almost four years the Company had been unsuccessful in removing the Senecas. In addition, Congress, short on money and under ongoing pressure from antiremovalists, continued to drag its feet on funding the Buffalo Creek Treaty. The Ogden Company saw compromise as its best opportunity to actually get its hands on at least some Seneca lands. When negotiations began, the Company made several propositions that would have given it possession of all of the Senecas' New York lands. However, the Hicksites countered by emphatically stating that they would not accept any deal that did not keep the Cattaraugus and Allegheny Reservations in Seneca possession. Ultimately the Ogden Company capitulated and took a deal that would give them the Buffalo and Tonawanda Reservations.[92] The new agreement stipulated that in exchange for those sites, the Senecas would be allowed to keep the Cattaraugus and Allegheny Reservations. Senecas living at Buffalo and Tonawanda could remove west, or relocate to Cattaraugus and Allegheny. Orthodox Quakers were suspicious of the deal and feared that it might be an Ogden ploy to acquire all Seneca lands. They feared the Company might pressure the Senecas to cede their remaining reservations, and therefore advised the Natives to reject the deal and reconcile themselves to removal. The Senecas, however, chose not to pursue this course and with the notable exception of those who lived at Tonawanda,[93] voted for compromise. The tribe signed the "Compromise Treaty" or the second Treaty of Buffalo Creek on May 20, 1842.[94]

The efforts then to prevent Seneca removal yielded some tangible results. True, the signing of the Compromise Treaty displaced and dispersed many Haudenosaunees. Some Senecas went west to what would become Kansas; some emigrated to the St. Regis Reservation in Canada, and still others moved to the Cattaraugus and Allegheny Reservations. However, unlike the failure of the antiremoval campaign of 1829–1830 to protect the lands of the Cherokees and the other "civilized tribes" of the American South, the joint efforts of the Senecas and Quakers preserved two of the Senecas' four reservations. This victory kept a substantial amount of land in Seneca hands and therefore many Senecas remained in New York. In 1846 the Senecas would secure yet more land through purchase. In addition, President Tyler would preside over a new treaty in which the Senecas bought over a third of the Tonawanda Reservation from the Ogden Company.[95]

* * *

In important ways the outcome of the Senecas' fight against Removal paralleled what had happened in the south. In both instances, antiremovalists for the most part failed to stop Removal. Moreover, in both cases, Native antiremovalists based their efforts on a worldview that was at base relational. They would work in alliance with white Americans and they would claim that the reciprocal obligations Native communities and the United States had to each other demanded that the Americans not forcibly dispossess them of their lands. Removal was an insane policy born from a heinous calculus in which one group could be ripped from its home so as to satisfy the insatiable demands for more resources (or for what in the nineteenth century was termed "improvement") of another. Natives thought that perhaps through emotionally laden, as well as erudite, reminders of the connections and mutual obligations between them on the one hand and white Americans and the United States on the other, such a catastrophic and deluded policy might not come to fruition. They were unfortunately incorrect.

Yet it is also clear from the outcomes of Removal that unfolded in the two cases examined that relationality and reciprocity did not disappear. Native nations and the United States continued to be in political and social relation to one another, and reciprocity continued to lay at the center of those relationships. In the inhumane world in which the United States had stolen Native lands, it would now, in return for those lands, "protect" Native lands in the west or guarantee that the Senecas' remaining New York lands would not be acquired against their will. Why did the Cherokees, the Senecas, and others agree to such a situation? The answer is because from Native perspectives relationality could not be extinguished or made to entirely disappear as it was fundamental to the constitution of the world. No matter how unhealthy those relationships were, they nonetheless remained. Natives like Elias Boudinot and others would arrive at the same conclusion after Removal was enacted — that they must use and leverage their relations to the United States as far as they could regardless of how diseased those relationships were. They therefore "agreed" to Removal and its associated treaties because this was both all they could do and because such actions aligned with their understandings of the world. As already stated, they returned to relationality and reciprocity; indeed, they never abandoned them.

The antiremoval campaigns of the 1820s, 1830s, and 1840s mediated the expression of an important Indigenous form of thought within a settler colonial context. Natives had twice allied with white Americans to prosecute heated, national, political campaigns in which they promulgated detailed defenses of Native rights, and carried those defenses directly to the highest officials of the US government. These arguments were based on the idea that as long-standing allies with ongoing relationships and agreements, white Americans were bound to their Indigenous partners to meet their needs. Even though antiremoval largely failed, the movement broadcast through the public sphere the Indigenous idea that reciprocity lay at the heart of healthy and mutually beneficial relationships. Though the United States failed to abide by this idea or by its agreements, Native peoples continued to adhere to relationality and reciprocity. This after all was central to what it meant to be Indigenous.

Notes

1. Here I follow other scholars who have examined how political discourse functioned through the public sphere. For example, I like Colin Wells, see the discussions in the public sphere as engaging topics that go beyond simply what is overtly discussed in published texts. See Colin Wells, *The Devil and Doctor Dwight: Satire and Theology in the Early American Republic* (Chapel Hill, NC: University of North Carolina Press, 2002). Hence, while antiremoval literature was most clearly about rights and the prevention of Removal, the underlying subtext was about reciprocal duties. I depart

from scholars of previous generations who understood Native American participation in the public sphere as reactive to their fears of ineluctable "disappearance." See, for example, Robert A. Ferguson, *The American Enlightenment, 1750–1820* (Cambridge, MA: Harvard University Press, 1997), 164–6. Natives feared heinous mistreatment at the hands of policies like Removal. However, their engagement with the public sphere was not solely governed by such worries. Rather, their engagement with the public sphere in the cases examined here helped reproduced Indigeneity through reliance upon ontological understandings of reciprocity. For other work on the functioning of the public sphere in early America, see Michael Warner, *The Letters of the Republic: Publication and the Public Sphere in Eighteenth-Century America* (Cambridge, MA: Harvard University Press, 1990).

2. James Robinson to PYMIC, September 16, 1821, AA41, Box 2, Folder 3, #128, Correspondence of PYMIC, Records of PYMIC, Quaker Collection, Special Collections, Haverford College, Philadelphia, PA.

3. Seneca Deputation to Philadelphia Yearly Meeting Indian Committee, December 12, 1819, AA41, Box 1, #83, Records of PYMIC, Quaker Collection, Special Collections, Haverford College, Philadelphia, PA.

4. John Ross, George Lowrey, Major Ridge, and Elijah Hicks to President James Monroe, January 19, 1824, in Moulton, *The Papers of Chief John Ross, Vol. 1*, 59–61. My emphasis.

5. New York Yearly Meeting Indian Committee to the New York Yearly Meeting, January 1, 1819, AA41, Box 3, #56, Letters of NYMIC, Correspondence of PYMIC, Quaker Collection, Special Collections, Haverford College, Philadelphia, PA.

6. Elias Hicks to Clark, January 29, 1822, ABCFM 18.3.1 v. 3, American Board of Commissioners for Foreign Missions Records, Houghton Library, Harvard University, Cambridge, MA.

7. "Seneca Indians No. 1," *The New York Daily Advertiser*, 2, no. 489 (November 4, 1818), available online through the Archive of Americana published by Readex, America's Historical Newspapers, http//infoweb.newsbank.com.

8. John Lowry, Jon Walker, The Ridge, Richard Taylor, John Ross, and Cheucunsenee to William Crawford, March 12, 1816, in Moulton, *The Papers of Chief John Ross*, 26–7.

9. John Ross, George Lowrey, Major Ridge, and Elijah Hicks to John C. Calhoun, February 11, 1824, in Moulton, *The Papers of Chief John Ross*, 66.

10. Andrew Jackson, First Annual Message to Congress, December 8, 1829, accessed through the American Presidency Project at www.presidency.ucsd.edu/ws/index.php?pid=29471

11. See Laura Edwards, *The People and Their Peace: Legal Culture and the Transformation of Inequality in the Post-Revolutionary South* (Chapel Hill, NC: University of North Carolina Press, 2009). Edwards argued that the emerging state-centered legal system codified law in objective statutes, deposited the ultimate authority to interpret the law in state supreme courts, and focused on the protection of an individual's rights. Moreover, she contended that the new legal system increased inequality through its focus on rights as some groups, particularly white men, were thought to possess rights, whereas others, such as slaves, were cast as holding no rights at all. The law worked in favor of those who possessed rights and disenfranchised those who did not. I complicate this narrative by arguing that just as the law's focus on rights could strengthen inequality, it could also work to reduce it. Those who did not have rights could argue for them, as various Indians and their white allies did, and if successful in gaining recognition of those rights, they could then leverage them in their interests. Indians of course are not the only ones who have argued for and acquired rights. Women, black Americans, gay and lesbian Americans, and others have all sought to reduce or efface inequality through exercise of rights.

12. "Indian Tribes," in Smith Robert, ed., *The Friend*, 7, no. 48 (September 5, 1835), 383, Special Collections, Haverford College, Philadelphia, PA.

13. These numbers are taken from *The Friend*, 2, no. 34 (June 6, 1829), 266, Special Collections, Haverford College, Philadelphia, PA.

14. The numbers for Philadelphia area Quakers come from *The Friend* 2, no. 18 (February 14, 1829), Special Collections, Haverford College, Philadelphia, PA.

15. Alisse Portnoy, *Their Right to Speak: Women's Activism in the Indian and Slave Debates* (Cambridge, MA: Harvard University Press, 2005).

16. John Ross, Major Ridge, George Lowrey, and Elijah Hicks to Joseph Gales & William Seaton, April 20, 1824 in Moulton, *The Papers of Chief John Ross*, 79.

17. Jeremiah Evarts to Cephas Washburn, August 9, 1829, ABC 1.01 v. 8, American Board of Commissioners for Foreign Missions Records, Houghton Library, Harvard University, Cambridge, MA.

18. John Ross and George Lowrey Annual Message to the Cherokee Nation, October 14, 1829, in Moulton, *The Papers of Chief John Ross*, 172.

19. Robert Campbell, "Memorial to the Honourable President and Members of the Senate of the State of Georgia," *The Friend*, 2, no. 34 (June 6, 1829), 265, Special Collections, Haverford College, Philadelphia, PA.

20. Introduction to a Memorial of the New England Yearly Meeting in Smith, ed., *The Friend*, 3, no. 25 (April 3, 1830), 200, Special Collections, Haverford College, Philadelphia, PA.

21. John Ross to Jeremiah Evarts, April 6, 1830, in Moulton, *The Papers of Chief John Ross*, 188.

22. Cherokee Memorial, in Smith, ed., *The Friend*, 3, no. 19 (February 20, 1830), 152, Special Collections, Haverford College, Philadelphia, PA.

23. Ibid.

24. A Cherokee Farmer, "Letter to the Editor of the Cherokee Phoenix," *Cherokee Phoenix*, 2, no. 1 (March 18, 1829). Cherokee Phoenix 1828–1829, AN 151.N43 C56 Item 1, Special Collections, Northeastern Oklahoma State University, Tahlequah, OK.

25. "The Duties of Christians Towards the Aborigines of This Country," printed in *the Cherokee Phoenix*, 2, no. 32 (November 11, 1829). Cherokee Phoenix 1828–1829, AN 151.N43 C56, Item 1, Special Collections, Northeastern Oklahoma State University, Tahlequah, OK.

26. John Ross to George Lowrey, William Hicks, Lewis Ross, Richard Taylor, Joseph Vann, and William S. Coodey, November 27, 1829, in Moulton, *The Papers of Chief John Ross*, 178.

27. Memorial of John Ross, Richard Taylor, David Gunter, & William S. Coodey, Representatives of the Cherokee Nation of Indians in the *Cherokee Phoenix and Indians' Advocate*, 2, no. 11 (June 17, 1829), Special Collections, Northeastern Oklahoma State University, Tahlequah, OK.

28. Annual Message of John Ross to the Cherokee National Council, October 14, 1829, in Moulton, *The Papers of Chief John Ross*, 170. My emphasis.

29. John Ross and George Lowrey, "Annual Message to the Cherokee Nation, 1829," October 14, 1829 in Moulton, *The Papers of Chief John Ross*, 169–72.

30. Jeremiah Evarts, "William Penn Essay VIII," in Prucha, *Cherokee Removal*, 94.

31. Memorial of the Philadelphia Orthodox Quakers, January 11, 1830, published in Smith, ed., *The Friend*, 3, no. 15 (January 23, 1830), 116, Special Collections, Haverford College, Philadelphia, PA.

32. Philadelphia Orthodox Quakers in Smith, ed., *The Friend*, 3, no. 15 (January 23, 1830), 114–15. Emphasis in the original.

33. Jeremiah Evarts, "William Penn Essay No. II," in Prucha, *Cherokee Removal*, 57–8.

34. John Ross to Jeremiah Evarts, April 6, 1830, in Moulton, *The Papers of Chief John Ross*, 187.

35. John Ross, George Lowrey, and Elijah Hicks to President John Quincy Adams March 12, 1825 in Moulton, *The Papers of Chief John Ross*, 104. Emphasis in the original.

36. Ibid.

37. Memorial of a Delegation from the Cherokee Indians presented to Congress January 18, 1831, Phillips Pamphlet Collection, Folder 7311, Western History Collection, University of Oklahoma, Norman, OK.

38. Frelinghuysen to the Senate in Watson, *Jackson vs. Clay*, 174.

39. New England Yearly Meeting, "Memorial to the Senate and House of Representatives of the United States of American in Congress Assembled," dated March 3, 1830, in Smith, ed., *The Friend*, 3, no. 25 (April 3, 1830), 199, Special Collections, Haverford College, Philadelphia, PA.

40. R. Taylor, John Ridge, and W.S. Coodey, "Memorial of a Delegation from the Cherokee Indians," January 18, 1831, Folder 7311, Phillips Pamphlet Collection, Western History Collection, University of Oklahoma, Norman, OK.

41. The bill passed on May 26, 1830 by a vote of 102 to 97; Francis Paul Prucha, *The Great Father: The United States Government and the American Indians*, Volume 1 (Lincoln, NE: University of Nebraska Press, 1984), 206.

42. Elias Boudinot, Cherokee Phoenix, February 21, 1828, quoted in Theda Perdue, *Cherokee Editor: The Writings of Elias Boudinot* (Athens, GA: University of Georgia Press, 1996), 93.

43. "Another Marriage of an Indian with a White Girl Contemplated," *Sentinel and Witness*, 3, no. 131 (June 29, 1825), 3, Middletown, CT, Early American Newspapers, America's Historical Newspapers, https://infoweb-newsbank-com.uri.idm.oclc.org/apps/readex/doc?p=EANX&t=state%3ACT%21USA%2B-%2BConnecticut&sort=YMD_date%3AA&f=advanced&val-base-0=Elias%20Boudinot&fld-base-0=ocrtext&fld-nav-0=YMD_date&val-nav-0=1825%20-%201826&docref=image/v2%3A124956311564BED2%40EANX-1282C28B4E6AB450%402387807-1282C28B75615FF0%402-1282C28C604DCE50%40Another%2BMarriage%2Bof%2Ban%2BIndian%2Bwith%2Ba%2BWhite%2BGirl%2BContemplated&firsthit=yes. Accessed October 18, 2019

44. Isaiah Bruce, the American Eagle, June 1825, in Perdue, *Cherokee Editor*, 9.

45. Harriett Gold to Herman and Flora Gold Vaill, June 25, 1825, in Theresa Gaul, *To Marry an Indian: The Marriage of Harriett Gold and Elias Boudinot in Letters, 1823–1839* (Chapel Hill, NC: University of North Carolina Press, 2006), 84.

46. Daniel Brinsmade to Herman and Flora Gold Vaill, June 29, 1825, in Gaul, *To Marry an Indian*, 89.

47. Herman Vaill to Harriet Gold, June 29, 1825, in Gaul, *To Marry an Indian*, 92–3.

48. Ibid.

49. Ibid. Emphasis in the original.

50. Lyman Beecher, Timothy Stone, Joseph Harvey, and Philo Swift in the *Litchfield Eagle*, Vol. 62, no. 3217 (July 6, 1825), New London, CT, Early American Newspapers, America's Historical Newspapers, https://infoweb-newsbank-com.uri.idm.oclc.org/apps/readex/doc?p=EANX&t=state%3ACT%21USA%2B-%2BConnecticut&sort=YMD_date%3AA&f=advanced&val-base-0=Elias%20Boudinot&fld-base-0=ocrtext&fld-nav-0=YMD_date&val-nav-0=1825%20-%201826&docref=image/v2%3A1036CCAC76876960%40EANX-12C8A5D090E10F68%402387814-12C8A5D0B1F97CD0%402-12C8A5D18F721618%40The%2Bfollowing%2BAppears%2Bin%2Bthe%2BLast%2BReport%2Bof%2Bthe%2BMission%2BSchool%2Bat%2BCornwall.%2BLitchfield%2BEagle&firsthit=yes. Accessed October 18, 2019.

51. Jeremiah Evarts to Rev. Dr. Chapin, July 5, 1825, ABCFM 1.01 v. 5, American Board of Commissioners for Foreign Missions Records, Houghton Library, Harvard University, Cambridge, MA.

52. John Ross to "The Committee and Council in General Council Convened" in Perdue, *Cherokee Editor*, 165–6.

53. Elias Boudinot, February 5, 1836, in Perdue, *Cherokee Editor*, 191.

54. Elias Boudinot, October 2, 1832, in Perdue, *Cherokee Editor*, 175–6.

55. Elias Boudinot to John Ross, December 4, 1836, in Perdue, *Cherokee Editor*, 225. Emphasis in the original.

56. Ibid., 224.

57. Ibid., 220.

58. Ibid., 218.

59. Ibid., 220. Emphasis in the original.

60. Removal of the Six Nations was part of larger efforts by the US government to remove Natives from east of the Mississippi River. The proposed treaty stipulated that the exchange of the Wisconsin land for the tract in Kansas was authorized under the Indian Removal Act: a law that provided the United States government with the legal authority to enter into land exchange agreements with Natives.

61. The preemption right was a right to Indian lands in New York. This right derived from a dispute between Massachusetts and New York. After the Revolutionary War, both states claimed lands in what is today western New York. They settled their dispute in 1787. Massachusetts agreed to give up its claim and allow New York to take the land. Massachusetts reserved a "preemption right" to any Indian lands in New York, which meant that if Indians vacated New York lands, Massachusetts would have title to them. Subsequently, Massachusetts sold its preemption right to the Holland Land Company. The Holland Company then sold the right to the Ogden Land Company. The Ogden Company wanted to remove the Seneca so that they could exercise the preemption right. See Mary Conable, "A Steady Enemy: The Ogden Land Company and the Seneca Indians" (Ph.D. dissertation, University of Rochester, Rochester, NY, 1994).

62. Protest of the delegation from the Seneca Nation in the State of New York against the ratification of the Buffalo Treaty, March 20, 1838, AA 44, Folder 6, #55, Records of the Philadelphia Yearly Meeting Indian Committee (Orthodox), Quaker Collection, Special Collections, Haverford College, Philadelphia, PA.

63. Governor Blacksnake, John Pierce, Sky Pierce, Jacob Blacksnake to Philadelphia Yearly Meeting October 31, 1838, AA41 Box 1, #92, Letters of Seneca to PYMIC 1801–49, Correspondence of PYMIC, Records of PYMIC, Quaker Collection, Special Collections, Haverford College, Philadelphia, PA.

64. See Conable, "A Steady Enemy," 83.

65. See Conable, Chapter 3.

66. For biographical information on Joseph Elkinton, see "Elkinton, Joseph, 1794–1868," in the Dictionary of Quaker Biography, Quaker Collection, Special Collections, Haverford College, Philadelphia, PA. Also see Elkinton's obituary in *The Friend*, 41, no. 27 (February 29, 1868), Quaker Collection, Special Collections, Haverford College, Philadelphia, PA.

67. "To the Committee for the Gradual Civilization and Improvement of the Indian Natives," April 12, 1838, AA42, #70, Legal, Land, Legislative, Records of PYMIC, Quaker Collection, Special Collections, Haverford College, Philadelphia, PA.

68. "Petition of the Chiefs of the Seneca Nation to the Honourable Samuel Prentiss Member of United States Senate," February 28, 1838, AA44, Folder 5, #47, Records of PYMIC, Quaker Collection, Special Collections, Haverford College, Philadelphia, PA.

69. Ibid.

70. Information on Quaker efforts to copy and distribute the antiremoval memorials is contained in Subcommittee to PYMIC, April 12, 1838, AA42, #70, p. 6 of the document, Land, Legal, Legislative, Records of PYMIC, Quaker Collection, Special Collections, Haverford College, Philadelphia, PA.

71. Quaker records indicate that of the approximately 2300 Seneca living on the four reservations, 1813 opposed removal. See "Statistical Documents Prepared at the Several Reservations," AA44, Folder 5, January–February, 1838, Legal, Land, Legislative, Records of PYMIC, Quaker Collection, Special Collections, Haverford College, Philadelphia, PA.

72. Protest of the Delegation from the Seneca Nation in the State of New York against the ratification of the Buffalo Treaty, March 20, 1838, AA44, Folder 6, #55, Records of PYMIC, Quaker Collection, Special Collections, Haverford College, Philadelphia, PA.

73. Ibid.

74. "Citizens of the County of Chatauque to the Honourable the Senate of the United States," February 1838, AA44, Folder 5, #28, Records of PYMIC, Quaker Collection, Special Collections, Haverford College, Philadelphia, PA.

75. "Address of the Seneca to the President," unknown date between 1838 and 1842, AA44 Folder, 5, #57, Records of PYMIC, Quaker Collection, Special Collections, Haverford College, Philadelphia, PA.

76. "Petition of the Chiefs and Warriors of the Allegheny Against Making a Treaty," August 17, 1837, AA44, Folder 4, #140, Records of PYMIC, Quaker Collection, Special Collections, Haverford College, Philadelphia, PA.

77. "Address of the Seneca to the President," unknown date between 1838 and 1842, AA44, Folder 5, #57, Records of PYMIC, Quaker Collection, Special Collections, Haverford College, Philadelphia, PA.

78. "Memorial of the Committee for the Gradual Civilization and Improvement of the Indian Natives," March 12, 1838, AA44, Folder 6, #51, Records of PYMIC, Quaker Collection, Special Collections, Haverford College, Philadelphia, PA.

79. New York Yearly Meeting Indian Committee to New York Yearly Meeting, January 1, 1819, AA41 Box 3, "Letters of the New York Yearly Meeting Indian Committee," #56, Correspondence of PYMIC, Records of PYMIC, Quaker Collection, Special Collections, Haverford College, Philadelphia, PA.

80. "Memorial of the General Committee of the Yearly Meeting of Friends of the States of New York and Vermont and Parts Adjacent, Charged with the Subject of Promoting the Civilization and the Welfare of the Indians," February 5, 1838, AA44, Folder 5, #141, Records of PYMIC, Quaker Collection, Special Collections, Haverford College, Philadelphia, PA.

81. "Seneca to His Excellency Martin Van Buren President of the United States," March 20, 1838, AA44, Folder 6, #76, Records of PYMIC, Quaker Collection, Special Collections, Haverford College, Philadelphia, PA.

82. "Petition of the Chiefs and Warriors of the Allegheny Against Making a Treaty," August 17, 1837, AA44, Folder 4, #140, Records of PYMIC, Quaker Collection, Special Collections, Haverford College, Philadelphia, PA.

83. "Address of the Seneca to the President," unknown date between 1838 and 1842, AA44, Folder 5, #57, Records of PYMIC, Quaker Collection, Special Collections, Haverford College, Philadelphia, PA.

84. Subcommittee to PYMIC, April 12, 1838, AA42, #70, p. 6 of the document, Legal, Land, Legislative, Records of PYMIC, 7, Quaker Collection, Special Collections, Haverford College, Philadelphia, PA.

85. "Speech of Ambrose H. Sevier of Arkansas, in the U.S. Senate," March 17, 1840 in Robert Smith, ed., *The Friend: A Religious and Literary Journal*, 13, no. 33, Quaker Collection, Special Collections, Haverford College, Philadelphia, PA.

86. "Speech of Ambrose H. Sevier of Arkansas, in the U.S. Senate," March 17, 1840, in Smith, *The Friend*, Quaker Collection, Special Collections, Haverford College, Philadelphia, PA.

87. These numbers come from two sources, one written by the Seneca and another by a white man named R.B. Heacock who lived in the Buffalo area. Heacock reported 17 chiefs had signed, while the Senecas reported 16. See "Letter from R.B. Heacock stating that deception and fraud had been used in obtaining the assent of the chiefs to the treaty with the New York Indians, as amended by the resolution of the Senate of the 11th of June, 1838," January 23, 1839, AA44, Folder 8, #101, Records of PYMIC, Quaker Collection, Special Collections, Haverford College, Philadelphia, PA. Also see "Seneca Delegation to President Van Buren," January 25, 1839, AA41.1, Folder 12,

#103, Records of PYMIC, Quaker Collection, Special Collections, Haverford College, Philadelphia, PA.

88. "Seneca Delegation to President Van Buren," January 25, 1839, AA41.1, Folder 12, #103, Records of PYMIC, Quaker Collection, Special Collections, Haverford College, Philadelphia, PA.

89. For the names of the Seneca delegation, see Governor Blacksnake, John Pierce, Sky, Perce, and Jacob Blacksnake to the Philadelphia Yearly Meeting, October 31, 1838, AA41, Box 1, #92, Correspondence of PYMIC, Records of PYMIC, Quaker Collection, Special Collections, Haverford College. For corroboration that the subcommittee of Bettle, Elkinton, and Evans visited Washington, see "PYMIC to the Chiefs and Warriors of the Seneca Nation," April 24, 1839, AA41.1, Folder 12, #129, Records of PYMIC, Quaker Collection, Special Collections, Haverford College, Philadelphia, PA.

90. Conable, "A Steady Enemy," Ph.D. dissertation, 214–16.

91. Undated (probably June 1840) and unsigned letter of the Philadelphia Quakers to "the Seneca Indians residing in the State of New York," AA41.1, Folder 11, #8, Records of PYMIC, Quaker Collection, Special Collections, Haverford College, Philadelphia, PA.

92. Robert Scotton to PYMIC, April 25, 1842, Indian Records, Vols. 1–10, AB 30, 1841–1850, Records of PYMIC, Quaker Collection, Special Collections, Haverford College, Philadelphia, PA.

93. The tribe did not give the Tonawanda branch the chance to vote because they knew the Tonawanda would never accept the cession of their reservation.

94. The Tonawanda Seneca fought the treaty and the majority refused to remove. Their struggle against removal is another story. Through a treaty agreement, the Tonawanda ended up buying about 30 percent of their reservation from the Ogden Company in 1856.

95. For a thorough discussion of the political history of the Tonawanda struggle to keep their reservation, see Conable, "A Steady Enemy," Chapter 9, "The Tonawanda Exception, 1842–1857," 283–324.

5 Christian Bonds

Choctaw Male Authority and the Politics of Choctaw–United States Relations, 1831–1859

When the Choctaws left Mississippi, they carried with them cultural baggage that made the journey west all the more difficult. The Choctaws associated the west with the dead. The sun traveled west and plummeted down into the horizon on its daily cycle of life and death, and souls of departed individuals replicated this cycle by migrating to that same horizon upon their demise. The Choctaw origin story moreover recounted that long ago "the people" had fled from the west and wandered until they were instructed by spiritual beings to stop at a place named Nanih Waiya, a sacred mound located in what is today Mississippi that came to mark the center of the Choctaws' universe. The Choctaws consequently considered the regions beyond their homeland perilous — a belief their origin story compounded by explaining that if the Choctaws were ever to relocate, they would be struck by suffering, disease, and death. This prediction seemed eerily to come true after the signing of the Treaty of Dancing Rabbit Creek as an estimated 3000–4000 Choctaws perished on the journey to Indian Territory.[1] Yet, despite this extreme communal pain and the emotional and cultural trauma created by the US policy of Removal, the Choctaws survived their forced relocation to the west. And as Donna Akers has explained, they were able to rebuild a new nation in the west as they re-created life in the "land of death."[2] But the Choctaw nation in the west was not a mirror image of what it had been in the east.

Rather, Choctaw elites took decided measures to reshape the nation in ways that would reduce the possibility for further conflict with white Americans and with the United States. Upon first glance, the motivation for this might appear purely pragmatic. After all, few, if any, Choctaws believed that their move west truly separated them from white Americans, insulated them from the larger sociocultural and economic world dominated by American power, or made them safe from land-grabbing settlers. As described in Chapter 4, antiremovalists — and of course Choctaws among them — often argued directly against pro-removalists who claimed that migration would offer the Indians protection by putting distance between themselves and white populations. It might therefore seem that Choctaw leaders sought to bring into closer alignment Choctaw society and culture with that of broader American civilization in order to protect themselves against potential attempts by white Americans to erode Choctaw sovereignty or to take land. It can appear that Choctaw leaders might have simply been employing a strategy to hedge against any unforeseen machinations against the Choctaw nation. While this contention formed one important influence on the behavior of Choctaw elites, on its own it is an oversimplified characterization of Choctaw actions in the post-Removal period. More to the point, it paints those actions as reactionary and consequently leads to the conclusion that the Choctaws predominantly capitulated to the imperial onslaught of the American nation state. If we assume only this position, we miss the totality of the historical context by eliding from our view the ways that Choctaw Indigeneity shaped their understandings of their circumstances.

Removal was a rupture of the Choctaws from the land, a disembodiment of the people from their place. As such it was a tearing asunder of the prime relationship — the Choctaws and Nanih Waiya — that lay at the foundation of the world the Choctaws inhabited. The rupture of the people from their place reverberated in the unraveling of the social fabric made from the mesh of relationships that constituted the Choctaws' universe. Removal then was not simply a geographical movement from east to west, but rather a profound dislocation whose consequences were immanent throughout the Choctaws' universe. Its result was a ubiquitous unbalancing of relationships, the result of which in turn was widespread unhealth. Even though the Choctaws technically "agreed" to Removal, their removal was at base a breakdown in the relationship between themselves and the United States. This breakdown jeopardized the other relationships that made up the Choctaws' world. In this circumstance, it was imperative that the Choctaws rebuild their relationships and regain health.

This is the context we need to assume in order to understand the Choctaws' actions in the post-Removal period. They faced a pressing need to rebuild healthy relationships. As the Choctaws rebuilt their world in the west, they sought *balance*. In the simplest sense, balance meant the creation of healthy relationships. The immediate aftermath of Removal posed problems both internally among the Choctaws themselves and externally between the Choctaws and the United States. The severe trauma of Removal, exacerbated by the cultural connotations with which the Choctaws associated the west and by the understanding of the world as relational in structure, obviously deeply and ubiquitously disrupted the ligaments that bound Choctaw society. In these circumstances, the Choctaws began the work of rebalancing — or restoring to health — the internal social bonds of their society and the external political relationship between themselves and the United States. The Choctaws sought not merely "survival" in the west, but a healthy flourishing of the Choctaws as Indigenous people on their new lands.

Christianity was important to both these efforts as the Choctaws used the religion as a medium through which to achieve the balance they wished to achieve. We will examine two examples of this phenomenon. First, the Choctaws leveraged the religion to help rebuild social bonds and in particular the social authority needed to correct destructive antisocial behavior by Choctaw youths. And second, Choctaw political leaders exploited their participation in Christianity to attempt to influence to their benefit Choctaw relations with the United States and with white Americans.

These processes were deeply significant because as with all things Indigenous they were never disconnected from the land. Indeed, these efforts were specifically about connecting to the new lands the Choctaws occupied in the west. The building of healthy relationships between the Choctaws themselves started anew the process of creating a web of healthy relationships on and through the land. And the efforts to form a better relationship with the United States, one that would not ultimately subject the Choctaws to an exercise of American power that would displace once again the Choctaws from their new lands, was also about solidifying the Choctaws' presence on their lands. The Choctaws' regeneration in the west should be understood as a positive feedback process built on balance. As the Choctaws built new healthy relationships with each other, this in turn gave them an enhanced ability to simultaneously forge a better political relationship with the United States. The first process replanted the Choctaws into the land, and the second one would hopefully secure the Choctaws in their place by foreclosing upon the possibility of another destructive uprooting by the United States. In this way, the Choctaws' actions — whose objective was the attainment of balance — was one way that the Choctaws rebuilt an Indigenous connection to the new lands upon which they were settled. Finally, these processes were neo-autochthonous in that the balance they were meant to produce, flowed, in part at least, through a medium, Christianity, that was not Indigenous in origin.

***

Christianity had made inroads among the Choctaws prior to Removal and maintained a presence among them after their migration to Indian Territory. The Choctaws, like the Cherokees, in fact took the initiative to ensure that the religion would retain its influence after Removal. Even though many Choctaws had grown disillusioned with Christian missionaries, and some leaders such as Mushulatubbee expressly requested that no preachers enter the new Choctaw nation,[3] others asked the missionaries (particularly Cyrus Kingsbury and the erudite Cyrus Byington) to follow them west. They did so in part because the American Board missionaries had proven their worth to the Choctaws through the staunch support they had provided in the fight against Removal. Though both Cyrus Kingsbury and Cyrus Byington did not immediately travel west with the emigrating Natives, the American Board, with the support of Choctaw leadership, quickly reestablished their Choctaw mission in Indian Territory after Removal. By 1832 two new mission stations had opened in the west: one at Bethabara under the care of missionary Loring S. Williams, and the other at Wheelock with Alfred Wright as missionary. The following year, Ebenezer Hotchkins opened a new station at Clear Creek.[4] However, just as had been the case before Removal, the vast majority of Choctaws did not profess themselves Christians in the tumultuous period immediately following the forced move west. Numbers of Choctaw Christians remained low, perhaps only 200 to 300 out of a population of approximately 10,000.

Nor did the number of Choctaw Christians appreciably increase during the remainder of the 1830s. Most Choctaws were simply not willing to adopt a new religion and abandon Native beliefs. Though Christianity held a presence in the Choctaw nation, it was by no means central to the lives of the majority of Choctaws.

By the mid-1840s, however, the number of Choctaw Christians would begin to grow. Even though the numbers during the antebellum era would never amount to a large percentage of the total Choctaw population, they increased substantially in comparison to where they had been during the 1830s. By the early 1850s, there were over 1000 Choctaw Christians. Table 5.1 shows the increase in congregants between the years 1844 and 1850.

This data reveals growing Choctaw interest in Christianity that went beyond simply obtaining membership in the church as many Choctaws sought deeper, more personal involvement in their churches. In each year recorded, many Choctaws chose to undergo rituals connected to church fellowship and took either oral or written exams in order to become "communicants" or official church members who could partake in ritual salvation. Many were also baptized and had their children christened. Finally, Choctaw church members donated significant amounts of money to the American Board's Choctaw mission. The Natives' interest in Christianity in turn resulted in an increase in the number of ABCFM churches in the Choctaw nation. By 1844 there were six churches — located at Pine Ridge, Wheelock, Mountain Fork, Mayhew, Chickasaw, and Mount Pleasant. By 1846 two new churches, one at Good Water and the other at Sixtowns, were added. And in the Choctaw mission's 1850 annual report, the missionaries recorded ten churches within the nation.[5]

What explains increased Choctaw interest in Christianity? After all, by 1850 almost 10 percent of the Choctaw population west of the Mississippi was connected to the church. Two factors provide an explanation. The first is pragmatic. Because many of the American Board churches ran Sunday schools in which Choctaw children learned to speak English and read the Bible, the missionaries and their churches offered an avenue to an education and thus to vital skills that many Choctaws believed would help them contend with the changed world they faced in the post-Removal era. Among the most important of these skills were the chance to become literate (in both English and Choctaw) and the ability to learn

Table 5.1 Choctaw Members in the Churches of the American Board of Commissioners for Foreign Missions

Year	Total Members	Added on Exam	Added on Letters	Adult Baptisms	Child Baptisms	Black Members	Choctaw Donations
1844	524	No data	No data	No data	No data	No data	No data
1845	600	85	26	67	81	No data	$658.68
1846	645	96	138	58	47	No data	$1358.56
1848	846	153	6	129	98	No data	$518.69
1850	1100	182	20	149	111	108	$881.30

Source: The data for this table comes from ABC 18.3.4 v. 6, numbers 11, 48, 49, 50, and 51, Papers of the American Board of Commissioners for Foreign Mission, Houghton Library, Harvard University.

to speak English, which in turn provided opportunity for Choctaw children to become more familiar with white American culture. Language skills in particular were prized as they helped the Choctaws protect themselves from being cheated by whites in economic exchanges such as working as wage laborers or bartering. The Choctaws consequently perceived education as empowering and sought access to it in the mission churches.

The second, and for us more consequential, reason some Choctaws turned to Christianity was to address the societal chaos created by Removal. As Donna Akers has explained, the years following forced relocation were extraordinarily damaging to Choctaw social structure, especially because US policies toward the Choctaws had the effect of eroding the social power of matrilineal clans. Principally, the insistence on the part of American officials to attach family authority to fathers and to vest land ownership in male heads of households ran contrary to the matriarchal authority of Choctaw practices. Because the United States worked to shift social and economic power from female to male hands, clans lost the social clout they had traditionally wielded. The result was a decay of social order occasioned by an erosion of extended kinship bonds. This led to increased crime, particularly violent crime, as clans were less able to restrain young men from antisocial behavior.[6] To make matters worse, the Choctaw government seemed powerless to reign in crime. As the American Board missionaries explained, there was "a great want of . . . decision on the part of the Authorities of the nation," as "murders and other outrages are frequent." They added that there were "few or no punishments" for crime, which induced "both old and young desperadoes to see what exploits they can perform, thinking that whatever they may do they will escape with impunity."[7] In response, some Choctaws used Christianity as a medium through which to counter this chaotic social state by binding together individuals into a community through common belief and shared ritual. These benefits provided a strong inducement for some Choctaws to adopt the religion.

The opening in 1848 of the Mount Zion church under the Choctaw preacher Pliny Fisk highlights how both access to education and efforts to contend with social disorder drove some Choctaws to the Christian religion. Fisk, who was a "licentiate" (a Native pastor who had been licensed to preach by the ABCFM missionaries), moved to the village that would house the Mount Zion church at the request of four Choctaw brothers who had attended the mission church at Wheelock. Fisk may have been genuinely pious, but this was not the case for the four brothers. According to the missionaries, these brothers were most interested not in religion but in literacy as they had "learned to read our Choctaw books . . . and wished to teach their offspring what they had themselves learned." Even though the missionaries ultimately read the Choctaws' desire to read as evidence of their burgeoning piety, the evidence suggests that the primary motivation for their embrace of Christianity was more worldly than spiritual. The four Choctaw brothers had used the church to become literate and now wanted to pass on this skill to their children — a contention supported by the fact that none of the brothers "made a profession of their faith in Christ, yet they determined to have a school and the preaching of the gospel in their new location." Such a refusal to profess faith suggests that listening to the preaching of the gospel was the trade-off made for the opportunity to acquire education.[8]

The Mount Zion church, however, is also revealing of Choctaw efforts to rebuild social cohesion in the post-Removal era, specifically through the opportunity and the structure Christianity provided for the exercise of male authority. As the clans' power waned and women lost some of their long-standing social authority, Choctaw men used the church to fill the vacuum and acquire social power. The opening of the Mount Zion church was in fact a direct result of the authority of Choctaw men — authority that they had obtained by rising to social prominence within the American Board churches. Fisk had become a preacher, and two of the four brothers who founded the church at Mount Zion had, since 1844, served in the church at Wheelock as its "faithful and useful elders." The brothers and Fisk parlayed their standing in the church to strike out on their own and settle an unoccupied part of the country where they would lead not only a church but "adjacent villages" too. They became spiritual as well as political leaders, and in truth successful leaders as the new church at Mount Zion had grown to "sixty one" members only a year after it opened. In short order the church had become a focal point of the new village that had sprung up around it. Again, the reason why stems from the opportunity the church provided for the Choctaws to cement new social bonds. Missionary observations specifically mentioned that the Choctaws desired to rebuild attenuated connections between the generations. They reported that, the Natives were "determined to remove to some unoccupied part of the country, where their little ones . . . could be more easily controlled and more readily brought under instruction." As male church authorities, Choctaw men leveraged their positions to exercise authority in aspects of Choctaw life that were vital to social cohesion such as the upbringing and teaching of children. In this way, the Choctaw Christian church became a vehicle for a reestablishment of balance that centered on the reconstruction of intergenerational social bonds predicted on the authority of men. Moreover, that this reconstruction of bonds happened on "some unoccupied part of the country" is important. The Choctaws' rebuilding of social bonds was incomplete without the re-creation of integration between the people and the land. By removing to land that was yet to be settled, the Choctaws' connection to each other and to the land would happen simultaneously, strengthening the entire web of relationships that linked peoples and place.

It is also important to point out that this process did not require the Choctaws to break from other older elements of their heritage. Indeed, the quest to achieve healthy, balanced relationships was at the center of Choctaw participation in Christianity. The Choctaws who congregated at the Mount Zion church, in other words, were not cultural apostates who had turned away from older Choctaw practices as they became more devoted to Christianity. Missionary lamentations on the behavior of the Mount Zion Choctaws attest to this. For example, the missionaries found the Choctaw ballgame to be morally offensive and they sternly advised Choctaw Christians to give it up. Despite such admonishments, the missionaries lamented that the Choctaws of Mount Zion lived "in a neighborhood where the people were much given to ball-plays and other amusements." Choctaw cultural practices (as with seminal conceptualizations like balance) persisted alongside their new religious practice. The Choctaws did not find them mutually exclusive even if white preachers who served as their ostensive guides in Christian practice did.[9] Just as importantly, the ongoing play of the ballgame was yet another social practice that connected the Choctaws of Mount Zion to each and helped rebuild relationships that had been decimated by Removal. Again, Christianity was a medium that provided the context for the reexpression of Choctaw beliefs and behaviors whose goal was the creation of healthy relationships between the people and the land upon which they lived.

***

In addition to rebuilding internal social bonds, the Choctaws used the church to mediate the construction of bonds between the Choctaw nation and white Americans. This is clear from how their political leaders used Choctaw participation in Christianity as a potent tool to create cohesion between themselves and white Americans. In the middle of the nineteenth century when many white Americans adhered to a racial logic that clearly demarcated non-whites as putative subordinates, the ability of the Choctaws to point to a shared religion between themselves and other Americans acted both as an enormous challenge to supposed Choctaw inferiority and as medium that bound the Choctaws to other Americans. If the Choctaws were to not only survive in, but also to thrive in, an environment in which white belief in their racial superiority was ubiquitous and the political and economic power of the United States reigned, they would need to dismantle the stark contrasts that many white Americans had drawn between themselves and "Indians." For savvy Choctaw elites, theirs, as well as their people's participation in Christianity, served as an instrument to obtain such a goal.

Choctaw Christians like Joseph Dukes consequently often made hyperbolic statements that predicated the future survival of the Choctaw people on their turn to Christianity. "It seems to me," he wrote,

> [that] the Choctaws have come to a point where they will either pursue a course for their prosperity or their downfall. Means of education are abundant, intelligence increasing every day, what will all these avail unless it has religion at the bottom of it. . . . How vastly important then that the education of the youths be conducted solely on religious principles.[10]

According to Dukes, only a national system to promote religious education would ensure the survival of the Choctaws. He, like Pliny Fisk and the brothers who had founded Mount Zion church, envisioned ways to balance the relationship between the Choctaws and white Americans that leveraged Christianity as an ecology vital to the health of the Choctaws' social experience. For Pliny Fisk, this had meant the construction of social bonds among Choctaws themselves. For Dukes, it signaled the advancement of the Choctaw nation within the context created by the presence of American empire. Dukes saw Christianity as central to the Choctaws' ability to relate to the United States in ways that would ensure their persistence under an imperial context.

In his work on the secular, philosopher Talal Asad has argued that the secular and the religious were often interdependent despite the fact that they were customarily conceived as opposites in a variety of binary systems. In his examination of democratic liberalism, he claimed that Christianity and the secular (in the form of democratic liberal politics of the modern era) informed one another through interdependent myths centered on the theme of redemption. The first (religious) myth was that Christ's death served to redeem all of humanity. The second (secular) myth was that the world must be redeemed through the rise and perpetuation of a political order that valued democratic systems and individual rights. This political order moreover arises in a two-step process. First, individuals redeem themselves through application of self-discipline that leads to acceptance of the values of modern liberal politics, and second they introduce and then enforce adoption of this modern liberal political order on others. Asad further argued that missionary Christianity "fused" the two myths within the contexts of European global empires through the development of an ideological foundation that held that the people of the world needed to be transformed through their introduction to Christianity so that Christ's sacrifice of his own death could in fact redeem the world. And as we know, the "civilization" projects European, and later Euro-American, settlers imposed upon Indigenous peoples included secular reeducation elements that sought to convey belief in rights, democracy, and other hallmarks of a modern liberal political order.

Asad's discussion focused on how European subjects melded religious and secular redemption myths through evangelical Christianity, but they of course were not the only people capable of wielding Christianity in this way. It appears that the Choctaws engaged in their own variant of the process described by Asad. They were of course not looking to embrace the redemptive messages of the "Christianization" and "civilization" processes of American settler colonialism, but rather strategically using them as media through which to create a healthier relationship between themselves and the United States. Instead of a relationship whose defining characteristic was racial hierarchy (that had of course resulted in the destructive consequent of forced removal), they sought to forge one that was more humane. In other words, shared identity as Christians could promote, it was hoped, a better relationship in which the Choctaws would not be subject to destructive abuses of power on the part of the United States. In this way, the Choctaws sought balance through their engagement with Christianity. In the sociopolitical context that interested men like Dukes, it meant using their positions as Christians to influence the political processes between the Choctaw nation and the United States. Generally, they argued that that state — the United States — and that that state's citizenry — Americans — needed to respect and support the struggles undertaken by Christian Choctaws to secure political, economic, and social rights. For our purposes, the degree to which the US and white Americans supported the Choctaws in these demands is not as important as the fact that the Choctaws made them in the first place. In simply claiming the power to make the demand, the Choctaws worked to influence the central external political relationship that their community occupied — that between itself and the United States.

It was this process of attempting to strengthen their political position relative to the United States that led Choctaw leaders to personally assume Christian identities and to cast the Choctaws as a Christian nation even though only a minority of Choctaws had embraced Christianity. These leaders made a point of employing Christian language and practice, and they took pains to reference Christian ideology as they discharged their official duties. For example, the Choctaws infused Christian ritual into a formal meeting they called in order to honor US Choctaw Agent William Armstrong shortly after his death in 1847. For starters they asked that long-time resident minister to the Choctaws Cyrus Kingsbury open the meeting with a prayer. The meeting delegates then added their own invocation to the Christian god. "It has pleased Almighty God in his [illegible word] holy Providence, to remove by death, William Armstrong." This meeting also served as a wake, for which the Choctaw David Folsom delivered a eulogy laden with Christian language and theology. He praised Armstrong for his "good counsel" and lauded him for his advice that "the chief desire of any man should be 'to act honorably in all things and prepare for the world to come.'" Here Folsom showed deft understanding of the Christian doctrine that linked good works on Earth to the afterlife. He further underscored this Christian-inspired subtext by characterizing Armstrong's words as "good preaching."[11] By using religion in his characterization of Armstrong, Folsom sought to show that he, and by extension the Choctaw people, respected and understood Christian precepts because they themselves had become Christians.

There was again a strategic political element that compelled Choctaw politicians like Folsom to focus on Choctaw participation in the Christian religion. Christianity served as an important aspect of Choctaw identity that men like Folsom could leverage as they discharged public duties to legitimize and empower Choctaw efforts to influence sociopolitical relations with the United States to their benefit. In the case of Folsom's eulogy, he used it as a springboard from which he and the Choctaws sought to erode the strength of racial prejudices against "Indians" dominant in mid-nineteenth-century America. It was for precisely this reason that in his eulogy, Folsom followed references to Christianity with an idealized portrait of Armstrong. Folsom painted Armstrong as an exemplar of good relations between the Choctaws and white Americans exactly because (according to Folsom at least) race did not enter into Armstrong's mediations of disputes between the two groups. In his eulogy, Folsom explained that Armstrong "manifested a lively interest in our [Choctaw] welfare," and that "whenever there was a dispute between a Choctaw and a white man, he always satisfactorily adjusted it." Moreover, Armstrong "was an honest man," who saw to it that "every thing was straight," and who as Choctaw Agent made sure that "all money was paid as it should be." The eulogy's intersections of Christian references and its description of Armstrong as a paradigm of virtuous interracial relations laid bare not just the more obvious argument that as peoples tied by a common religion white Americans must respect Choctaw needs and treat them fairly, but also a less obvious but just as important effort by a Choctaw to state that uncritical acquiescence by white Americans to a damaging racial ideology that subordinated Natives to white Americans was not a position they must putatively adopt.

This important underlying effort to exert their own influence on race relations in American society explains why the Choctaws widely publicized Folsom's eulogy of Armstrong. They sent copies to various newspapers, including the *Arkansas Intelligencer*, *The Cherokee Advocate*, and the *Washington Telegraph*. Their aim was grander than just trying to achieve better treatment for the Choctaws — they highlighted their identity as Christians to legitimize their right to articulate a vision of social relations that would challenge the racism that had acted as a significant ideological underpinning of the heinous mistreatment Natives had to that point in time faced in the United States.[12] For our purposes here, what these actions show is that the Choctaws used Christianity to work toward building social bonds in ways that produced a healthier relationship, one not defined by ongoing maltreatment of the Choctaws at the hands of the United States.

By the mid-1840s, Christianity had gained increased importance among the Choctaws. It provided access to education, a framework for social cohesion, new avenues of male authority, and contributed to a new element of Choctaw identity that Natives used in efforts to influence the countenance of sociopolitical relations between the Choctaws and the United States. The significance of Christianity was not lost on Choctaw political leaders who worked to ensure that it would maintain a presence within the nation, and remain a part of Choctaw identity. This is most evident through the concerted actions Choctaw leaders took to preserve relations with American Board missionaries.

In the early 1850s, an incident occurred in which an American Board missionary was treated violently by a disgruntled Choctaw man. The American Board voiced their concern and displeasure by drafting a letter of complaint to the Choctaw National Council. The Council responded with a conciliatory missive that showed contrition and articulated the hope that this unpleasant event would not jeopardize Choctaw relations with the Board. Drawing attention to the significance of good relations between themselves and the missionaries, the Choctaws explained that a resolution of the matter and the maintenance of warm relations would have "an important bearing on us as a people." They then agreed with the Board's demand that its missionaries be secure and free from violence while resident within the Choctaw nation. But the main purpose of the Council's letter was not just to guarantee that preachers would be safe from the threat of violence, but rather to ensure that the American Board would continue to maintain a presence and a mission among the Choctaws. The Choctaws wrote:

> We do sincerely hope that this circumstance . . . will not be the occasion of interrupting the harmony which has so long existed between us. We hope that it will not divert from its accustomed channel any of that generous and enlightened cooperation we have enjoyed in past years.

The Choctaws acknowledged their long-standing relationship with the Board, and they made clear that they wanted it to persist. Their reasons for so doing were equally salient. The mission went a long way toward legitimizing the Choctaw claim to a Christian identity as it demonstrated an active Choctaw desire to be Christian. Moreover, the Board and its missionaries provided a vital link between the Choctaw people and American Christians who were sympathetic to the Choctaws precisely because they were, from white perspectives, shedding paganism and embracing Christianity. The Choctaws wanted to maintain the support of these "friends of the Red Man." "We do sincerely hope," they wrote "that this unhappy occurrence will not in any way operate on the minds of the Christian public to our disadvantage." This hope was a direct reflection of the fact — understood all too well by the Choctaws — that a Choctaw Christian identity, white Christian support for the Choctaws, and Choctaw ability to wield influence on the course of their relations with white Americans were all intertwined, and that keeping them so would only help the Choctaws advocate for their interests.[13]

***

Removal had caused severe traumatization and dislocation for the Choctaws. Some contended with these experiences by drawing on their participation in Christianity in order to work toward securing their communities in the west. Drawing on the religion as a structure for male authority functioned as an instrument to counter chaotic social forces that found expression in antisocial and criminal behavior of some young male Choctaws in the immediate post-Removal period. Meanwhile, Choctaw political leaders used Choctaw participation in Christianity to draw political and social bonds between the Choctaw nation and the United States. Shared Christianity could serve as a base for a healthier relationship, and it was hoped by Choctaw leaders that this would go some way toward creating a political relationship between the two nations in which Choctaw dispossession from their new western lands would not be contemplated by the United States.

Through these processes, the Choctaws worked to achieve balance — to become healthy — through exploitation of their participation in Christianity. This was one example of the work of regeneration undertaken by the Choctaws in the wake of Removal. The efforts to secure the Choctaws both from social dislocations internal to their society and from further land dispossession at the hands of the United States would help facilitate ongoing Choctaw presence in the west. Christianity served as a medium through which to achieve the balance needed for the flourishing of Choctaw Indigeneity in the context of the modern United States.

Notes

1. Donna Akers, *Living in the Land of Death: The Choctaw Nation, 1830–1860* (Ann Arbor, MI: University of Michigan Press, 2004).
2. Ibid.
3. Ibid., 104.
4. "MISSIONS: GREECE. 1827. CONSTANTINOPLE. 1831. SYRIA. 1821. SMYRNA. 1833. NESTORIANS IN PERSIA. 1833. BOMBAY. 1814. CEYLON. 1816. SIAM. 1831. CHINA. 1830. INDIAN ARCHIPELAGO. 1833. SANDWICH ISLANDS. 1820 HAWAII. MAUI. MOLOKAI. OAHU. KAUAI. PATAGONIA. 1833. WEST

AFRICA. 1833. CHEROKEES. EAST OF THE MISSISSIPPI. 1817. ARKANSAS CHEROKEES. 1820. CHICKASAWS. 1821. CHOCTAWS. 1818. EAST OF THE MISSISSIPPI. CHOCTAWS OF RED RIVER. CREEKS. 1832. OSAGES. 1820. STOCKBRIDGE INDIANS. 1828. MACKINAW. 1823. OJIBWAS. MAUMEE. 1822. NEW YORK INDIANS." The Missionary Herald, Containing the Proceedings of the American Board of Commissioners for Foreign Missions (1821–1906), January 1, 1834, 5, www.proquest.com/. Accessed March 30, 2011.

5. I took these numbers from ABC 18.3.4 v. 6, Numbers 11, 48, and 50, American Board of Commissioners for Foreign Mission Records, Houghton Library, Harvard University, Cambridge, MA.

6. Akers, *Living in the Land of Death*, 107–9.

7. "Report of the Choctaw Mission, 1850," ABC 18.3.4 v. 6, Number 11, American Board of Commissioners for Foreign Mission Records, Houghton Library, Harvard University, Cambridge, MA.

8. "Choctaws. Letter from Mr. Wright, July 17, 1849, A New Church Organized" in *The Missionary Herald, Containing the Proceedings of the American Board of Commissioners for Foreign Missions*, October 1849; 45, 10, the American Periodicals Series Online, http://proquest.umi.com. Accessed March 31, 2011.

9. Ibid.

10. Joseph Dukes to Rev. A. Gleason, March 20, 1846, ABC 18.3.4 v. 6, #137, American Board of Commissioners for Foreign Missions Records, Houghton Library, Harvard University, Cambridge, MA.

11. "A Meeting in the Choctaw Nation. Death of Maj. WM. Armstrong," *The Arkansas Intelligencer*, 6, no. 20 (June 26, 1847) (Van Buren, AR), Early American Newspapers, America's Historical Newspapers. http://infoweb.newsbank.com. Accessed March 31, 2011.

12. Ibid.

13. George Hawkins, Cornelius McCurtain, George Folsom, Chiefs of the Choctaw Nation; Joseph Dukes, David Folsom, National Judges, Thomson McHenry, and two others Trustees to the Prudential Committee of the ABCFM, November 5, 1852, ABC 18.3.4 v. 6, #77, American Board of Commissioners for Foreign Mission Records, Houghton Library, Harvard University, Cambridge, MA.

Epilogue

Under severe distress and subject to ongoing inhumane treatment, Native peoples reproduced their communities and regenerated Indigeneity. What then did it mean to be Indigenous under the settler state and its imperial ambitions during the late eighteenth to mid-nineteenth centuries? It meant the continued expression of Indigenous ways of being. The stories told in the preceding chapters have worked to reveal how this sustained expression of Indigeneity unfolded. What they shared was a process of rearticulation, and therefore reanimation, of Indigeneity. This process — termed "neo-autochthony" — comprised the planting of Indigenous conceptualizations into non-Native cultural structures. This process subverted the logic of the settler society's drive for Indigenous "assimilation." Instead of the eventual erasure of Indigeneity through Native peoples' adoption of the practices of the American settler society, Native peoples used the very institutions — those that for white Americans were assumed to be the tools to extinguish Indigeneity — as media in which to express concepts seminal to Indigenous worldviews. In this way Native peoples found new "spaces," in addition to the land upon which Indigeneity originated, to manifest Native ways of thinking, and hence of being. The result was the regeneration of Indigeneity in an era in which non-Natives had generally assumed the inevitable "disappearance" of the "Indian."

Natives were indeed victimized, but they were not only victims. Natives "survived," but they did much more than that — they actively and creatively reproduced Indigeneity in novel ways. This matters immensely for our understanding of the history. Except for scholars of Indigenous studies, the history of Native North America has generally been told both in popular culture and by professional historians as a tragedy centered on the brutal genocide of Native Americans. There is good reason for this of course as Natives were subjected to repeated attempts at genocide. Moreover, they were dispossessed of their lands — just genocide in another form. As Bob Marley explained in his song "Buffalo Soldier," there was "a war for America."[1] And if measuring by who holds the lands, Natives indeed lost. As I have on more than one occasion been told by colleagues, Natives "were a defeated people."

No, they were militarily defeated for the most part, and yes lost most of the land. But a "defeated *people*?" No, today there are Indigenous groups all throughout the continent that have distinct Native identities and unique cultures. They are directly connected to their ancestors (some of whom are the historical Native actors discussed in the preceding chapters) in a chain, or a *kobade*, to use Leanne Simpson's Anishinaabemowin word.[2] What are the links that make up that chain? One link is the neo-autochthony examined in this book. But there are many others, and they are vital and central elements of the story of Indigenous America. Scholars and historians must uncover them and tell these histories. In addition to describing the horrors of genocides underwritten and unleased by settler colonialism, they must also tell how Native peoples maneuvered and used these contexts to reproduce both themselves and Indigeneity itself. If we fail to do so, we miss — and worse elide — whole histories, and in so doing lend support to a reification of the settler colonial effort to erase Indigeneity. Learning and telling the histories of Indigenous regeneration is a vital element of resurgence.

Requiem for the Holocene, Happy Birthday Indigeneity

It comes down not to the land and not to the people, but to the relationships between the land and all of its people both human and non-human (all of the living beings). Indigeneity is about the relationships among all of these, and more specifically about ensuring that those relationships are as healthy as possible so as to reproduce life. Roxanne Dunbar-Ortiz has explained in her book *An Indigenous Peoples History of the United States* that the story of American history is "wrong . . . in its essence," by which she meant that American history as it is normally told does not place settler colonialism as the central defining characteristic or driving force behind American history.[3] We need to add that the essence of settler colonialism is by its very structure destructive. This is because one of its central features is subordination or erasure of Indigenous peoples, and more, of Indigeneity itself. By attacking Indigeneity, it attacks the relationships between and among the people, and between the people and the land. In part, it does so by replacing relationality with individualism and by obscuring the interconnections between peoples and place. It does so by substituting "the people" for rampant and almost completely unrestrained pursuit of self-interest. Settler colonialism is a sociopolitical structure in which atomized and disconnected individuals pursue their self-interest in competition with each other as they strive to accumulate the resources (the land for instance) everyone wants. This is the opposite of Indigeneity as it centers on consumption and depletion rather than on regeneration. It is ultimately untenable as resources dwindle and individuals find it increasingly difficult to find purpose in an unrelenting drive for self-interest. The destructive ethos of settler colonialism then reverberates back on colonizers, ultimately consuming them too. This is the point at which we find ourselves in the beginning of the second decade of the twenty-first century.

The signs are everywhere. They include the rise of right wing populism around the globe, massive income inequality, seemingly daily mass shootings in the United States, the accelerating sixth mass extinction event, and even popular culture — for instance, the band The Offspring's song "The Kids Aren't Alright" chronicles the suicides, unemployment, and general despair of a neighborhood's kids who as youth were once full of hope. "What the hell is going on?" an exasperated Bryan "Dexter" Holland, the lead singer, asks.[4]

The biggest sign is of course climate change. As we experience the winter of 2020 with little to no snow in southern Scandinavia, ever-increasing and more violent extreme weather events around the globe, and continuing disruptions to the ability of flora and fauna to adapt and survive, there is little doubt of the existential nature of the crisis we face. This is really no surprise as the last few centuries have witnessed the ongoing severing of the relationships between the people and the land as the land became commoditized and its Indigenous inhabitants (both human and non-human) displaced. In these processes everything has a consequence. Everything goes somewhere, there are no "externalities." Indigeneity is about regeneration, but colonialism is about consumption. Climate change is the predictable result of the latter.

That Indigenous peoples reproduced Indigeneity through the experience of settler colonialism is therefore doubly important. It is important not just for our understanding of history, but for our present and immediate future. The concepts, values, and practices of Indigenous ontologies are important as recipes to begin to address and redress the woes that have been created as consequences of settler colonialism. They are not a panacea, but they provide a different paradigm, a different ontic, and a different way of being that can help us produce health rather than illness.[5] As Jodi Byrd has explained, our task is to make a world for us all, including "Natives, settlers, and arrivants."[6] Indigeneity is about relationships, connections, responsibilities, balance, and health. These are the ingredients for the regeneration of life. We are all Indigenous to somewhere. Let's root ourselves anew and find our purpose in contributing to healing and regenerating life on our land.

Notes

1. "Buffalo Soldier," *Confrontation*. Tuff Gong/Island, 1983. Bob Marley and the Wailers, Bob Marley and Noel "King Sporty" Williams, 1978.
2. Leanne Betasamosake Simpson, *As We Have Always Done: Indigenous Freedom Through Radical Resurgence* (Minneapolis, MN: University of Minnesota Press, 2017), 8.
3. Roxanne Dunbar-Oritiz, *An Indigenous Peoples History of the United States* (Boston: Beacon Press, 2015), 2.
4. "The Kids Aren't Alright," *Americana*. Columbia Records, 1998. The Offspring, Dexter Holland, 1998.
5. I am not the first scholar to point out the utility of Indigenous ways of being to address the environmental issues the world faces today. For monograph length treatments of this subject, see Daniel Wildcat, *Red Alert* (Golden, CO: Fulcum Publishing, 2009); and Melissa K. Nelson and Daniel Shilling, eds., *Traditional Ecological Knowledge: Learning From Indigenous Practices for Environmental Sustainability* (Cambridge, UK: Cambridge University Press, 2018).
6. See Jodi Byrd, *The Transit of Empire: Indigenous Critiques of Colonialism* (Minneapolis, MN: University of Minnesota Press, 2011), 229.

Bibliography

Manuscript Collections

American Board of Commissioners for Foreign Missions Records, Houghton Library, Harvard University, Cambridge, MA.

Archive Collection, Mattatuck Museum, Waterbury, CT.

Cherokee Documents, Special Collections, Northeastern Oklahoma State University, Tahlequah, OK.

Cherokee Phoenix, Special Collections, Northeastern Oklahoma State University, Tahlequah, OK.

Cherokee Phoenix and Indians' Advocate, Special Collections, Northeastern Oklahoma State University, Tahlequah, OK.

Collection, Special Collections, Haverford College, Philadelphia, PA.

Correspondence of Philadelphia Yearly Meeting Indian Committee, Special Collections, Quaker Collection, Haverford College, Philadelphia, PA.

Cyrus Kingsbury Collection, Western History Collection, University of Oklahoma, Norman, OK.

Dictionary of Quaker Biography, Special Collections, Haverford College, Philadelphia, PA.

The Friend, Special Collections, Haverford College, Philadelphia, PA.

Jay L. Hargett Papers, Western History Collection, University of Oklahoma, Norman, OK.

John Drew Papers, Gilcrease Museum, Tulsa, OK.

Peter Pitchlynn Papers, Gilcrease Museum, Tulsa, OK.

Phillips Pamphlet Collection, Western History Collection, University of Oklahoma, Norman, OK.

Quaker Necrology, Special Collections, Haverford College, Philadelphia, PA.

Records of the Philadelphia Yearly Meeting Indian Committee (Orthodox), Quaker.

Roberta Robey Collection, Minor Archives, Western History Collection, University of Oklahoma, Norman, OK.

Published Manuscript Collections

The American Presidency Project. Andrew Jackson, First Annual Message to Congress, December 8, 1829. www.presidency.ucsd.edu/ws/index.php?pid=29471

Bernd, Peyer, ed. *The Elders Wrote: An Anthology of Early Prose by North American Indians, 1768–1831*. Berlin, Germany: Reimer, 1982.

Durant, A.R. *Constitution and Laws of the Choctaw Nation together with the Treaties of 1837, 1855, 1865, and 1866*. Wilmington, DE: Scholarly Resources, Inc, 1973.

Guilds, John Caldwell, and Hudson, Charles, eds. *An Early and Strong Sympathy: The Indian Writings of William Gilmore Simms*. Columbia, SC: University of South Carolina Press, 2003.

Gaul, Theresa Strouth, ed. *To Marry an Indian: The Marriage of Harriett Gold & Elias Boudinot in Letters, 1823–1839*. Chapel Hill, NC: University of North Carolina Press, 2005.

Moulton, Gary E. *The Papers of Chief John Ross*. Norman, OK: University of Oklahoma Press, 1985.

Murray, Laura, ed. *To Do Good to My Indian Brethren: The Writings of Joseph Johnson, 1751–1776*. Amherst, MA: University of Massachusetts Press, 1998.

Perdue, Theda. *Cherokee Editor: The Writings of Elias Boudinot*. Athens, GA: University of Georgia Press, 1996.

Phillips, Joyce B., and Phillips, Paul Gary. *The Brainerd Journal: A Mission to the Cherokee 1817–1823*. Lincoln, NE: University of Nebraska Press, 1998.

Prucha, Francis Paul. *Cherokee Removal: The William Penn Essays and Other Writings by Jeremiah Evarts*. Nashville, TN: University of Tennessee Press, 1982.

———. *The Great Father: The United States Government and the American Indians*, Volume 1. Lincoln, NE: University of Nebraska Press, 1984.

Scholarly Resources, Inc. *The Constitutions and Laws of the American Indian Tribes*, Volume 5. Wilmington, DE: Rowman and Littlefield Publishers, 1973.

Watson, Harry. *Andrew Jackson vs. Henry Clay: Democracy and Development in Antebellum America*. Boston and New York: Bedford and St. Martin's Press, 1998.

Whipple, Charles. *Relation of the American Board of Commissioners for Foreign Missions to Slavery*. New York: Negro Universities Press, 1969.

Online Collections

The American Presidency Project. www.presidency.ucsd.edu/ws/index.php?pid=29471

Biographical Directory of the United States Congress. http://bioguide.congress.gov/scripts/biodisplay.pl?index=W000724

Early American Newspapers, America's Historical Newspapers. https://infoweb-newsbank-com.uri.idm.oclc.org/apps/readex/welcome?p=EANX

Evans Early American Imprint Series, Evans TCP. https://quod.lib.umich.edu/e/evans/N09814.0001.001?rgn=main;view=fulltext

Evans Early American Imprint Series I, Evans 1639–1800, Readex, America's Historical Newspapers. https://infoweb-newsbank-com.uri.idm.oclc.org/apps/readex/?p=EANX

Georgia Historical Newspapers. http://neptune3.galib.uga.edu/ssp/cgi-bin/tei-news-idx.pl?sessionid=7f000001&type=years&id=CHRKPHNX

The Occom Circle, Digital Archive, Dartmouth College, Hannover, NH. https://collections.dartmouth.edu/occom/html/ctx/personography/personography.html

Proquest, American Periodical Series. www.proquest.com

Books

Akers, Donna. *Living in the Land of Death: The Choctaw Nation, 1830–1860*. Ann Arbor, MI: University of Michigan Press, 2004.

Alfred, Taiaiake. *Peace, Power, Righteousness: An Indigenous Manifesto*. Oxford: Oxford University Press, 2009.

Banner, Stuart. *How the Indians Lost Their Land: Law and Power on the Frontier*. Cambridge, MA: Harvard University Press, 2007.

Bastien, Betty. *Blackfoot Ways of Knowing: The Worldview of the Siksikaitsitapi*. Calgary: University of Calgary Press, 2004.

Blackhawk, Ned. *Violence over the Land: Indians and Empires in the Early American West*. Cambridge, MA: Harvard University Press, 2006.

Bouton, Terry. *Taming Democracy: "The People," the Founders, and the Troubled Ending of the American Revolution*. Oxford: Oxford University Press, 2009.

Brooks, James. *Captives and Cousins: Slavery, Kinship, and Community in the Southwest Borderlands*. Chapel Hill, NC: University of North Carolina Press, 2002.

Brooks, Lisa. *The Common Pot: The Recovery of Native Space in the Northeast*. Minneapolis, MN: University of Minnesota Press, 2008.

Butler, Jon. *Awash in a Sea of Faith: Christianizing the American People*. Cambridge, MA: Harvard University Press, 1990.

Byrd, Jodi A. *The Transit of Empire: Indigenous Critiques of Colonialism*. Minneapolis, MN: University of Minnesota Press, 2011.

Calloway, Colin G. *First Peoples: A Documentary Survey of American Indian History*, third edition. Boston: Bedford and St. Martin's, 2008.

Castiglia, Christopher. *Interior States: Institutional Consciousness and the Inner Life of Democracy in the Antebellum United States*. Durham, NC: Duke University Press, 2008.

Cipolla, Craig N. *Becoming Brothertown: Native American Ethnogenesis and Endurance in the Modern World*. Tucson, AZ: University of Arizona Press, 2013.

Cogley, Richard. *John Eliot's Mission to the Indians before King Philip's War*. Cambridge, MA: Harvard University Press, 1999.

Cook-Lynn, Elizabeth. *Anti-Indianism in Modern America: A Voice from Tatekeya's Earth*. Urbana, IL: University of Illinois Press, 2001.

———. *New Indians, Old Wars*. Urbana, IL: University of Illinois Press, 2007.

Coulthard, Glen Sean. *Red Skin, White Masks: Rejecting the Colonial Politics of Recognition*. Minneapolis, MN: University of Minnesota Press, 2014.

Dillon, Elizabeth. *New World Drama: The Performative Commons in the Atlantic World, 1649–1849*. Durham, NC: Duke University Press, 2014.

Dippie, Brian W. *The Vanishing American: White Attitudes and U.S. Indian Policy*. Middletown, CT: Wesleyan University Press, 1982.

Donald, Leland. *Aboriginal Slavery on the Northwest Coast of North America*. Berkeley, CA: University of California Press, 1997.

Dowd, Gregory. *A Spirited Resistance: The North American Indian Struggle for Unity, 1745–1815*. Cambridge and New York: Cambridge University Press, 1991.

Dunbar-Ortiz, Roxanne. *An Indigenous Peoples History of the United States*. Boston: Beacon Press, 2015.

Duval, Kathleen. *The Native Ground: Indians and Colonists in the Heart of the Continent*. Philadelphia: University of Pennsylvania Press, 2006.

Edmunds, R. David. *Tecumseh and the Quest for Indian Leadership*. Boston: Little, Brown, 1984.

Edwards, Laura. *The People and Their Peace: Legal Culture and the Transformation of Inequality in the Post-Revolutionary South*. Chapel Hill, NC: University of North Carolina Press, 2009.

Ferguson, Robert A. *The American Enlightenment, 1750–1820*. Cambridge, MA: Harvard University Press, 1997.

Foner, Eric. *Reconstruction Revolution, 1863–1877*. New York: Harper & Row, 1988.

Gallay, Alan. *The Indian Slave Trade: The Rise of the English Empire in the American South*. New Haven, CT: Yale University Press, 2002.

Garrison, Tim Alan. *The Legal Ideology of Removal: The Southern Judiciary and the Sovereignty of Native American Nations*. Athens, GA: University of Georgia Press, 2002.

Gutierrez, Ramon A. *When Jesus Came the Corn Mothers Went Away: Marriage, Sexuality and Power in New Mexico, 1500–1846*. Palo Alto, CA: Stanford University Press, 1991.

Hall, John W. *Uncommon Defense: Indian Allies in the Black Hawk War*. Cambridge, MA: Harvard University Press, 2009.

Halliburton, R., Jr. *Red over Black: Black Slavery among the Cherokee Indians*. Westport, CT: Greenwood Press, 1977.

Hamalainen, Pekka. *The Comanche Empire*. New Haven, CT: Yale University Press, 2009.

Hamilton, Geoff. *A New Continent of Liberty: Eunomia in Native American Literature from Occom to Erdich*. Charlottesville, VA: University of Virginia Press, 2019.

Hauptman, Laurence M. *Conspiracy of Interests: Iroquois Dispossession and the Rise of New York State*. Syracuse, NY: Syracuse University Press, 1999.

Henry, Kevin. *Peaceable Kingdom Lost: The Paxton Boys and the Destruction of William Penn's Holy Experiment*. Oxford: Oxford University Press, 2009.

Heyrman, Christine. *Southern Cross: The Beginnings of the Bible Belt*. New York and Chapel Hill, NC: University of North Carolina Press, 1998.

Hinderaker, Eric. *Elusive Empires: Constructing Colonialism in the Ohio Valley, 1763–1800*. Cambridge: Cambridge University Press, 1997.

Horsman, Reginald. *Race and Manifest Destiny: The Origins of American Racial Anglo-Saxonism*. Cambridge, MA: Harvard University Press, 1981.

Izumi Ishii, Izumi. *Bad Fruits of the Civilized Tree: Alcohol & the Sovereignty of the Cherokee Nation*. Lincoln, NE: University of Nebraska Press, 2008.

Jarvis, Brad D.E. *The Brothertown Nation of Indians: Landownership and Nationalism in Early America, 1740–1840*. Lincoln, NE: University of Nebraska Press, 2010.

Johnson, Paul. *A Shopkeeper's Millennium: Society and Revivals in Rochester, New York, 1815–1837*. New York: Hill and Wang, 1978.

Johnson, Paul, and Wilentz, Sean. *The Kingdom of Mathias*. Oxford and New York: Oxford University Press, 1994.

Jordon, Ryan. *Slavery and the Meetinghouse: The Quakers and the Abolitionists Dilemma, 1820–1865*. Bloomington and Indianapolis, IN: University of Indiana Press, 2007.

Kaplan, Amy. *The Anarchy of Empire in the Making of U.S. Culture*. Cambridge, MA: Harvard University Press, 2002.

Kelly, Duncan. *The Propriety of Liberty: Persons, Passions, and Judgement in Modern Political Thought*. Princeton, NJ: Princeton University Press, 2010.

Kidwell, Clara Sue. *Choctaws and Missionaries in Mississippi, 1818–1918*. Norman, OK: University of Oklahoma Press, 1995.

———. *Choctaws in Oklahoma*. Norman, OK: University of Oklahoma Press, 2007.

Klein, Rachel. *Unification of a Slave State: The Rise of the Planter Class in the South Carolina Backcountry, 1760–1808*. Chapel Hill, NC: University of North Carolina Press, 1990.

Krauthammer, Barbara. *Black Slaves, Indian Masters: Slavery, Emancipation, and Citizenship in the Native American South*. Chapel Hill, NC: University of North Carolina Press, 2015.

Larson, Rebecca. *Daughters of Light: Quaker Women Preaching and Prophesying in the Colonies and Abroad, 1700–1775*. Chapel Hill, NC: University of North Carolina Press, 2000.

Lepore, Jill. *The Name of War: King Phillip's War and the Origins of American Identity.* New York: Vintage Books, 1999.

Lipman, Andrew. *The Saltwater Frontier: Indians and the Contest for the American Coast.* New Haven, CT: Yale University Press, 2015.

Lyons, Scott Richard. *X-Marks: Native Signatures of Assent.* Minneapolis, MN: University of Minnesota Press, 2010.

Mann, Barbara Alice. *George Washington's War on Native America.* Lincoln, NE: University of Nebraska Press, 2009.

McCurry, Stephanie. *Masters of Small Worlds: Yeoman Households, Gender Relations, and the Political Culture of the Antebellum South Carolina Lowcountry.* Oxford: Oxford University Press, 1995.

McDonnell, Michael. *Masters of Empire: Great Lakes Indians and the Making of America.* New York, NY: Hill and Wang, 2015.

Meranze, Michael. *Laboratories of Virtue: Punishment, Revolution, and Authority in Philadelphia, 1760–1835.* Chapel Hill, NC: University of North Carolina Press, 1996.

Mihesuah, Devon. *Cultivating the Rosebuds: The Education of Women at the Cherokee Female Seminary, 1851–1909.* Urbana, IL: University of Illinois Press, 1993.

Miles, Tiya. *The House on Diamond Hill: A Cherokee Plantation Story.* Chapel Hill, NC: University of North Carolina Press, 2012.

———. *Ties That Bind: The Story of an Afro-Cherokee Family in Slavery and Freedom.* Berkeley, CA: University of California Press, 2006.

Minges, Patrick. *Slavery in the Cherokee Nation: The Keetowah Society and the Defining of a People, 1855–1867.* New York: Routledge, 2003.

Nelson, Melissa K., and Shilling, Daniel, eds. *Traditional Ecological Knowledge: Learning from Indigenous Practices for Environmental Sustainability.* Cambridge, UK: Cambridge University Press, 2018.

Nichols, Andrew. *Red Gentlemen & White Savages: Indians, Federalist, and the Search for Order on the American Frontier.* Charlottesville, VA: University of Virginia Press, 2008.

Perdue, Theda. *Slavery and the Evolution of Cherokee Society, 1540–1866.* Knoxville, TN: University of Tennessee Press, 1979.

Pfister, Joel. *The Yale Indian: The Education of Henry Roe Cloud.* Durham, NC: University of North Carolina Press, 2009.

Portnoy, Alisse. *Their Right to Speak: Women's Activism in the Indian and Slave Debates.* Cambridge, MA: Harvard University Press, 2005.

Pravilova, Ekaterina. *A Public Empire: Property and the Quest for the Common Good in Imperial Russia.* Princeton, NJ: Princeton University Press, 2018.

Prucha, Francis Paul. *The Great Father: The United States Government and the American Indians,* Volume 1. Lincoln, NE: University of Nebraska Press, 1984.

Richter, Daniel. *Facing East from Indian Country: A Native History of Early America.* Cambridge, MA: Harvard University Press, 2001.

———. *The Ordeal of the Longhouse: The Peoples of the Iroquois League in the Era of European Colonization.* Chapel Hill, NC: University of North Carolina Press, 1992.

Rifkin, Mark. *Manifesting American: The Imperial Construction of U.S. National Space.* Oxford: Oxford University Press, 2009.

Rothman, Adam. *Slave Country: American Expansion and the Origins of the Deep South.* Cambridge, MA: Harvard University Press, 2005.

Rushforth, Brett. *Bonds of Alliance: Indigenous and Atlantic Slaveries in New France.* Chapel Hill, NC: University of North Carolina Press, 2014.

Ryan, Mary. *Cradle of the Middle Class: The Family in Oneida County, New York 1790–1865*. Cambridge, UK: Cambridge University Press, 1983.

Ryan, Susan. *The Grammar of Good Intentions: Race and the Antebellum Culture of Benevolence*. Ithaca, NY: Cornell University Press, 2003.

Santi, Enrico Mario. *Fernando Ortiz: contrapunteo y transculturacion*. Puebla, Mexico: Editorial Colibri, 2001.

Satz, Ronald. *American Indian Policy in the Jacksonian Era*. Lincoln, NE: University of Nebraska Press, 1975.

Saunt, Claudio. *A New Order of Things: Property, Power, and the Transformation of the Creek Indians, 1733–1816*. Cambridge, UK and New York: Cambridge University Press, 1999.

Sheehan, Bernard W. *Seeds of Extinction: Jeffersonian Philanthropy and the American Indian*. Chapel Hill, NC: University of North Carolina Press, 1973.

Silver, Peter. *Our Savage Neighbors: How Indian War Transformed Early America*. New York: Norton, 2009.

Silverman, David J. *Red Brethren: The Brothertown and Stockbridge Indians and the Problem of Race in Early America*. Ithaca, NY: Cornell University Press, 2015.

Simpson, Audra. *Mohawk Interruptus: Political Life across the Borders of Settler States*. Durham, NC: Duke University Press, 2014.

Simpson, Betasamosake Leanne. *As We Have Always Done: Indigenous Freedom through Radical Resurgence*. Minneapolis, MN: University of Minnesota Press, 2017.

Smith, Timothy. *Revivalism and Social Reform: American Protestantism on the Eve of the Civil War*. Baltimore, MD: Johns Hopkins University Press, 1980.

Snyder, Christina. *Great Crossings: Indians, Settlers, and Slaves in the Age of Jackson*. Oxford, UK: Oxford University Press, 2017.

Spangler, Jewel. *Virginians Reborn: Anglican Monopoly, Evangelical Dissent, and the Rise of the Baptists in the Late Eighteenth Century*. Charlottesville, VA: University of Virginia Press, 2008.

Sturm, Circe. *Blood Politics: Race, Culture and Identity in the Cherokee Nation of Oklahoma*. Berkeley, CA: University of California Press, 2002.

Tallbear, Kim. *Native American DNA: Tribal Belonging and the False Promise of Genetic Science*. Minneapolis, MN: University of Minnesota Press, 2013.

Taylor, Alan. *The Divided Ground: Indians, Settlers, and the Northern Borderland of the American Revolution*. New York: Alfred A. Knopf, 2006.

Viola, Herman J. *Thomas L. McKenney: Architect of America's Early Indian Policy, 1816–1830*. Chicago: Sage Books, 1974.

Wallace, Anthony. *The Death and Rebirth of the Seneca*. New York: Vintage Books, 1970.

Walters, Ronald. *American Reformers: 1815–1860*. New York: Hill and Yang, 1978.

Warner, Micael. *The Letters of the Republic: Publication and the Public Sphere in Eighteenth-Century America*. Cambridge, MA: Harvard University Press, 1990.

Weddle, Meredith Baldwin. *Walking in the Way of Peace: Quaker Pacifism in the Seventeenth Century*. Oxford: Oxford University Press, 2001.

Wells, Colin. *The Devil and Dr. Dwight: Satire and Theology in the Early American Republic*. Chapel Hill, NC: University of North Carolina Press, 2002.

West, Elliott. *The Last Indian War: The Nez Perce Story*. Oxford: Oxford University Press, 2009.

White, Richard. *The Middle Ground: Indians, Empires, and Republics in the Great Lakes Region, 1650–1815*. Cambridge and New York: Cambridge University Press, 1991.

Wildcat, Daniel. *Red Alert*. Golden, CO: Fulcum Publishing, 2009.

Wolfe, Patrick. *Settler Colonialism and the Transformation of Anthropology: The Politics and Poetics of an Ethnographic Event*. London: Continuum, 1998.

Wood, Gordon. *The Radicalism of the American Revolution*. New York: Vintage Books, 1993.

Yarbrough, Fay A. *Race and the Cherokee Nation: Sovereignty in the Nineteenth Century*. Philadelphia: University of Pennsylvania Press, 2008.

Articles

Chiles, Katy L. "On Becoming Colored in Occom and Wheatley's Early America," *Periodical of the American Language Association (PMLA)*, 123, no. 5, Special Topic: Comparative Racialization (October 2008), 1398–1417.

Furstenberg, Francois. "The Significance of the Trans-Appalachian Frontier in Atlantic History," *The American Historical Review*, 113, no. 3 (June 2008), 647–77.

Hershberger, Mary. "Mobilizing Women, Anticipating Abolition: The Struggle against Indian Removal in the 1830s," *The Journal of American History*, 86, no. 1 (1999), 15–40.

Rushforth, Brett. "'A Little Flesh We Offer You': The Origins of Indian Slavery in New France," *The William and Mary Quarterly*, 60, no. 4 (October 2003), 777–808.

Dissertations

Conable, Mary. "A Steady Enemy: The Ogden Land Company and the Seneca Indians," PhD diss., University of Rochester, 1994.

Songs

"Buffalo Soldier," *Confrontation*. Tuff Gong/Island, 1983. Bob Marley and the Wailers, Bob Marley and Noel "King Sporty" Williams, 1978.

"The Kids Aren't Alright," *Americana*. Columbia Records, 1998. The Offspring, Dexter Holland, 1998.